# THE SELF-RELIANCE MANIFESTO

# THE SELF-RELIANCE MANIFESTO

# MANIFESTO

## HOW TO SURVIVE
## ANYTHING ANYWHERE

### LEN McDOUGALL

The following sections first appeared in a different format in *The Outdoors Almanac* Len MCDougall (Burford Books): "Advanced Orienteering," "Weather," and "Tracking Wildlife." "Knots" is excerpted from *Everyday Knots* by Geoffrey Budworth (Thalamus Publishing).

Skyhorse Publishing books may be purchased in bulk at special discounts for sales promotion, corporate gifts, fund-raising, or educational purposes. Special editions can also be created to specifications. For details, contact the Special Sales Department, Skyhorse Publishing, 307 West 36th Street, 11th Floor, New York, NY 10018 or info@skyhorsepublishing.com.

Skyhorse® and Skyhorse Publishing® are registered trademarks of Skyhorse Publishing, Inc.®, a Delaware corporation.

Visit our website at www.skyhorsepublishing.com.

10 9 8 7 6 5 4 3 2 1

2013 edition printed for Barnes & Noble, Inc.
ISBN: 978-1-4351-4628-0

Paperback ISBN: 978-1-61608-061-7

Library of Congress Cataloging-in-Publication Data is available on file.

Printed in China

## WARNING AND DISCLAIMER

The author had no part in creating the plants sections, pages 200–271. Poisonous plants sometimes resemble edible plants, and they frequently grow side by side. It is the reader's responsibility to properly identify and correctly use the plants described in this book.

In addition, the author and publisher assume no responsibility for injuries of any kind, including death, arising from the use or misuse of any of the instructions, tools, advice, or tips contained in this book. Many of the tactics and techniques described in these pages require substantial training and/or professional advice or supervision in order to perform them safely.

This book is dedicated to Chakota, the thoroughbred timber wolf who taught me so much about life and the world in the years we spent together, most of which I am only now beginning to appreciate.

# Contents

Introduction                          1

Fire                                 10
Water                                28
Food                                 48
Shelter                             104
Medicine                            128
Security and Defense                142
Coping with Disasters               180

APPENDICES                          198
   Edible Plants                  200
   Poisonous Plants               260
   Knots                          272
   Tracking                       284

Index                               304

# THE SELF-RELIANCE MANIFESTO

x

# Introduction

Recent history has shown that there is need for a clear, easily followed how-to manual with instructions for coping with the most common challenges in the aftermath of a natural or man-made disaster. After Hurricane Katrina devastated New Orleans, citizens who had ignored orders to evacuate clustered onto rooftops, begging overflying helicopters for water; and the resulting epidemic of cholera proved that thirsty people will eventually drink the most foul water. The carnage that followed the earthquake that shattered Port au-Prince, Haiti, was the stuff of nightmares, with hungry, thirsty people and crying children shuffling past piles of decaying, often unidentified corpses while waiting for help from a government that was itself in shambles. These and other horrors from mudslides, volcanoes, and torrential rainfalls have clearly shown that even in this age of technological wonder, the ability to fend for oneself in times of tribulation is less than it could be.

As anyone who watches world news can see almost daily, there is a growing laundry list of potentially horrendous catastrophes stacking up. From inhabited islands sinking off the coast of India to almost unbelievable earthquakes in Chile to giant asteroids hurtling toward our planet at incredible velocities, we earthlings—all of us, of every species—are joined together in a dangerous game over which we have no control. If one of the monstrous solar flares,

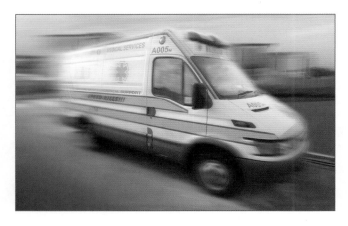

History has shown that emergency services are often overwhelmed in a major disaster, and it pays to be as self-reliant as possible during such times.

super-volcanoes, towering tsunamis, or "dirty" radiation bombs that scientists warn us about become a reality, any or all of us might be forced to deal with a world without modern conveniences.

Contrary to the image created by scriptwriters and newscasters, dedicated "survivalists"—most of whom dislike that title—do not believe in the end of the world. In fact, survivalists may be the most optimistic people, because they refuse to believe in an end of days, and they actively take steps to ensure that they and their loved ones will prevail against whatever disaster may befall them. A survivor's mindset typically doesn't trust governmental authorities to save him or her from catastrophe—or even to tell him the truth about an impending disaster. Whether that outlook is prudent or paranoid, it is a fact that both the Office of Homeland Security and its Federal Emergency Management Administration have recommended that Americans stock food, water, and other supplies sufficient to endure at least three days without public services or outside help.

In a major disaster, there is no way governmental authorities could assist, or even reach, every citizen in need of help. The hard reality is that in the aftermath of any major natural or man-made disaster, you and your loved ones will probably be on your own, at least for a while. You need to know, or have reference to, easily followed instructions for dealing effectively with the problems most commonly encountered when the lights go out and faucets stop flowing.

## THE SURVIVOR'S PHILOSOPHY

There are several misconceptions about survival and the people who live that lifestyle. First is the label of paranoia that has been applied to everyone who seeks self-sufficiency by politicians and media personalities who (I believe) don't comprehend the possibility of a disaster severe enough to close local restaurants and the other trappings of an urban lifestyle. It appears to have been forgotten that just a few generations have passed since people who lived through the Great Depression and World War II canned their own vegetables from truck gardens, hunted and butchered their own meats, and stocked up on supplies before each winter. Those were people who had experienced deprivation first-hand, and they had disliked it enough to guard against it.

One real misconception is that a survivalist must be tough-minded and physically hardened. This belief is common among military instructors and a few civilian survival schools that claim to push students beyond the "false limits they have set for themselves" and into some mythical sense of enlightenment. Unnecessary hardship has no place in real-world survival, and both military and civilian survival trainees have died when their instructors pushed them too far.

Prize fighters know that it isn't always a knockout punch that wins the fight; veteran boxers recognize that every blow, even a light one, saps some of an opponent's strength. The same applies to a survival scenario. A person who is well rested and fed is better able to face physical obstacles and to resist infectious pathogens than one who is weakened by hunger, thirst, or pain.

Toughness and physical fitness mean nothing when the enemies are hypothermia or dehydration, and the most rugged man's man can be in mortal danger if hypoglycemia causes him to pass out while negotiating a narrow cliff ledge. There will likely be sufficient hardships to tax your physical and mental resources without voluntarily adding more.

Another mistaken notion about survivalists is that they are paramilitary types who yearn for combat. It should go without saying that warfare is the antithesis of survival,

While causes are debated, there is no arguing that natural disasters have wrought havoc around the world.

and a person who means to prolong the lives of himself or herself and his or her family will keep as far from flying bullets and violence as possible. A survivor's kit should indeed include firearms and other weapons, but primarily for hunting or fishing for food. Fire-fights are the domain of armies that can afford to expend more ammunition than a person who is outfitted for survival can carry.

This is not to say that a disaster survivor should be unwilling or unprepared to fight—quite the contrary. In the aftermath of Hurricane Katrina it took less than three days for hungry, thirsty youths to band into roving gangs who forcibly stole what they could from other victims. The same happened after the massive 2010 earthquake in Haiti, and it would be unreasonable to believe that mobs of predators wouldn't form in the wake of any major disaster. Taking a lesson from the French Foreign Legion, it behooves a survivalist to possess the will, the skill, and the means to instantly counterattack adversaries with enough force to break their resolve. History has proved that a gang cannot be bargained with; but it has also shown that a smaller force can convince marauders to break off an assault if it can swiftly and effectively hurt them.

## PRIORITIES IN A REAL SURVIVAL SITUATION

Not so long ago it was common for people who had known deprivation in real life to have a root cellar stocked with canned foods.

Authorities on wilderness survival have always tried to come up with hard-and-fast rules about coping with a real life survival situation. People like rules because rules provide the security of knowing what to do without thinking.

Problem is, a wilderness doesn't abide by rules that we humans invent. Nature is fluid, always in motion, always changing, ever evolving. Animals deal with those changes by having their own onboard tools, weapons, environmental protection, and super acute senses.

Humans have virtually none of those things. For us, the fight-or-flight instinct is self-destructive; we can't outrun even a raccoon, we have no claws for climbing to safety, we carry no bodily weapons, and pound-for-pound we're the weakest species on the planet. A simple rainstorm can kill us with hypothermia.

Our weapon is that great big brain we're all born having. Fight-or-flight is useless to us, but being a chess player can save your life. By planning and strategizing, we can see into

the future; we can look at a tree and see shelter, a boat, snares, fishing poles, bow and arrow, spear. . . . A victim sees only what is there, but a survivor sees opportunities to create.

What is most important in a survival scenario? That depends entirely on the situation. You can't shoot your way out of a blizzard. The old saw about food being least important because it'll take three months to starve doesn't have much meaning to someone on the verge of passing out from hypoglycemia while on treacherous footing.

No human is tough enough to go toe-to-toe with nature, and the naked-into-the-woods philosophy has never been subscribed to by any humans who actually live in the wild. And the slogan "The more you know, the less you carry" isn't entirely realistic either. "The more you know, the better equipped you will be" would be more accurate. Nature can be a harsh judge, unforgiving of inadequacies and weakness.

The best lightning rod for your protection is your own spine.
—*Ralph Waldo Emerson*

# Fire

## THE NEED FOR FIRE

**V**eteran survival instructors know that no outdoor skill is more likely to save your life anywhere on earth than the ability to make fire. Any environment with a temperature below 98.6 degrees Fahrenheit will steal body heat unless a person is insulated against it. Soldiers in the Vietnam War learned that even tropical Southeast Asia was dangerously cold and miserable during the monsoon season, and visitors to deserts or mountains discover that sweltering days are followed by bone-chilling nights. Add a drenching rain, and a 90-degree day feels like 70; throw in a 10 mph wind, and the felt temperature falls to about 50.

Even when hypothermia isn't severe enough to kill a victim outright, each exposure to heat–sapping conditions dents the victim's energy reserves and immune system. A chill lowers the body's defenses sufficiently for an otherwise harmless virus to gain a foothold, and an immune system that is already compromised by a shivering body that has diverted available calories to generating heat now has to battle an infection. You don't have to actually freeze to death to die of hypothermia. Fire not only enables a person to endure the coldest temperatures, but also helps to maintain a strong body in other ways as well. Boiling and cooking kills harmful organisms in water and food, a bright fire can be seen from many miles on a dark night, and smoke is a clear signal against a daytime sky. Most animals steer clear of fire, and—maybe most importantly—a crackling blaze makes the most dismal situation seem less frightening.

## MAKING FIRE

Any experienced survival instructor can affirm that friction-type fire drills and bow-and-drill fire starters are impractical in a real-world scenario, where the times a fire is most needed are likely to be when conditions are most prohibitive for lighting one. A bow-and-drill is almost impossible to make and use in a cold rain, and to stubbornly waste energy trying to make it work does not enhance one's chances of survival. A bow-and-drill isn't entirely useless, and it doesn't hurt to practice making fire with one—if only to show yourself how difficult it is to master. But there are more effective alternatives, and several of these should be incorporated into every home, car, or wilderness survival kit.

## FIRE-MAKING TOOLS

For decades my primary wilderness fire-making tool has been the Strike Force flint-and-steel ($17) from Ultimate Survival Technologies. Sparks from its large flint rod have never failed to make fire, and waterproof tinder cube in the tool's handle helps to guarantee that it never will. In recent years the Strike Force has been joined by the smaller one-hand-operated Blast Match, and the even smaller Sparkie. Similar sparking tools can be found in ready-made survival knife kits.

Any temperature below 98.6 degrees Fahrenheit is capable of inducing hypothermia, and survival instructors agree that no survival skill is likely to be more valuable than the ability to make fire under any conditions.

# FIRE

The ability to dry and warm one's feet prevents a crippling affliction known as trench foot, and is just one of the potentially lifesaving services provided by fire.

Disposable butane lighters have been cheap, reliable, and lightweight fire-makers for decades.

A good wetting will take the small flint striker out of action until it dries, so it pays to have several spread throughout your just-in-case gear in protective ziplock bags. When its butane is gone, the lighter can still strike a fire if you remove its metal hood and apply its weak spark to finely frayed tissue or cotton batting. Priced at less than $1 apiece, disposable lighters offer the advantage of numbers, because lighters can be strewn throughout a person's immediate world, increasing the likelihood that one will be available when needed.

A bulkier but more functional alternative to throwaway gas lighters are the long-barrel versions, like those seen most often used for igniting gas and charcoal grills. With long exhaust tubes that keep flames several inches from the hand, these lighters help protect against being burned, but also give users an extended reach for re-lighting the pilot lights of gas appliances and lighting jarred candles whose wicks have burned beyond reach of a match or conventional lighter.

Today's fire-starting tools can virtually ensure you the ability to make fire in any weather.

A higher quality alternative to disposable butane lighters are refillable models, especially long-barrel types like Zippo's Outdoor Utility Lighter, or OUL.

Liquid-fuel lighters ($15) have been a mainstay of emergency fire-making outfits for nearly a century. My survival outfits carry one of these with a small bottle of fuel—enough for weeks of regular use—and a package of replacement flints. Actual burn time on a fill-up is just a minute or so, and a lighter is not suitable for use as a candle, but it can ignite dozens of fires between refills. If regular fuel is unavailable, I've substituted white gas, unleaded gasoline, and even isopropyl alcohol.

Matches are a must in survival kits. "Lifeboat" matches with waterproof over-size heads (about fifteen-cents per match) are probably best, but wooden kitchen matches or paper book matches in a watertight pill bottle can be stored for years. Just remember that these latter types require their own strikers to ignite, and be sure to include those in the bottle, too.

The Sparkie flint-and-steel one-hand fire-starting tool is small enough to carry everywhere, yet effective enough to make fire under almost any conditions.

## TINDER MATERIALS

Once you have a reliable ignitor, you need a tinder that lights easily and burns hot enough to ignite small twigs or other kindling into a self-sustaining blaze. Most natural environments–including city parks and vacant lots—provide ample tinder materials. Dry grass is an ideal tinder that flames at the touch of a flame or hot spark. The outer, peeling bark from white, yellow, and silver birch trees contains flammable oils that burn energetically. Reindeer moss lichens, found in open sandy and rocky places around the world, are food, medicine, and outstanding tinder when crunchy-dry. Sticky sap, or "pitch," leaked from woodpecker and other holes in living conifers was the active ingredient in the pitch

torches of old. Dried pine needles scraped from the ground below the pine trees that shed them also contain flammable pitch oils, and will ignite at the touch of a flame. Very small dead pine twigs, none much larger than a pencil lead, can be bundled together in one hand, and their ends ignited like a torch using the flame of a lighter.

Most dry leaves do not burn well, and trying to make fire with them is generally a waste of time.

Namesake of the pitch torch that lighted the way for generations prior to lanterns, sticky, congealed pine sap from shallow wounds in conifer bark is flammable and long-burning, antiseptic, and sticky enough to serve as adhesive.

The best natural tinders are airy, and those that are not should be made that way by rolling them forcefully between your palms until individual plant fibers separate. A "bird's nest" of tangled fibers will always light more easily and burn hotter than a solid piece of any combustible material.

Civilized environments provide paper, Styrofoam, and other flammable materials, but you'll be most secure with a no-fail tinder that can be carried in your pocket at all times. Manufactured tinder sticks, ribbons, and pastes can be found in sporting goods stores, and there are home-brewed tinders—like cotton balls saturated with petroleum jelly—but my long-time favorite is the fire wick.

## THE FIRE WICK

The most basic type of fire wick consists of thick cotton packaging string that has been saturated with molten paraffin, cooled and hardened, then cut to convenient lengths. The string used must be cotton, not nylon or rayon, because synthetics don't burn well or cleanly and emit poisonous gases.

The fire wick, shown here burning atop snow, is waterproof, easily lighted, and downright cheap to make.

To make fire wicks, just lower several feet of cotton string carefully into a metal vessel in which a pound of paraffin (canning wax) has been heated to a liquid. Paraffin is sold in most supermarkets for about a dollar per pound. Alternately, you can melt the stubs of candles, which works just as well but gives the wicks whatever scents or dyes were in the candle wax.

Use caution when melting paraffin; do it in a well-ventilated space where there are few flammables and plenty of fresh air. Wear gloves when handling hot wax, and never allow paraffin to get hot enough to smoke, because smoke means that it is about to burst into flames. If that happens, don't panic; the wax is still safely contained. Simply cover the melting pot with a loose-fitting lid to smother the fire, and remove it from the heat.

Next, pluck one end of the string from the melting pot with pliers—always do this in a place where you won't mind wax drippings. Pull the string outward in a straight line, letting it drag over the pot's rim, until the entire length is laid out in a straight line. Allow the wax-soaked string to cool and harden (5 minutes or less), then cut the stiffened string into sections with a sharp knife or scissors. Package the completed fire wicks into pill bottles or zip-lock bags (the wicks are unaffected by water), and scatter them throughout your gear. I even carry them in the toolbox, where they've come in handy for re-lighting gas furnaces and other pilot lights.

A good alternative to cotton string is wool felt weatherstripping, or old felt pac-boot liners cut into sections. Fire wicks made from these burn longer because they absorb

more paraffin. Again, use only felt made from pure wool, because some is comprised of synthetic fibers that don't burn well and give off soot and toxic gases.

To use a fire wick, you'll need a butane or liquid-fuel lighter, but I've had success igniting well-frayed fire wicks using only sparks from flint-and-steel tools. The trick is to fray the fire wick into an airy mass of very fine fibers that ignites at the touch of a hot spark or flame.

## MANUFACTURED TINDERS

If wet weather makes natural tinders difficult to light, ready-made chemical fire starters like military Hexamine and Trioxane tablets can be had cheaply from brick-and-mortar, mail order, or online Army-Navy stores. Or you might opt for the patented "WetFire" tinder cubes from Ultimate Survival Technologies. All of these ignite at the touch of a flame or hot spark, regardless of weather.

Practical reasons for excavating a shallow depression to hold a campfire include ensuring that it is sited on non-flammable soil, keeping hot embers from blowing away, reducing its visibility if desired, and for quickly extinguishing the fire by smothering it with loose soil from the pit's perimeter.

## BUILDING A FIRE

When building a fire, "build" is the operative word. The secret to starting a fire quickly and efficiently is to start small. Begin by creating a "fire pit," which may not actually be a pit, but an open area of bare dirt, at least 3 feet square, from which all flammable ground litter has been scraped with the edge of a boot sole. Next, lay a platform of sticks placed parallel to one another on the ground, where the platform will support and protect your fledgling fire from moisture in the earth below.

Lay the tinder you'll use onto the platform and set it afire. Add more

Start your fire small, slowly building it larger as small pieces of wood placed onto the tinder begin to catch.

tinder as needed until you have a small but strong blaze. Slowly build a cone of kindling—dead twigs, pencil-thick or smaller—around the perimeter of the flaming tinder. Add larger sticks as the fledgling fire grows, until you've achieved a crackling blaze.

In wet conditions, note that wood lying on the ground will be wettest. When making fire in rain, the driest kindling sticks will be dead twigs that are still attached to their parent trees, where overhead canopies shield them from falling water and gravity helps to shed rain that does reach them. In a hard rain, it helps to use this same principle for laying your fire, building a protective, water-shedding tipi "roof" of kindling sticks over the tinder atop the platform before lighting it.

If the tinder pile smokes but does not flame, kneel down and place your pursed lips as close to the smoking ember as possible, and very gently blow into the tinder until the ember begins to glow. Do not blow hard; the objective is to force-feed air into the spark, increasing its burn rate and temperature until it becomes hot enough to ignite the tinder into flame; a prolonged, gentle blow is best.

When the kindling tipi is flaming strongly, add more and larger twigs to the cone until a bed of glowing red embers forms below, atop the tinder platform you laid at the start. With a good bed of embers, begin laying additional sticks side by side to form a "furnace pile." The parallel configuration of the furnace pile maximizes your fire's usefulness by creating grooves into which added lengths of wood can lay and be stable enough to hold a cooking vessel. When the cooking is done and you want the fire to throw as much heat and light as possible, just lay more lengths of wood on top, until the pile looks like a pyramid when viewed from the ends. This configuration causes a fire to burn as evenly and efficiently as possible, while enabling its user to build it large and hot without fear of losing control over it.

Used by aboriginal peoples the world over, the tipi method of arranging kindling over flaming tinder is the most efficient configuration for applying maximum heat over the greatest area of the kindling.

## GATHERING FIREWOOD

Movies typically show gathered firewood in convenient lengths, but that isn't realistic or effective for fires in real life. Even if you had the means to cut or break large limbs and logs into neat pieces, the net gain isn't worth the energy expended to do so. Instead, lay long pieces of wood onto the fire so that their centers burn through. Then place the burned ends of either half onto the fire, feeding the lengths inward as the ends are consumed.

## THE BOW-AND-DRILL

In the three-day Basic Survival courses I teach, I ignore the bow-and-drill fire starter that has been so romanticized as the fire-making tool of a real survival expert. Its components are time-consuming to select and manufacture, and it is a difficult tool to use, especially under the cold, wet conditions in which you'll most desperately need the warmth of a fire as quickly as you can get one started. It is almost guaranteed that the tool will not work in a freezing rain, and it's just as certain that relying on the bow-and-drill in such weather can cost you your life. It was not relied on by early frontiersmen who went nowhere without their flint-and-steel tinderboxes, or by the native people who wasted no time adopting flint-and-steel for themselves. Today there are too many effective pocket-size fire starters available to not have at least one of them at all times.

In most places, there will be enough dead wood from trees and shrubs to sustain a fire sufficient for cooking, warmth, or signaling.

Despite all that, it is an axiom of survival that he with the most options wins, and in a real-world scenario, you cannot have too many methods of getting a fire started. By all means, practice making and using a bow-and-drill. Just don't bet your life on it.

The principle of a bow-and-drill is easy to grasp: A wooden spindle, or drill, is fashioned from dry softwood, then rotated on a "fireboard" of dried deadwood with downward pressure against the drill's top end to maximize friction. The objective is to produce abrasion sufficient to create a mound of powdered wood, then enough heat to make that powdered "char" smolder. The smoldering char is then covered with a fine, easily lighted tinder material, and coaxed to a flame by gently blowing into the smoking tinder to accelerate combustion.

Construction of a bow-and-drill is also simple, although prohibitively time consuming under emergency conditions. The tool has five components: the bow, the bowstring, the handle, the fireboard, and the drill. The ideal drill should be dead and dry, even gray and a little dry-rotted, about 8 inches long, an inch in diameter, and round and straight to minimize wobble during rotation. The bottom (drill) portion is whittled to a dull point and the top is rounded as smoothly as possible. Use an abrasive stone to smooth imperfections from the finished drill.

The drill's top spins inside a palm-size handle made from dried wood, about 3 inches wide by 6 inches long by 2 inches thick. Handles are best made from hardwood, which will not abrade so easily, thus creating less friction against the top of the drill and allowing it to spin more easily. Edges should be rounded and smoothed to fit comfortably in your palm. Using the point of your knife as a drill, dig out and shape a concave detent that matches the top, rounded portion of the drill. To make the two pieces more compatible, rotate the drill under hand pressure in the hole of the handle. The addition of a little sand will help

to smooth the rough surfaces in the hole. If possible, the finished handle detent should be lubricated with candle wax or grease to minimize friction between drill top and handle.

The fireboard is made from a slab of dry weathered-gray wood about 6 inches wide by 12 inches long and roughly 1 inch thick, as flat as possible on both sides. It's usually easiest to make a fireboard by splitting slabs from a section of dead, half-rotted log or stump with a stout knife or hatchet. When you find a suitable candidate, drill a conical hole into its edge using the tip of the knife. The hole should be about one-half inch deep and sized to accept and hold the bottom, friction-bearing end of the drill. The exact location of the hole on the board isn't critical, but it should be about ⅛ inch from the outside of the board at its widest point.

When the hole is finished, cut a downward-sloping notch into the ⅛-inch of wood that remains between its edge and the outside of the board, slightly deeper and narrower than the drill hole. This notch serves as a chute to channel hot, powdered char onto the tinder.

The bow is made from a green branch of any springy wood. It should ideally be about 1 inch in diameter by 2 feet long. Notch both ends crosswise with a shallow groove to help hold the bowstring in place. If the bow has a natural curve, use it to your advantage.

The bowstring can be made from nearly any type of sturdy cord. I prefer thick cord with woven outer casings—like bootlace or parachute cord—because these offer more traction against the drill shaft with less slippage. Tie one end to the bow using a slipknot, making sure that the cord fits securely into the notch, and lock it in place with a timber-hitch. Pull the string until it's taut, but not so tight that it flexes the bow. Tie the free end to the oppo-

When the weather is cold or wet, a long-burning fire of very large dead tree trunks might be desired; burn them in half, do not expend valuable energy hacking or sawing them into pieces.

Cooking steaks on a flat rock that is heated from below, like a prehistoric griddle.

site end of the bow, again making certain that it nestles snugly into the groove.

With the components assembled, hold the bow horizontal to the ground in the right hand, and place the drill, rounded end up, between the bow and the string. Wrap the string around the drill one time and place the pointed end of the drill into the hole in the fireboard. I prefer to wrap the drill so that it is to the inside, between bowstring and bow, because this increases drill stability during use.

Place the handle on top of the drill with the left hand, making sure that the rounded top of the drill sits loosely but securely into the hole in the handle. Kneel with your right knee resting on the ground and your left foot on the fireboard to hold it in place. Rest your left elbow on your left knee and press downward firmly, but not hard, on the handle. With the bow held horizontal to the fireboard, begin moving it back and forth with a smooth, easy sawing motion. The drill will spin in one direction, then the other, with each stroke forward and backward. If the drill doesn't spin freely, decrease downward pressure on the handle.

As the drill spins against the fireboard it will heat up from friction. A sprinkling of dry sand into the fireboard hole helps to maximize friction. As you continue to work the bow back and forth, the drill tip will begin to smoke, and charred-brown wood powder will accumulate in the fireboard's drill hole. As hot char fills the drill hole, it will fall through the notch and onto the pile of dried tinder (crushed dry grass, cotton fibers, powdered reindeer moss) placed directly below the notch opening. When enough char falls onto the tinder, it will begin to smoke.

When the tinder is smoking freely, lay the bow and drill to one side and

If your home is in outer suburbia or a rural area, you might want to consider an LP (Low Pressure) propane-fired kitchen range, which continues to operate without electricity until its pressure tank is depleted.

gather the tinder in your cupped palms. Very softly blow into the pile through pursed lips; a prolonged, gentle blow is best—too strong, and you'll extinguish the coal. When the tinder catches fire, lay the flaming mass gently onto a small platform made by placing dead sticks parallel to one another on the ground, and add more dry tinder.

Next, pile very small (less than a pencil's diameter) dry twigs tipi-fashion on top of the burning tinder, being careful not to compress the tinder under too much weight that can inhibit burning, or even extinguish your fire. As the small twigs begin to flame, add more and larger sticks until a bed of coals underneath makes the fire self-sustaining.

## THE COOKING FIRE

The Furnace Pile method of arranging burning wood described above is ideal for cooking because it provides stable, flat surfaces on which to rest a pot. The intensity of the heat coming through between solid pieces of wood can be adjusted by increasing or decreasing the space between them. Hot coals, not flame, do most of the actual cooking. Be aware that a wood fire is much hotter than a kitchen range, and that cooking surfaces burn away; always pay close attention to cooking food, and if you must divert your attention, remove the food from direct contact with your fire.

Fire ensures that meals can be served hot when temperatures are cold, and that food will be free of pathogenic organisms.

## THE HEATING FIRE

The furnace pile is an ideal configuration for heating, because it can be adjusted for height, length, and intensity. By "growing" the fire's bed of coals to body length, and feeding it with similar-length pieces of dead wood, a person can lie next to the fire—at a safe distance of at least 4 feet—and be warmed by radiated heat sufficient to permit several hours of restful sleep. Large-diameter, even damp and half-rotted logs are best, because they burn slowly and more

No matter how cold the temperature, a warm fire can fend off hypothermia.

When a hatch of blood-drinking flies or mosquitoes fills the air, avoiding as many bites as possible is a genuine imperative, and smudge fires may become a way of life in summer.

steadily, but you must have a healthy fire beneath them when they are added. Remember that the earth itself is an efficient heat sink, and always lay a pallet of parallel sticks, or use a closed-cell sleeping pad to keep your body off the ground.

## SMUDGE FIRES

A smudge fire is usually a small fire with a hot bed of embers that is built near where people are living. It is partially smothered with armfuls of green or wet foliage that generate thick plumes of smoke before catching fire. A smudge fire's purpose is to drive back the hordes of biting mosquitoes and flies that emerge not only from wilderness swamps, but also from old tires, culverts, storm sewers, even puddles of rain water in asphalt pot holes. The worst plague of mosquito-borne yellow fever in U.S. history occurred not in a jungle swamp, but in New York City at the turn of the twentieth century.

In practice, several small fires are built in fire pits a dozen yards upwind from a person's area of activity. When the hot embers are covered with damp green ferns, grasses, pine boughs, or even half-rotted logs, the embers will generate smoke from the poorly burning fuel. Biting insects are repelled by smoke, and in concentrations that are lower than what most people consider intolerable. The preferred fuel for smudge fires is of course wood and vegetation, but when biting insects and the diseases they introduce to communities threaten to be epidemic, anything that produces smoke is acceptable, including asphalt shingles and tires, both of which produce voluminous—and toxic—black smoke when they burn.

## THE COAL BED

Restful sleep is always needed, and in a survival situation where your body's resources are being taxed, it can be critical to avoiding a downward spiral of fatigue, lethargy, apathy, illness, and finally death. Being cold while sleeping robs a body of rest, so it is imperative that a person stay warm throughout the night.

The Coal Bed is a time-honored technique for getting a warm night's sleep outdoors. Construction is as simple as excavating a body-size depression to a depth of 6 inches, then building a fire in its bottom. Spread the fire throughout the length and breadth of the depression until its bottom is covered with hot coals. Re-cover the depression with the soil excavated from it, and then lie on top, gaining warmth from below by heated earth from the slowly cooling embers.

In winter, it might be necessary to build a body-size fire atop the snow to melt downward to and then thaw the frozen earth below before it can be excavated. One caveat is to make certain that all embers are in the depression, below ground level, and covered with at least 4 inches of non-flammable dirt or sand.

# BED WARMERS

In the days when all homes were heated by a wood-fueled fire, it was common practice to keep a football-size stone next to the hearth or stove, where it would absorb heat from the fire. At bedtime, the stone was often placed at the foot of the bed to ward off cold toes all night. A caveat is to never heat any stone that has been underwater, because even the hardest stone absorbs moisture, and it is not uncommon for trapped steam to cause a stone to explode with the force of a grenade. Stones wet from rain or short submersion in water are safe to heat.

A variation on the stone warmer is the water-bottle warmer that I teach winter-survival students. A simple canteen or water bottle filled with hot (not boiling) water, and perhaps wrapped in a shirt if it's too hot, will retain warmth all night. An added bonus is that there is also warm water for drinking or coffee in the morning.

Banking a fire to make it smolder for long periods, ready to be revived when a hot fire is needed, is a valuable part of knowing how to use fire.

# BANKING A FIRE

If you're in a stationary situation where a wood-fueled fire is part of daily life, whether it's a fireplace or a campfire, you'll need to "bank" that fire during periods when it must be left unattended. In principle, banking a fire means reducing it to the equivalent of a slow idle, in which it smolders at a low heat, consuming minimal fuel, but can be coaxed back to a hot flame quickly and easily.

In practice, a fire is banked by placing a log that is too large—or even too wet and half-rotted—to burn atop a bed of hot embers. All wood should be parallel to provide a stable grooved platform that keeps banking logs from rolling away as they are slowly consumed from below. A well-banked fire will smolder until the embers below consume the banking log above enough to form a gap that is too wide for combustion to continue; then it will simply die.

# THE TRENCH STOVE

When I was a kid, a practical lightweight backpack cookstove didn't exist, and all meals cooked in a wilderness were prepared over a wood fire. It was overkill to make a conventional campfire every time you wanted to heat beans and coffee for lunch. What hunters and hikers needed was a small source of concentrated heat that could be quickly lighted and easily extinguished without leaving a trace. This need was answered with simple affair known as the trench stove.

A trench stove begins with a narrow concave groove dug into the earth. Sometimes called a "boot heel stove, " because in softer soils it can be scraped out with a boot heel, this round-bottom slit is at least 6 inches deep at its center, 12 inches in length, and about 4 inches wide. Sides should be smooth and straight to help direct generated heat. Be sure to site your trench stove out of the wind and scrape away flammable materials around the trench to a distance of at least 1 foot, then use the dirt excavated from it to fashion a low fire break around the hole's perimeter. Lay a platform of dry finger-thick sticks side by side to form a floor at the trench bottom; this will shield your small cookfire from moisture in the soil.

Lay your tinder atop the fire bed and ignite it, then place a loose cone of very small kindling sticks tipi-fashion around the flame. Add larger kindling sticks as those below catch fire, but avoid adding too much wood too quickly, thus smothering the fledgling fire before it can become self-sustaining. When the bottom of the trench becomes covered with red coals, you're ready to cook.

Using a trench stove is like cooking with any liquid- or gas-fueled camping stove. Simply set your cookpot across the trench, where it is supported on both sides while its center is heated from below. The trench enables the fire to draft oxygen from either end, and permits adding more fuel from either side without disturbing the cookpot. Stir

Hibachis and barbecue grills can be pressed into service as urban cookstoves when public utilities stop working during a crisis.

frequently, because a trench stove generates considerable heat.

Extinguishing a trench stove is also simple; just scrape live embers and smoldering material to the center of the trench and refill the hole with the same dirt that came out of it. If possible, pour a liter or so of water onto the coals prior to refilling the trench, but even without this added insurance, the chance of a buried fire re-igniting is nil.

Finally, smooth over the fill dirt and sprinkle dead leaves, ferns, twigs, and other local debris onto the site. Sealing the stove beneath several inches of soil and camouflage makes residual food odors difficult for animals to detect, and hides visual evidence from people you might not want to know that you've been there.

## URBAN COOKFIRES

Urban and suburban survivalists can ensure that they have the means to cook and to boil water by including a charcoal-type barbecue grill or hibachi in their just-in-case outfits. Either of these cookers can be fueled by traditional charcoal briquets, or with dead wood from trees and shrubs. Do not use dismantled wood furniture for cooking food, because it inevitably contains lacquers, varnishes, glues, and other preservatives that are toxic when burned, and can impart an unpleasant taste to foods cooked over it. If you use charcoal, include a bottle of starting fluid in your kit. Barring that, the longer-burning briquets can be ignited by laying a small wood fire beneath them first.

Common-sense cautions when using a barbecue grill under emergency conditions include using the unit only in a well-ventilated area—never inside a dwelling—never building a fire too hot or too large. Never burn toxic materials like tarpaper or plastic, and keep the grill closed whenever possible.

Multifuel cookstoves designed for camping can burn gasoline, alcohol, even kerosene, but they should always be used outdoors.

# Water

## IMPORTANCE OF WATER

**D**rinking water is critical in any survival situation, because no one can live more than a few days without it. Water is necessary for cell reproduction, to flush toxins from the bloodstream, to maintain a functional body temperature in both hot and cold temperatures, and for proper digestion. The first symptom of dehydration is dark yellow urine often with a musky odor of concentrated toxins. Worsening symptoms include constipation caused by lack of lubricating fluids, diverticulitis with abdominal pain and nausea, then intestinal blockage with headache, fatigue, fever, and death from toxemia.

## WATER FROM PRECIPITATION

Rain or snow that falls through the smog cover of industrialized places is known to contain airborne pollutants like sulfuric acid, but no pathogenic organisms are known to exist in falling precipitation. The volume of precipitation collected can be increased by spreading a poncho or tarpaulin at a slight horizontal angle, then placing a vessel under its lowest point to catch runoff. Absorbent clothing—especially cotton—may be used to collect rain by wringing water from saturated fabric into a container.

No one lives more than a few increasingly miserable days without water, and there are a multitude of ailments that stem from not getting enough to drink.

Fresh snow is safe to use as drinking water, but "hardpack" snow that has laid on the ground for several days or longer, or ice covering bodies of water, may contain dormant and still-infectious parasites. To avoid gathering snow that might harbor parasites left there by or washed there from animal feces, take only the first 1–2 inches of powder for drinking water, and try to boil whatever snow you use for cooking or drinking purposes.

## THE DANGERS OF UNTREATED WATER

The Food and Drug Administration estimates that 370,000 Americans contract waterborne parasites annually, and the Center for Disease Control claims that 80 percent of us will be afflicted at least once within our lifetimes. Parasites are not exclusive to third-world nations, or to the poor, and they are much more common, and more easily contracted, than is generally believed.

Feces are the source of most parasites, whether aquatic or terrestrial. Most animals do not defecate directly into their own drinking water, but runoff from melting snow and rain guarantees that eggs (oocysts) from parasites will be washed into streams and lakes, just as they have evolved to do. Science is still discovering animals that live in a drop of natural water, but three that campers and backpackers in North America should be concerned with are *Giardia lamblia*, *Cryptosporidium parvum*, and *Cyclospora cayentanensis*. These digestive tract parasites remain infectious year-round and are not killed by freezing. In addition, the Fish and Wildlife Service has issued warnings that tapeworms, which are not aquatic, might still be contracted from waters on Lake Superior's Isle Royale National Park, their eggs washed there from infected wolf scats. In some tropical climes, you can add to these heart, liver, and lung flukes (worms) that even today kill thousands of people each year.

One in every thousand Americans contracts a waterborne parasite every year, and every case is a terrible, often dangerous experience that is best avoided.

The greatest human fear of waterborne pathogens stems from their microscopic size, and our inability to detect their presence. Not every sip of water harbors parasites, but all streams, ponds, and lakes contain them. Flowing water is not parasite-free, regardless of current speed or remoteness. The only safe natural water sources are spring heads, where subterranean water flows directly from the earth, and even then only at the source, before the spring has flowed far enough to be tainted by runoff from surrounding terrain.

Adding to the arcane nature of parasites, two or more hikers might drink from the same waters, and only one will become infected. Explanations could be that one did not ingest parasites, or that his or her immune system was strong enough to repel invaders before they could get a foothold in the intestines. Some people may become immune to parasites they've already survived—a good argument for maintaining a strong immune system—but even an adapted immune system can be overwhelmed if the number of parasites ingested is high.

Waterborne pathogens are not killed by freezing and can lie dormant for months encased in ice.

## CHEMICAL WATER DISINFECTANTS

Iodine tablets are still widely sold as water disinfectants in camping supply and army surplus stores, but they are not recommended for serious survival because they do not kill some of the most dangerous parasites. Iodine kills bacteria (typhoid, cholera), flagellates (giardia), and viruses (hepatitis), but not cysts (cryptosporidium) or flatworms (tapeworms)—the latter of which may be infectious as eggs, or as free-swimming flukes.

Most aquatic parasites are carried to water from infected feces by rain or snow runoff, and no body of water on earth is free of them.

31

While neither chlorine nor iodine are proof against some of the most common aquatic pathogens, chlorine-dioxide tablets can kill all dangerous organisms in water. (*Photo courtesy Katadyn USA*)

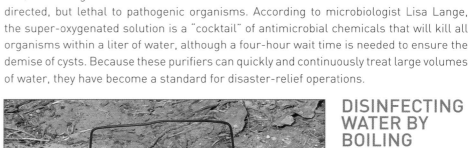

Chlorine—sometimes sold in the form of halazone tablets—kills viruses and bacteria, but not cysts or all flagellates.

Recently rendering both those chemicals obsolete as water treatments are chlorine dioxide tablets made from a cocktail of sodium chlorite and sodium dichloroisocyanurate dihydrate, like the Micropur MP1 tablets from Katadyn. Each Micropur tab treats 1 liter of water, killing giardia, bacteria, and viruses within fifteen minutes, but requires a four-hour wait to ensure the demise of tough cysts.

Similar to Micropur tablets is the new electro-chemical purifier, like MSR's MIOX, which promises "municipal-grade" water in the field. The MIOX uses watch batteries to ionize a chamber filled with untreated water and salt, converting those elements to chemicals that are safe for humans once diluted as directed, but lethal to pathogenic organisms. According to microbiologist Lisa Lange, the super-oxygenated solution is a "cocktail" of antimicrobial chemicals that will kill all organisms within a liter of water, although a four-hour wait time is needed to ensure the demise of cysts. Because these purifiers can quickly and continuously treat large volumes of water, they have become a standard for disaster-relief operations.

Almost the stuff of science fiction, MSR's MIOX purifier uses untreated water, ordinary salt, and electrical current from wafer batteries to create a super-chlorinated cocktail that is lethal to all harmful organisms in natural water.

## DISINFECTING WATER BY BOILING

An age-old method of killing all aquatic patho-

Boiling suspect water has always worked to kill harmful pathogens, but does not reduce or remove heavy metals or chemicals that contaminate the groundwater of many urban places.

gens is to heat the water they inhabit to a rolling boil for one minute. In reality, virtually every organism will be killed before the water reaches 180 degrees Fahrenheit, but the boiling point of 212 degrees provides visual confirmation that a lethal temperature has been reached. The Environmental Protection Agency (www.epa.gov) confirms that even heat resistant hepatitis viruses (rarely encountered in nature) are killed after boiling for one minute.

## WATER FILTERS

The downside of treating water with chemicals or with heat is that neither removes or reduces toxins. Germs and parasites can be made harmless by killing them, but in the aftermath of a disaster, it can be expected that even natural waters will be polluted with heavy metals, fertilizers, pesticides, and petrochemicals. The most convenient tool for addressing this problem is a backpack-type water filter, and I believe one of these should be in every kitchen and automobile, as well as in every backpack.

Invented almost a century ago, the portable water filter has truly come into its own only in recent years.

The simplest explanation of what a water filter does is that it uses external pressure to force raw water through a semi-permeable cartridge whose pores are too small for bacteria and parasitic organisms to penetrate—a process known as "reverse osmosis." Some do this with a two-stage pump that draws in raw water, then drives it through a filter cartridge; some do it by squeezing water contained in a flexible bottle through a filter; some use the force of gravity to filter water under its own weight. Some have ceramic filter cartridges, and some are made from paper and fiberglass. All water filters are manufactured following EPA guidelines that require they remove bacteria, cysts, and flagellates, and that they also strain out up to 80 percent of harmful chemicals. They do not remove sub-microscopic viruses, but these are seldom encountered away from

Disassembled for drying after a trip afield, MSR's MiniWorks water filter with long-lived ceramic cartridge is representative of the reliable simplicity that makes modern water filters a must-have in the home and the backpack.

civilization and are easily killed by additional treatment with chlorine or iodine. Some water filter kits include viricide chemicals, either in a stage of the water filter itself, or in a separate bottle.

Which filter is best depends on the anticipated need. Paper-filter models are least expensive, and slowest to clog because of increased surface area, but they have an average life of 200 gallons. Ceramic filters are much easier to clog with silt, but the unit can be disassembled, the filter cleaned, and the filter returned to service in a couple of minutes; ceramic filters have an almost infinite use life (they do not need to be scrubbed with the abrasive pad provided to clean them), but can break if dropped onto a hard

Simplest and lightest of portable water filters is the personal all-in-one squeeze bottle type; just fill it with untreated water, and squeeze potable water from the drinking spout.

surface. Squeeze-bottle filters are excellent for traveling light, fast, or—especially—by small boat, because you simply dip the bottle into raw water, screw on the cap with attached filter cartridge, and squeeze the bottle to obtain potable water from its drinking tube.

## DISTILLED WATER

Distilled water is the result of using heat to evaporate raw water into its two component gases, hydrogen and oxygen, then channeling those gases into a confined space where they cool, recombine, and condense back into water. Being lighter than particulate

The Katadyn Combi is one example of a high-volume, ceramic-element portable water filter that is suited for groups, but can also be fitted to kitchen faucets should municipal water become unsafe to drink.

matter, the component gases rise alone, leaving everything else behind, then re-mix to form pure water after cooling. The advantage of a water still is that it can transform seawater, sewer-fouled flood waters, extremely toxic coolant from automobile radiators, scummy pond water, even mud, into potable water.

## BASIC SOLAR STILL

The simplest distillation device, manufactured solar stills have long been standard equipment for U.S. Navy life rafts, and they have been recommended in virtually every wilderness survival manual in print. A solar still uses the sun's warmth to evaporate untreated water, trapping its component gases against a transparent or

translucent waterproof membrane. There they cool and condense back into water, which drips into a container below.

A solar still can be as uncomplicated as digging a hole in the ground, setting a metal soup can at its bottom, and covering the hole with a sheet of clear plastic. As daytime temperatures cool after sunset, oxygen and hydrogen trapped by the plastic membrane condense against its underside. A weight (stone) placed in the membrane's center makes it cone-shaped, and gravity causes condensed droplets to slide downward into the container below.

A solar still is most effective when constructed with a clear plastic membrane that permits maximum sunlight to penetrate, and it works best in arid conditions, where air isn't saturated by evaporated moisture. Under desert conditions (hot, dry days and cool nights), a solar still—or several of them—can keep a person alive.

Whether heated by the sun or over a low fire (metal cans only), condensation stills can be made from just a 6-foot length of hose and almost any spouted bottle or container—including 2-liter soda bottles—and any of these will deliver a constant supply of drinking water.

## CONDENSATION STILLS

A more efficient variation of the basic solar still is the solar condensation still. Start by filling an enclosed container—a metal or plastic gasoline or jerry can with a pour spout is ideal—half full of contaminated water, leaving sufficient air space to allow maximum

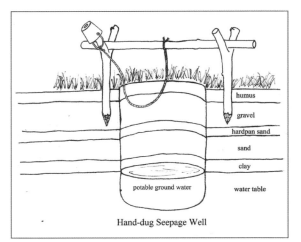

Hand-dug Seepage Well

A seepage well is simply a hole dug straight down to the water table.

condensation. Slide a 4- to 6-foot section of garden hose over the can's pour spot; in most instances the hose will fit snugly without modification, but it may be taped or hose-clamped to the spout to help ensure that no vapors can escape except through the open end of the hose. Wrap the hose into a single coil, tying or taping it to hold that form. Make sure that the coil is at the bottom (see illustration) to permit gravity to trap any heavier-than-air particles that might somehow be forced into the hose. Finally, set the half-full container onto a roof, or any other sunny, hot surface, and place the end of the hose into a container.

# HEATED CONDENSATION STILL

A solar still is passive, reliant on sunlight and humidity levels, but a heated condensation still uses applied heat to actively evaporate contaminated water, enabling it to continuously produce drinking water. This condensation still is fundamentally the same as the solar type, except that it requires a steel gasoline-type can because it uses the heat of a low fire to actively evaporate raw water. Again, the can's pour spout serves as an output for condensed water, and should be lengthened with a garden-hose extension that is long enough to accommodate a loop for trapping particles that might be forced into the hose by heat.

Because it can operate nonstop twenty-four hours a day for as long as fuel and raw water are available, a heated condensation still is ideal for producing drinking water for a group. Safety warnings include never heating water to a boil, and never permitting the container to go dry; either could cause unsafe pressures to develop inside the container, causing it to split at its seam, or even to explode. If the can begins to bulge even slightly, remove it from heat immediately.

## SEEPAGE WELLS

More than one piece of survival literature advises

Two L-shaped wires set into PVC tubes and held parallel to the ground cross one another when passing over underground water sources where it might be suitable to dig or drive a well.

that it's better to drink untreated water than to die of thirst. That's debatable; petrochemicals and other toxins found in urban floodwaters can cause serious illness by themselves, and having a parasite under conditions that already tax bodily resources to the limit can be lethal. The best course of action is to suffer neither malady.

Seepage wells have been used since the first human settlements were built. Known in lore as a village well, the nexus of community gossip, or in fables as a "wishing well," the seepage well is simply a hole dug straight down to the water table. Like a springhead, water that fills the bottom of the well pit is cold and potable because it has been filtered through many tons and feet of soil where no parasitic organisms can live.

Essentially a stout hollow nail with screened intake ports, the typical well point provides access to subterranean water at depths to and exceeding 50 feet.

Only a few generations have passed since the phrase "colder than a well-digger's ass" had genuine meaning to people who heard it, and although well diggers might have gone the way of the telegraph, the practice of digging a well is as viable today as it ever was. Even the most urban vacant lot in New York City can yield water if you can dig down to it. The trick is to find a place where water is close to the surface, and not inaccessible under bedrock or another impenetrable layer.

For those who have the gift, a "divining rod" of two steel wires (e.g., coat hanger wire) bent into L shapes and held horizontal to the ground will indicate where water is close to the surface by crossing over one another to form an X. No one can explain why divination works, or why it works for some people and not others (it doesn't work for me), but I've witnessed more than a few well drillers find water this way. Barring that, look for clues like birch trees, horsetails, or other plants that must grow where water is close to the surface.

If you're near to a lake or stream, creating a seepage well is as simple as digging a hole straight down at a distance of no less than two meters from the water's edge. Topsoil that might be contaminated with feces and terrestrial parasites (tapeworms, hookworms, et al.) should be tossed well away from the hole to prevent contaminants from falling inside. When the hole begins to fill with water, continue digging until you've created a pool deep enough to dip water from without stirring mud from the bottom.

Water that fills a seepage well is safe to drink immediately, but in finer soils it might take a full day for sediment to settle. While it may be free of parasites, most people cannot drink muddy water without triggering their gag reflex, so until the water clears you will need to strain it through a cloth—a handkerchief, T-shirt, or sock. Also bear in mind

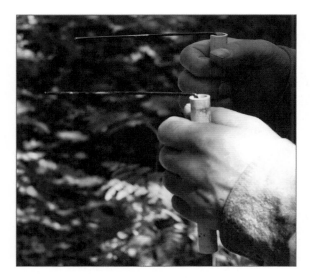

The physics behind why "divining" for buried water is successful are still unexplained, but the method has been finding good well sites for many centuries, and is still in use today.

that in agricultural and industrial areas there can be toxins in the water table that have leached there from the surface.

When creating a permanent seepage well, as at a cabin or long-term campsite, it will become necessary to build a wall around its opening to keep out frogs and rodents that will inevitably fall in, drown, and foul its waters. It will also need a roof to keep out bird droppings, and the potential parasites that they carry. These are the reasons that traditional village or "wishing" wells were walled and roofed.

Should an open-pit seepage well become fouled, it can be emptied of tainted water, and allowed to refill with freshwater. As bucket-brigade firefighters of old often discovered the hard way, taking too much water too quickly from even a reliable seepage well can cause it to go dry temporarily. By repeatedly pulling buckets of water from the pit, you can effectively replace bad water with fresh water, and if necessary, dig more sand from the bottom of the well to deepen it before it refills.

## DRIVING YOUR OWN FRESHWATER WELL

An improved version of the open seepage well is the driven well. In its simplest form, this method of bringing safe groundwater to the surface uses a pointed, rocket-shaped "well point" to drive downward through soil until it reaches the water table. The well point is hollow, with (usually) slotted holes along its barrel to allow water to flow into it. Inside, these holes are covered with a heavy mesh screen to keep out coarse sand and gravel.

With a hand-pump in your garden, you'll never run out of water.

A pilot hole for the well point is drilled using a steel hand-auger that screws into the earth while jamming loosened soil into its hollow body, and increasing the depth of a neat round hole 10 inches each time it is pulled up to be emptied.

The first step is to determine where will be the best place to sink your well—where the largest deposit of water lies nearest to the surface. The most time-honored method for determining that is through "divination" (mentioned briefly above). This unexplained yet remarkably effective means of locating subterranean water was once practiced by well-diggers using a y-shaped, green "twitch," preferably one made of willow. Water "witchers" would walk a selected area holding their branch twitches parallel to the earth; when the twitch began to vibrate or dip toward the earth of its own accord, there was water present underfoot. The more forceful the dips, the closer the water table.

Today's witchers tend to use a pair of L-shaped steel wires with equal-length sides about 6 inches long. To eliminate any chance of being influenced by the user, one side of each wire is placed inside a plastic PVC (water pipe) tube, and the tubes held vertical so that the free end of each wire is parallel to the ground. With tubes held at an even height with about 4 inches between them, the witcher walks his chosen area until the wires swivel toward one another and form an X. Below that X there is water close to the surface. The physics of water-witching have frustrated scientists for more than a century, but the fact is, it works, and the technique is still used by professional well drillers today.

There are several methods of getting a well point down to the water table, but the one most used by people in remote places today is the driving method, in which the point is driven downward like a nail. A nipple or pipe cap screwed snugly, but not tightly, onto the threaded end protects it from being damaged or deformed while being pounded from above. It is critical that neither the open end or the threads below it are harmed while the point is being pounded into the earth, or the end might not seal well with a mating coupling or the pump itself.

Begin by digging a pilot hole at least 2 feet deep using a hand auger or a shovel; the auger will make a pipe-size hole, but the wider shovel hole will require that soil be tamped around the well point to help hold it straight when pounding. A PVC casing placed over the well pipe—but kept above the point so that it doesn't inhibit water flow—keeps

loose dirt from falling in around the well pipe as it is driven downward.

Well hammers can be as simple as a sledge-hammer, or more preferably a large wooden mallet in softer soils. When punching through harder earth, some well drillers prefer a pile-driver weight (a pipe filled with concrete) suspended from a tripod from which it is hoisted upward, then dropped onto the capped well point. More physically demanding versions include "slam hammers" comprised of a heavy, flat-bottom iron weight with a long steel rod that extends from it and into the well pipe as a guide.

When the well point has been driven down until only about 10 inches remains above ground, remove the protective pipe cap and screw a 4-inch nipple (a collar with internal threads) over the exposed threads. Use pipe joint compound or Teflon plumber's tape (wound in the direction of the threads, clockwise) to ensure a watertight seal. Screw a 6-foot pipe that is threaded on both ends into the nipple—actual length of the pipe can vary, but it has to be short enough to reach the upper end (you'll probably want a step-ladder). Cap the upper end of the pipe, and pound it down until only about 10

Dropping a long, weighted string down the driven well pipe to test how far underwater a well point has penetrated.

inches remain above ground. Remove the cap, apply joint compound to the threads and screw on another nipple, then screw another length of pipe into the top of the nipple. Pound this pipe down, and repeat the process, making sure to seal every threaded connection with joint compound or Teflon tape.

The pipe should move visibly downward with each blow from your hammer. If it stops and refuses to sink farther after several blows, you

When a drop-string shows that the well-point is entirely submerged below the water table, attach, prime, and operate the pump until only clear water is produced.

might have hit a large rock. Do not continue hammering to force the pipe farther, or you might damage the well point. It's easier and safer to pull up the well point by gently wobbling the pipe back and forth to widen the hole as you pull upward, then to move the operation to another location.

When you reach the water table you will hear a hollow "bong" sound that issues from the pipe with every blow. To test it, remove the cap and drop a long string with a weight tied to its end (chalk line works well) down the well pipe until slack in the string tells you that the weight has reached the bottom of the well point. Draw the string back up, and measure how much of its length has been wetted to determine how deeply the well point has penetrated into the water table. To ensure good suction at the pump, it is important that the entire length of the perforated well point be immersed, and preferably at least 2 feet beyond that to account for seasonal variations in the water table.

When the drop-string is wetted to a length of at least 5 feet, it's time to screw on a pitcher pump (remember to seal the threads with pipe-dope or Teflon tape, or it might not draw efficiently). Prime the pump to create suction for its vacuum cylinder by pouring a cup of water into the pump's top, and jack the handle until water spurts from the pump with each downstroke. To be sure the well point is fully immersed in water, remove the pump, replace the cap, and hammer the pipe another 2 feet. Replace the pump, and jack the handle roughly 100 times to create a hollow filled with clear water around the well point. Alternately, you can use a portable electric water pump to create a water-filled cavity around the well point, and to test for a benchmark flow of 5 gallons per minute. When only clear water comes from the well spout, remove the pump and thread on a "check valve" between the well pipe below and the pump above; this will help to prevent water in the pipe from draining back down, reducing the need to prime the pump so often.

How deep your well needs to be of course depends on how deep the water table might be in a particular place. The depths to which manual pumps can operate is limited, depending on the type

Where ground water is untainted by chemicals leached from above, it will be drinkable directly from your well pump.

Dried, cracked silt-mud atop sand tells of water having recently been there, and the water table probably lies no more than a foot or two beneath the surface.

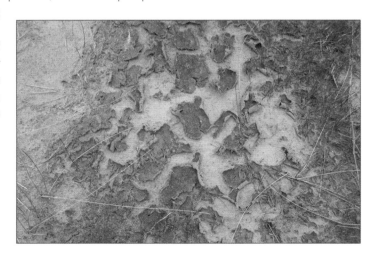

Coleman's propane-heated "Hot Water On Demand" unit is a very handy backup when utilities stop working, and there's even a shower attachment for personal hygiene and decontamination.

of pump, by the force of gravity and the length of its drawing stroke. In general, pitcher, jet, or centrifugal hand pumps are effective to a depth of 25 feet; larger stand pumps with draw cylinders will work to a depth of 50 feet.

Finally, check with authorities to be sure that there are no laws prohibiting wells where you live, and that the groundwater is not contaminated by toxic chemicals that have leached into it—this is not uncommon in more developed areas. Even where home wells are permitted, you will probably need to buy a building permit, and maybe have the finished well inspected and approved. Even with the red tape, a driven hand-pumped well is worth the hassle for the peace of mind it brings knowing that you can never run out of drinking water, come what may.

## DRIED WATER HOLES

African elephants know that places where water has pooled in the rainy season can still provide a life-sustaining drink. Low places where water had collected, from dusty river beds to ponds that have dried up under a hot summer sun, often have water just below their surfaces, protected from evaporation by an insulating layer of sand or dried mud. Digging down in a low spot at the bottom of a dried riverbed—usually identifiable as a ditch-like slot in the earth—will often reveal wet soil, and, beneath that, water. Look, too, for scales of dried mud that have cracked and curled upward from what had once been a pond bottom, or sand that has been arranged in concentric waves by lapping water that has since evaporated; you can often find water just a few inches below these places.

## WATER FROM TOILETS

Unless you have a water filter, mean to boil it, or both, avoid taking water from a toilet bowl, the way Hollywood shock-peddlers like to portray in their movies. The water in a toilet bowl—particularly the low-flow 1.6-gallon (6-liter) types, is probably not worth the effort to extract, and not worth the risk of disease it might carry.

The flush tank, however, is filled with tap water. It might have a slime of sediment, maybe even algae if it has been sitting for a while, but the water in it was safe to drink when it is filled. In fact, depending on the emergency—like chemical, biological, or nuclear fallout—the water in a covered toilet tank may be one of the safest sources of drinking water.

## WATER FROM HOT WATER HEATERS

Another safe source of potable water is the hot water tank found in nearly every home—including boilers found in apartment and commercial buildings. A typical residential hot water heater holds 50 gallons of water that is sealed from environmental contamination, and has already been heated to a temperature sufficient to kill most organisms. It might be necessary to filter drained water through a cloth to strain out lime and accumulated scale, but the water is potable without treatment.

## WATER FROM AUTOMOBILE RADIATORS

I watched a documentary on a respected channel that suggested emergency drinking water could be obtained from automobile radiators if it was strained through a cloth and then boiled. This small error is an example of how

Wide-mouthed bottles are better for use in freezing temperatures, because bottle necks can become blocked by ice.

survival instructors have a responsibility, a duty to their students to be correct, or else be silent. The diethylene glycol (DEG) and ethylene glycol used to make antifreeze are lethally toxic even in minute quantities, and there are slower-acting poisons from the lead-solder joints that seal radiators and their copper cores. Nor would I recommend trusting radiators containing "non-toxic" propylene glycol unless there were no alternatives. These poisons cannot be boiled away, or adequately removed by a backpack-type water filter. Unless you are going to distill it, water drained from the cooling or heating systems of any engine is not useful for making drinking water.

If you're thirsty, and you have water, drink it; hikers have died of dehydration while attempting to ration water. (*Photo courtesy Katadyn USA*)

## CANTEENS AND WATER BOTTLES

In a world where millions of resealeable, unbreakable, water-tight plastic containers are discarded every day, suitable canteens are everywhere. Chances are good of finding at least one beverage bottle in any car or truck, as well as garbage cans and dumpsters, and along roadways where some motorists incomprehensibly continue to toss empties from car windows. Wash bottles as thoroughly as possible, and use only food-grade containers, because plastics are in fact porous, and may absorb poisons that were in their original contents.

Storing water is one of the most critical, yet simplest and most inexpensive safeguards that anyone can take to prepare for almost any disaster.

Ready-made canteens include the G.I. 1-quart canteen, canvas case, and steel cup outfit that served well from World War II through the Vietnam War; this belt-carried system enables its owner to boil and cook with untreated water, then to transport it in a case that can be wetted to keep its contents about 20 degrees cooler than the outside air. Nalgene hiker bottles are lightweight and widemouthed to be better suited to freezing temps that block narrow spouts with ice. The newer stainless bottles also enable boiling of suspect water, but bottles and screw caps need to be tied together to be survival-ready. Or you might opt for a water bladder that can contain up to 2 liters of water, yet rolls up small enough to fit into a hip pocket when empty. Tips to remember with all of them is that half-filled canteens are advised in subfreezing temperatures, because sloshing water doesn't freeze easily; but remember too that the Vietnam War showed how the sloshing of a canteen can be heard by other people nearby.

In a real pinch, wetted rags, cotton clothing, even saturated foam rubber can be placed into a snack or other plastic bag. The bags themselves might not be sealed enough or sturdy enough to transport full of water, but absorbent material is kept saturated by impermeable plastic walls. To get a drink, focus a funnel from the bag opening into the mouth or into a container, and squeeze the bag to press water from the absorbent material inside.

## CONSERVING WATER

Never try to conserve drinking water, especially if your survival strategy entails traveling on foot. Desert hikers have been found dead of dehydration while carrying filled canteens, having denied themselves water until they were overcome by the effects of thirst and heat. Much like the cooling and heating systems of an automobile, a human

body cannot operate efficiently at reduced fluid levels, and forcing it to do so is flirting with potential breakdown of the whole machine. The best place to transport water is in your stomach, and the best strategy is to use what you need, then concentrate on finding more.

# STORING WATER

A person who must travel to escape from a civilization that is no longer inhabitable will need to know all of the aforementioned techniques for finding and purifying water, but storing water long term is a prudent strategy for remote cabins, seagoing boats, and even the most urban apartment. With cowardly terrorist threats looming over populated areas especially, most governments today recommend that their citizens store sufficient water and other commodities to endure several days without utilities. Having water on hand can be particularly critical in large cities, where an interruption of municipal utilities means loss of water not only for drinking, cooking, and bathing, but also for disposal of bodily wastes that can turn the most modern metropolis into a disease-ridden ghetto inside of a week.

Storing potable water is simple and virtually free; plain tap water has proved drinkable after eight years of storage in plastic fruit juice bottles in the corner of a basement. According to most survival authorities, basic drinking water requirements should be estimated at 2 gallons of water per person per day. In most instances an individual's bodily needs will range downward from there, but never forget that water is also needed for bathing—leprosy is one result of long-term lack of hygiene. Water will be needed for cooking and washing dishes, to refill toilet tanks for flushing, and for cleansing wounds. As vital as water is to life, and as critically scarce as it has proven to be in so many actual disasters, it would be difficult to have too much potable water stored.

Containers for storing water are many and inexpensive, or even free. Plastic jerry cans, usually colored blue to designate them as water cans, are made for water storage, and some even have spigot valves in their caps. Heavy-wall plastic juice jugs are ideal for water storage, and their smaller sizes ensure that only a small amount of water will be lost or contaminated if a container is breached; those same qualities make these containers well suited for use as canteens while traveling. Plastic soda bottles are acceptable for storing water but not as rugged. Avoid storing water in opaque plastic jugs, like those used for milk and some juices; these are extruded from a plastic that is made with corn starch to render the bottles biodegradable, and they will begin leaking in a few weeks. Never store water, or any consumable, in any plastic container that once held toxic substances; although they may be waterproof, plastics are actually porous, and most will absorb minute quantities of poisons stored in them.

Probably the best method of storing tap water is to fill a container with hot water right to the rim of its mouth, then screw its cap on snugly. As the already sterile hot water cools, it will contract minutely, creating a vacuum that ensures its contents cannot be contaminated, and effectively "canning" the water inside.

Raw water should of course be boiled or otherwise purified before storage. Again, filling storage bottles with hot (not boiling) water is most effective for sealing out contamination, and you can safely add three drops of tincture of iodine or chlorine bleach per liter to ensure the demise of bacteria or viruses. A simpler method is to drop a sodium chlorite tablet into each liter of raw water being stored to ensure that all pathogenic organisms inside are killed.

Stored drinking water should be kept in a cool, dry place, but there is no chance of algae or the growth of any other live organisms in containers that have been filled and sealed according to the preceding instructions. Cool, dry places (basements, closets) are probably the best storage spaces, but the only real concern is to prevent water from freezing, which could cause containers to split. Check water stores at least once a year, inspecting containers for leaks or damage, and replacing them as needed.

# Food

Some survival experts have claimed that because an average person will not die from starvation for more than two months, food is at the bottom of the list of survival priorities. I believe that it's a mistake to think in terms of sacrifice in any type of survival scenario. No one is too tough to die of thirst, hypothermia, or starvation, but almost everyone is already strong enough and tough enough to avoid falling victim to those problems.

I also believe that placing food at the bottom of the list is overly simplistic for other reasons. I've seen too many of my own survival students and companions become light-headed, and even faint, from the effects of low blood sugar (hypoglycemia), especially under challenging conditions, like cold rain or sub-zero windchills. One of those victims, my teenage nephew, fell unconscious into a blazing fire, and was saved from severe burns only by his saturated clothing.

## NUTRITIONAL NEEDS

In a modern world where diets have become a fashion in themselves and most of us have never known hunger beyond missing a meal or two, the real meaning of nutrition is muddled. Fat, for example, is a highly-prized nutritional requirement in the natural world, where animals and people do not suffer from arteriosclerosis caused by plaque buildup, which is caused by

Throughout history food has been highly valued, even worshipped, by humans, who knew that malnourishment was on the road to death.

eating more calories than a body burns as energy. Fat is coveted by wild predators, who crush skulls and bones of prey to eat fat-rich brains and marrow. It was valued by native tribes who ate buffalo fat even after it had gone rancid, and by frontiersmen who saved bacon fat for use as sandwich spread and called it "Indian butter." When the Lewis and Clark expedition ground to a halt in 1805, weak from dysentery and stomach pains, Sacajawea, the teenage Shoshone girl who accompanied them, melted their tallow (fat) candles in a pan and forced the men to drink the foul liquid; they felt better immediately. In a processed-food society, fat may be overused and a health hazard, but it is a critical component of the human diet, and you can't live for more than a few months without it.

Nor can we maintain the level of health needed to face tough times without proper vitamins. Sailors of old learned to include large amounts of citrus fruits in their ships' stores to ward off scurvy, a vitamin C deficiency that manifests itself with pain, internal bleeding, and weakened immune systems. Almost unheard of in the modern world, scurvy can occur after just a week or so without vitamin C, depending on how much is in a victim's system at the onset, and it is a potential problem for anyone in a survival situation. Fortunately, it is easily prevented, and cured, with a regular intake of food plants that are high in vitamin C.

Beriberi is a potentially serious illness caused by a deficiency of vitamin $B_1$ (thiamine). There are two major types of beriberi: Dry beriberi and the related Wernicke-Korsakoff syndrome cause damage to a victim's nervous system, with symptoms including difficulty speaking, inability to think, general pain, difficulty walking, numbness in extremities, uncontrollable eye movements, and vomiting. Wet beriberi symptoms include shortness of breath, increased heart rate, edema of the lower legs, and possibly heart attack. Drinking alcohol and high volumes of diuretics like coffee and tea can leach $B_1$ from the bloodstream.

Rickets is a softening or weakening of bones caused by insufficient intake of vitamin D, calcium, or phosphate. Vegetarian diets are known to be vitamin D deficient, and nursing mothers should be aware that breast milk does not contain sufficient levels of D to ward off childhood rickets (called osteomalacia). The human body can photosynthesize vitamin D from sunlight, which helps to explain the increased incidence of rickets among jail and prison inmates, miners, and factory workers who see little or no sunshine. An active outdoor lifestyle and a diet that includes dairy products are good defenses against brittle bones.

These are only a few of the ailments that occur from prolonged malnutrition—not to be confused with starvation, because victims of these and other deficiency-related illnesses have at times had plenty to eat, but did not have a diet that provided all the nutrients their bodies needed to maintain good health. The obvious preventative strategy is to be physically active, and to eat an omnivorous diet that includes vegetables and fruits, fish, poultry, and red meat. Readers should also be prepared for an indeterminate period of isolation, like being sealed inside a house with window and door sills duct-taped against radioactive or biological fallout. Having a broad range of food stores is prudent, but probably the most inexpensive guarantee of avoiding ailments caused by nutrient deficiencies is to include one to several bottles of over-the-counter multivitamin supplements, such as Centrum or One-A-Day.

## CANNED SURVIVAL FOODS

Although they could not have known the wealth of nutritional and other information that has since become common knowledge, the generation of Americans who lived through the Great Depression were probably the most capable survivors the world has seen. Those were hard times, when jobs and manufactured goods were both in short supply. Fortunately, most Americans were farmers then, and almost everyone knew how to hunt or grow edibles, then can, dry, or smoke them for long-term storage.

Even today there are rural places where grandmas fetch jars of freshly canned vegetables, fish, even meats from their root cellars. These people aren't any more paranoid than survivors of the Great Depression, and most don't anticipate that society will unravel; they are just people who've learned that it's smart to have a few meals on hand should the road to town get buried under snow, washed out by floods, or blocked by fallen trees. They understand from experience how unstable the luxuries so many of us take for granted really are, and they know the value of being prepared when you can't just go shopping for more of anything.

Canned foods are ideal for home survival pantries. At this time they are cheap, compact, durable, and have a verified storage life of at least

With a known shelf life of at least 25 years for most products, canned goods are the simplest and most economical means to ensure that even a high-rise urban apartment can contain a store of nutritious foods.

a quarter-century. Where I live, it's a way of life for year-round residents to store cases of canned foods each autumn, in preparation for winters that routinely exceed 20 feet of snowfall, and blizzards so intense that government snowplows are often withdrawn until skies clear. Many supermarkets run autumn case sales, in which twenty-four-can cases are offered at sometimes deeply discounted prices, and these are perhaps the ideal method for stockpiling canned goods. Alternately, you might opt to just add an extra can or two to your list each time you go shopping, then stash those away.

## STORING CANNED GOODS

Stored in a cool, dry place, as directed on their labels, today's rust-resistant, steel cans are lined with a polyethylene plastic, and more hermetically sealed than ever. For the sake of convenience, and as an added layer of protection, canned foods may be organized inside sealed plastic bags. Isolating cans this way helps to protect paper labels that

are notorious for coming off during long-term storage, and especially from floodwaters that are almost guaranteed to remove them, making it impossible to tell sweet peas from peaches. Confusion can be averted by labeling containers with permanent marker—GB for green beans, AS for applesauce, and so on. Some of the best storage containers are plastic "tote" boxes with snap-down covers, available at most department stores; these are available in different colors, allowing contents to be identified at a glance, they stack well, transport easily, and some can contain more than a hundred cans.

Double-protecting canned or dry foods, toilet tissue, clothing, and other items in a plastic snap-lid tote box or inside a tough plastic drum helps to ensure that they can weather most disasters intact.

## HAZARDS IN CANNED FOODS

A danger you need to be aware of when stockpiling canned goods is spoilage that might occur when the seal of a can is breached, exposing its contents to the outside and creating poisons that might not be detectable by smell or taste. One of the deadliest is a toxic protein created by the growth of *Clostridium botulinum* spores. Others are decay-borne bacteria like listeria and salmonella. Most organisms are killed by boiling at 100 degrees Celsius (212 degrees Fahrenheit), but the "exotoxin" that persists after botulism spores have been killed by heat can only be rendered harmless by a temperature of at least 350 degrees Fahrenheit.

When opening a can or jar of food for the first time, the interior should be a vacuum, and it should make a small sucking sound when its seal is broken—someone once referred to this sound as a "kiss of freshness." Be wary of cans that are dented, especially around their crimp-sealed rims. Tomato products that have gone bad are usually easy to spot, because they decay quickly and create internal gas pressure where there should be a vacuum, and contents typically flow out of a container when its lid is perforated. Never consume the contents of any jar or can that exhibits signs of internal pressure; jar lids should be concave (sucked inward) at their centers, never popped upward, and metal cans should never be bloated, with walls or ends bulging outward.

# HOME CANNING

Credit for discovering the secret of canning fresh-cooked foods to keep them edible for long periods is often given to French troops fighting during the Crimean War in the 1850s. Forced to march long distances across the Russian frontier with inadequate supply lines, French soldiers hurriedly dipped boiling soup from a camp cauldron and into wine bottles. To their surprise, soup in the corked bottles remained unspoiled for weeks under hot sun, and the science of canning food was born. Soon every rural family was bottling boiling-hot garden produce, meats, and fish in glass canning jars sealed with wax and screw-down lids as fare to see them through future lean times.

As canning evolved, it included pressure-cookers that enabled food in open jars to be super-heated beyond the 212-degrees Fahrenheit boiling point before they were sealed. When refrigeration wasn't possible and there were several days' worth of canning to be done, it was important to achieve such elevated temperatures to guard against botulism.

An expedient pressure cooker for super-heating foods can be made by placing a heavy skillet or other weight atop a covered pot.

My own experiments using fresh-cooked chili and soups have borne out what French troops learned so long ago. Even without a pressure cooker, boiling-hot foods ladled into jars—including pickle jars and other re-used bottles—have remained edible after three months (probably longer) of storage on an open-air shelf at room temperature.

Lightweight and compact, dried foods can serve as survival fare in a static setting, but are also ideal for traveling, especially on foot.

The key, as with any canned goods, is to achieve a vacuum-seal that sucks in the center of the jar's lid after cooling.

# DRIED FOODS

Dried foods are another recommended option for the home disaster-survival kit. Like canned goods, dry goods can have an almost indefinite storage life. Dried victuals don't have the added weight of water, and that means they can also serve as bug-out foods when a situation dictates packing up whatever you can carry and heading for a friendlier location. Generally speaking, one pound of dried food will supply adequate nutrition for one person for one day.

# RICE

Rice is the primary staple food for more than half of earth's human population, and the seeds of this aquatic grass have been proven in combat to be a first-rate survival food. Among the numerous vitamins and minerals contained in this humble grain are 130 calories and 2.4 grams of protein per 100 grams of rice. For up to several weeks an average person could remain healthy eating nothing but boiled rice—a fact borne out by thousands of tough Viet Cong soldiers in the 1960s and 1970s. The real beauty of rice as survival fare has always been its compatibility with virtually any other food, whether it be fresh fruits, foraged wild vegetables, fish, or meat. If you want to overcome rice's lack of vitamin C, for example, add wild blueberries or plantains. Kept dry and sealed in an airtight container, rice has remained edible for more than six years.

# BEANS

Beans are another top-notch survival food, and these dried bipolar seeds are even more nutritious than rice. A 100-gram portion of pinto beans provides 347 calories and more than 21 grams of protein—beans are one of the richest sources of protein in the vegetable kingdom. Although not as compatible with fruits and seafood as rice, beans are a great base for dishes with meat and vegetables. Personal experiences with red, black, pinto, navy, and kidney beans, and also split peas, have shown that when these dried seeds are contained inside watertight packages and stored as directed in a cool, dry place, shelf life is more than ten years (as long as I've ever stored them).

## PASTA

Pasta is another great lightweight option. A 100-gram serving contains 357 calories and 7.5 grams of protein. Make that pasta a box of macaroni-and-cheese, and the same serving size yields 368 calories with 15 grams of protein. One problem, as many backpackers can attest, is that pasta is typically packaged in cardboard boxes that offer little protection from the elements; after a few months in a backpack, macaroni changes from a healthy amber color to a sickly gray. Shelf life can be greatly increased by repackaging macaroni-and-cheese and other pastas into zip-lock freezer bags—with a moisture-absorbing silica-gel packet in each bag.

Pasta is a tasty and nutritious candidate for the disaster-survival larder, but cardboard packaging is not suited to long-term storage.

## DEHYDRATED POTATOES

The dehydrated scalloped and au gratin sliced potatoes found in almost every grocery store are tasty, nutritious, ultralight, and often overlooked survival foods. Providing 314 calories and 8.9 grams of protein per 100 grams, these have been a welcome addition to backpack fare for more than a decade, and are often mixed with wild vegetables and meats

to make them a complete meal. The cardboard boxes that contain them hold a hermetically-sealed plastic bag of sliced, dried potatoes, and a paper-foil packet of powder flavoring. Paper-foil packets are usually marked to identify their flavors, but if this is illegible or missing, mark the flavor on them with a permanent marker. The paper-foil packet does not stand up well to water, so both of the contents' packages are best removed from their box and stored inside a zip-lock plastic bag.

## BULK FOODS

Buying foods in bulk can be a money-saving method of stocking a survival pantry, but take a lesson from history. Early ocean-going sailing

ships, homesteaders, and wintering trappers all bought coffee, salt, flour, and other fare in quantities large enough to last through long periods when no re-supply was possible. Unfortunately, burlap, cheesecloth, and crockery offered poor protection against spoilage or infestation, and the history books are replete with sailors and backwoodsmen who were forced to eat weevil-ridden bread, or worse.

Today we discard as trash airtight, waterproof containers that long-term survivors of old would have paid almost any price to obtain, and these are ideal for reducing large volumes of food that were bought cheaply in bulk to more manageable portions. Wide-mouthed salsa bottles made of clear plastic are ideal for beans or macaroni; soda bottles filled with rice (use a funnel) are lightweight and permit easy metering when pouring out just enough of the grain for a meal. These and a wealth of throwaway containers like them can serve to make a large sack of flour transportable on foot, and having food stores individually portioned in a stationary setting helps to ensure that not all of them will be lost or contaminated should some unforeseen disaster occur.

## ESTIMATING FOOD NEEDS

Estimate the amount of food you have on hand using the 2,000-calories-per-day rule of thumb, and mix up meals to make them less boring, but also to help ensure that vitamins and minerals meet minimum daily requirements, as established by the Food and Drug Administration. Small cans are better for storage than large cans, because you lose less if one of them is damaged. How much food you keep on hand is a personal decision. The Office of Homeland Security has advised at least three days for each person in a household, because the Federal Emergency Management Agency figures that is the average time that it takes to restore goods and services to a stricken community. Some folks—me among them—think that might be a little too conservative (but then, grocery shopping for our household is a 130-mile round trip). It would be hard to have too much food stashed, but it's easy to not have enough, and by the time you need it, more might not be available. Besides, I kinda like knowing that I can help out a hungry neighbor, even one who right now thinks I'm a little paranoid.

## WILD FOODS

While I've never been too long away from the northern forests where I grew up, I went through a fairly typical nomadic phase as a young man. I spent one summer working for a steel-drum refurbishing company in Grand Rapids, Michigan, and even then, in the early 1980s, the city was a vastly different world than the one I'd known up north. It probably made a difference that my rented room was on the city's south side, where drug peddlers and homeless people sleeping in alleys mingled with three-piece suits on the edge of high rises and prosperity.

One feature that burned itself into my memory was the sight of famished "street people" lined up each day at noon and supper time in front of an obscure door that was marked only by small neon crucifix, waiting to get a hot dog or sandwich. Whatever else those people might have been, they were hungry, and they were fellow Americans. Most disturbing to me, these malnourished citizens whose very lives depended on handouts and charity were going hungry in the midst of a crop of wild vegetables sufficient to feed them all.

Cooking foods with a small amount of wood ashes helps to enhance their digestibility by breaking down proteins into usable amino acids.

## ENHANCING DIGESTIBILITY

It has been a practice among American Indians to add a handful of wood ashes to large pots of stew and other cooked dishes. The elements in wood ash help to break down complex proteins that are mostly indigestible to the human gut, which explains why the original recipe for hominy was to boil corn in water mixed with wood ash, and why many brands of dog kibble include wood ash in their lists of ingredients. By reducing tough vegetable fibers to usable amino acids from which our bodies can extract nutrition, even the roughest of non-toxic wild plants can be made to have at least some food value. For years I've routinely added a teaspoon of ashes from the cookfire per quart of boiling food when cooking for myself or for survival classes, but there are no officially sanctioned dosages.

## PLANTAINS

One of the most obvious and plentiful edible wild plants is a weed known as greater plantain or common plantain (*Plantago major*) that grows from almost every patch of dirt all over North America and Europe, and even from cracks in concrete and asphalt. This bane of gardeners and suburban lawn tenders everywhere was intentionally transported to North America from Eurasia half a millennium ago to serve as a fast-growing vegetable, and it has since established itself virtually everywhere. Able to thrive in the poorest soil, and in almost

Mature plantain with erect seed pods is a virtual multivitamin, and a respected home remedy for insects stings and bites, as well as poison ivy.

Rhubarb-like leaves of the plantain plant are rich in vitamins and iron, but are a little stringy, and best served boiled or steamed.

any climate, plantain is one of the fastest growing ground plants; a mature plant that is cut off at the roots will begin to replace itself with a whorl of new leaves within forty-eight hours.

Nutritionally, plantain is equally amazing. Closely related to spinach, plantain leaves are rich in vitamins A, C, several B vitamins, and iron. A 100-gram portion contains 510 calories, 1.30 grams of protein, and a broad spectrum of other dietary nutrients. When the plant matures, stalk-like seed pods that rise from its center are loaded with B vitamins. Taken as a whole, plantain is an almost complete multivitamin, including easily assimilated plant sugars (glucose and sucrose) and fiber. Some authorities have suggested that eating the seed pods will also bolster the body's natural insect-repellant skin oils with $B_{12}$, which is distasteful to biting bugs.

Plantains may be eaten uncooked, but adult leaves tend to be a little stringy, and seed pods are a bit tough. Preparation is as simple as boiling washed plants until tender, then serving the leaves as you would spinach, or the seed pods as you might green beans or asparagus. A little apple vinegar helps to liven the taste of cooked leaves, and I like them served hot with butter, salt, and pepper. Seed pods are good in stews and soups, stir-fry, or with melted cheese over them.

The value of plantain isn't limited to its culinary uses. An old and proven effective medicinal use of the crushed leaves is as a poultice bandaged directly onto bee and scorpion stings, spider and centipede bites, and infected lacerations. In non-sanctioned experiments with poison ivy sufferers, plantain poultices brought immediate relief from itching almost 100 percent of the time, although treatments needed to be repeated several times. Modern medicine has been somewhat reluctant to identify just how a poultice of plantain leaves draws out venom and infection, but the plant has been a useful home remedy for many generations.

Maybe best of all, common plantain is not only hardy enough to sprout up from cracks in asphalt and concrete, even gravel roadsides, it but also can tolerate a wide variety of climates. Plantains can be found in open places from Alaska through Mexico, from swamps to

Common plantain as it often appears in shaded swamps; the extra-long leaf stems reveal that this plant is stretching to reach sunlight.

semi-arid deserts. All of these qualities taken together make common plantain one of the first wild plants a survivor should learn to recognize and use.

## BRACKEN FERN

In the New World, one of the more important yet unsung plants that helped both native Americans and European immigrants to get along in the colossal forests of North America was the lowly bracken fern (*Pteridium aquilinum*). Native to nearly every wooded environment from Canada to Mexico, this abundant forest dweller is one of the most common summer sights on this continent.

The bracken fern is a true multi-purpose plant. From early spring to early summer, bracken fern shoots—called "fiddleheads" because the undeveloped foliage at the sprout's top resembles the ornately carved tuning end of a fine violin—are abundant wherever the plants grow. So long as the sprout's stem snaps crisply when you break it off, a fiddlehead can be used as food. Fiddleheads have an agreeable taste, similar to green beans. They're tender enough to be eaten raw, but have a slimy core that some people (me) find objectionable. Boiling takes away the sliminess, and makes shoots even more like green beans—I've served boiled fiddleheads in soups and other dishes, and no one has ever noticed until I pointed them out.

One of my favorite ways to prepare fiddleheads is to fry them in butter until the stems turn dark, and then serve them with salt and pepper. Or you might use the fried fiddleheads in an omelette, as a garnish for a baked potato, or in a gravy. You can even substitute fiddleheads for green beans in a green bean casserole.

One belief concerning fiddleheads as food is the practice of early tribal Americans to eat only boiled fiddleheads for three days before a hunt. Native Americans believed that saturating the body's digestive and other systems with whatever essences might be contained in bracken fern sprouts would remove body odors and make hunters undetectable by smell. There's no scientific data to back up that belief—no scientist has ever tested it—but the belief was widespread among tribes who'd had several millennia to try it.

Abundant in woodlands across America, bracken fern shoots, or "fiddleheads," have been a favored spring vegetable since before recorded history.

When a fern's fiddlehead is ripe for eating, it snaps off cleanly when bent.

Historians tell us that bracken fern roots were also eaten by Native Americans. The hardy black-barked roots extend horizontally several inches underground, and may support more than a half-dozen ferns per root—you can't wipe out a fern population by picking all of its fiddlehead sprouts. Reportedly, the rhizomes (roots) were roasted and eaten like hard bread sticks, or pounded into flour and used to make a bread dough.

Being food isn't the only service bracken ferns can render. Survival instructors agree that bracken ferns are just about the best bedding material, should you have to spend an unscheduled night in the woods without gear. Adult bracken fern foliage is toxic to livestock if eaten in large quantities—it contains an enzyme that destroys thiamine reserves—and that might also explain why a bed of brackens seems to be bug-free. Being plentiful wherever they grow allows survivors to lay a thick, soft bed that keeps body heat from being absorbed into the ground, and even to burrow into a pile of them, like a well-insulated coccoon, on a cold night. And stuffing wadded ferns into the torso and sleeves of a light jacket that you're wearing definitely decreases the amount of body heat lost through it.

In foul weather that makes building shelter a necessity, there's no better roof covering than adult brackens. Bundles of them placed stems-up in overlapping shingle-fashion (from bottom to top) will shed rain very well, block heat-stealing winds, and keep snow off while you sleep. An added bonus is that bracken ferns—even dry brown ones—aren't very flammable, and are unlikely to catch if a hot ember from your fire pops onto the shelter's roof.

Even though brackens don't make good tinder for building a fire, they can serve as an effective repellant against mosquitoes and biting flies. Armfuls of them thrown atop a campfire produce thick plumes of

Easy to identify by their long, unbranched stalks and frilly umbrella-like foliage, mature brackens are not edible, but there's no better bedding or shelter cover.

pleasant-smelling smoke that causes the most voracious insects to flee. This is also an excellent means of signaling overhead aircraft, should you be in need of rescue.

A word of warning: When gathering bracken ferns for any purpose, wear gloves, or barring that, cut stems with a knife. Do not pull against the stems barehanded, because they're comprised of rough, razor-sharp fibers that are guaranteed to cut your fingers—like a paper cut on steroids.

## BROADLEAF CATTAIL

The broadleaf, or common cattail, (*Typha latifolia*) is a wild edible that can be found along the shorelines of rivers, ponds, and marshes every month of the year. The tall, reed-like flower stalk with vertical green leaves that resemble giant blades of grass is familiar to most people, and easily recognizable in any season. Cattails grow in no more than a few inches of water, and in snow country their dead stalks and fluffy tufting seedheads have been used to help determine the safest places to walk on frozen waterways.

The edible parts of the cattail plant are its root, the whitish cores of young shoots, the green cigar-shaped seedhead that tops the long, straight stem in early summer, and heavy yellow pollen dust shaken from the spike-like flower atop the mature seedhead in mid to late summer. Young shoots sprout from the dormant root in early spring, even pushing

Found along freshwater shorelines across America, the common cattail has a long history as a survival food, as fiber for rope, and for weaving baskets.

upward through snow; by driving an index finger down into the mud alongside the sprout, then gripping the plat plant from above using the other three fingers, you can snap it sideways and break off the shoot above the root, which will then sprout another plant. Peel

New-grown spring cattail roots have been likened to potatoes, becoming tough and fibrous (but still marginally edible) in winter.

Dry reindeer moss crunches underfoot when you walk on it and is very flammable.

away the tough, fibrous leaves (themselves a good source of fiber for making rope), and the whitish cores can be eaten raw, boiled as an ingredient in other dishes, or steamed to create a dish known as "Russian asparagus." The raw shoots are crispy and pleasant-tasting, with a flavor that might be described as between celery and water chestnuts.

Rootstocks of the cattail can be eaten raw or boiled any time of the year, but only the new, tender taproots in spring actually bear resemblance to a vegetable. In winter the roots become tough and woody; some have likened them to potatoes, but there is little similarity beyond the fact that both contain starch. Winter rootstocks are moderately nutritious and generally palatable after boiling; probably the best way to prepare them as survival food is to roast or boil them for a half hour, then chew them up, swallowing what seems edible, and spitting out the rest.

Green, boiled seedheads are also considered survival fare. Usually roasted or boiled, the soft seed-bearing flesh is eaten like corn on the cob, down to the hard, hollow stem in their centers. Cooked seedheads are nutritious and digestible, but the taste is not one that makes most people want seconds, and the texture of the seedlings, which come apart when chewed, is only tolerable.

From May to July, male cattails produce large pollen-bearing spikes that rise from the center of the mature seedhead like yellow plumes. Large amounts of pollen can often be gathered from them by using a stick to lightly rap the seedheads while holding the flower directly over a container. When enough of the powder has been collected it can be mixed with water to make a batter that can be baked into cookies on a hot rock or in a mess tin. The pollen can also be used to thicken stews, or to enrich other dishes. One tip is to try to gather this and other pollens (pine and poplar trees produce large amounts of edible pollens in early summer) during a prolonged dry spell, because rains wash them away.

## REINDEER MOSS LICHENS

It's no secret that Hitler's Nazi scientists came too close to beating America and its allies to the atomic bomb. Less recognized are several attempts by British-equipped commandos to knock out a Norwegian heavy-water plant that produced the deuterium oxide needed to enrich uranium-235 to weapons-grade status. Protected inside a mountain, the plant was impervious to bombers or artillery; the only way to get to it was from inside.

In 1943, a small team of specially trained Norwegian-born commandos parachuted into that country's frozen north in a daring but dangerous daylight insertion. The commandos were spotted by a Nazi ski patrol even before their parachutes deployed. With the expertise of people born to ski, the little band of Norwegians escaped into the frigid mountain badlands, but were forced to abandon most of their equipment.

Reindeer moss describes a family of lichens that are found around the world, and which commonly possess impressive scientifically-verified nutritional and medicinal qualities.

Unable to hunt or to use their radio to call for an air drop, the harried band endured months of harsh near-arctic winter. By spring their pursuers had all but written them off as dead, so it came as a great surprise when an unexpectedly fit and healthy team of raiders sprang from the shadows one night and destroyed Hitler's chances of beating the Allies to an atomic weapon. I've repeated this great story a hundred times during survival classes, using it to impress upon students the potentially life-saving importance of the same wild food that kept those courageous Norwegians strong enough to accomplish their mission. That food is reindeer moss (*Cladina rangiferina*), a lichen that is neither moss nor fungus, but a primitive organism that falls between those classifications. Probably most people won't recognize it by name, but almost everyone will recall feeling dry beds of the gray, blue, or green stuff crunching underfoot as they walked through mostly barren fields. Or in wet weather, when the thirsty lichens absorb water like sponges, you might remember its soft, springy feel as you walked over it. The USDA recognizes eighteen species and subspecies of reindeer moss, but for our purposes here, they're all the same.

Found on every continent, extremely resistant to cold and drought, and hardy enough to flourish in places where green plants cannot, reindeer moss is a staple of not only caribou, but also most northern deer. In early spring, during the period when snow is melting, but green plants haven't yet sprouted, whitetails, elk, and other deer clear sometimes large areas of open sandy or rocky soil where reindeer moss grows in carpet-like beds. Despite being rich in vitamins A and C, and having more than twice the carbohydrates of potatoes, *C. rangiferina* is not a preferred deer food; it goes untouched when alternative foods are available. Reindeer moss is often the difference between living and dying when spring is especially cold or dry. It can also be a lifesaver for humans in the deep woods, because dried reindeer moss is one of nature's most flammable fire starters—something to keep in mind when making a campfire.

Nutritionally proven many times throughout history, reindeer moss has also had considerable value as a medicinal herb. Aboriginal cultures have used it as a poultice to ease the pain of arthritis, as a tea to break fevers, to treat jaundice, to loosen kidney stones, and even as a remedy for tuberculosis. In northern Europe it is still purposely fed to cows in the belief that it makes milk from them richer and creamier, and the Saami people in the region still harvest lichen crops as fodder for domestic reindeer herds.

While many of the medicinal qualities attributed to reindeer mosses have been neither accepted or disproved by science, it has been established that the lichens contain potent broad-spectrum antibiotic didymic acid for treatment of tuberculosis, and usnic acid for topical infections—and that they can rival penicillin in effectiveness. Most recently, reindeer moss has been added to modern medicine's arsenal against methicillin-resistant *Staphylococcus aureus* (MRSA).

Aside from their bitter taste, one problem with harvesting reindeer mosses as food or medicine has been their slow growth rate. That bed of lichens you walk over might

Whereas a simple snare is intended to catch and hold a prey animal, spring snares use the release of restrained force to actively strangle or break its victim's neck.

be more than a century old, and may require that much time to reestablish after being stripped away completely. Among the numerous countries that export ground lichens for the medical trade it's generally accepted that a harvest of 20 percent every five years is adequate to maintain healthy production.

Reindeer mosses exemplify how much we still don't know about nature. Who can say what miraculous cures or landmark discoveries might still be awaiting discovery within a single blade of grass?

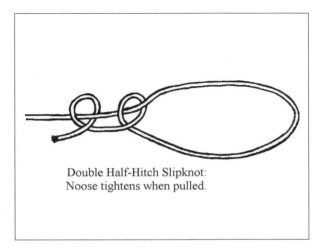

Double Half-Hitch Slipknot: Noose tightens when pulled.

## SIMPLE SNARES

Simple snares are nothing more complicated than easily-tightened nooses that are tied off to an anchor point and placed strategically to catch the neck or foot of a passing animal. Lacking fingers and the mental capacity for problem solving, animals that walk into a noose, then pull lightly until it constricts around them, will react to being trapped by instinctively attempting to flee, pulling the noose ever tighter, because they cannot conceive of loosening it. If the noose is around an animal's neck, it will usually kill itself by strangling or from breaking its neck. As elementary as the simple snare might seem to be, the principle behind it is sound in both theory and practice; Canadian northwoodsmen still hang strangling snares along rabbit trails in winter, and African poachers are too effective at catching elephants and rhinos using leg snares made of steel cable and attached log drags. Both methods can and do work to foot-snare flocks of geese and ducks on shore, to strangle squirrels and rabbits—or even to garrotte deer using fencing wire.

The best snare cord is man-made, and 100 feet or more of several diameters of string, cord, and rope are always handy to have in a home or car survival outfit. Another must-have is monofilament fishing line, and this slippery stuff is great for snares. Rawhide and braided plant fibers don't match the strength and abrasion resistance of synthetic cord, or the slipperiness that is critical to smooth, fast noose operation. Tensile strength should be matched to the weight of the animal being snared, as are noose diameters and snare heights. For smaller game, 10 feet per snare is usually more than sufficient.

## SPRING SNARES

A mainstay of movies and novels about wilderness survival, spring snares are never accurately portrayed in them, making this potentially valuable—if often overrated—hunting tool a thing of mystery and, inevitably, myths. The basic principle is simple: Spring snares restrain a bent green sapling or heavy weight whose force when released is sufficient to strangle or break the neck of an intended victim via an attached noose. This lethal energy is held in check by a trigger, a relay device that is capable of securing the force against it,

This easily remembered noose-knot can be suspended across game trails as a simple snare, or used in spring-type snares.

but tenuously enough to release the spring and attached noose with a small force applied in the correct place. Upon release, the force violently yanks the noose tight around its victim's neck, lifting it off the ground, or even decapitating large animals, depending on spring force and type of snare line used. By providing their own killing force, instead of relying on an animal's struggles to kill itself, spring snares are decidedly lethal.

The weak link in every spring snare is its trigger, the multi-component relay mechanism whose job it is to release pent-up spring force when its parts are separated by a gentler outside force. In a perfect world, a trigger disengages with only a light pull or push; in the real world it will be exposed to rain, wind, ice, and snow that could cause hang-ups or premature release.

This pencil snare employs two anchor stakes and a "pencil" trigger to loosely suspend a noose below, and at the same time restrain considerable spring force from a bent green sapling above.

## PENCIL SNARE

For simplicity, reliability, adaptability, and effectiveness, the classic pencil snare is probably the best survival snare for every environment. With two release points, or "sears," the pencil snare is twice as likely to trip, while at the same time stable enough to resist strong wind and hard rain. It can be easily constructed from any terrain where trees or woody shrubs grow, and its size and power can be regulated up or down to accommodate every animal from squirrels to deer. With a little creativity and a few variations, the pencil trigger can be employed for a variety of purposes, including deadfalls, trip wires, perimeter alarms, and even booby traps.

The parts of a pencil snare are simple to understand and easy to construct using only a knife. They include an appropriate-size snare cord, a pair of notched anchor stakes, and the "pencil" trigger that is restrained by the anchor stakes. Wooden components are easier to fashion and work best when made from dead wood that is dried to a hard gray, but still firm enough to whittle clean shavings from; green wood is softer, it's more difficult to whittle, splits easier, and is more subject to warping and freezing because of the moisture it contains. Again, size of the snare and components are determined by the size of the intended prey, but on average the anchor stakes are roughly 2 inches in diameter, about double the diameter of the pencil.

When cutting notches, follow the ageless wisdom of cutting away from yourself at all times, because being hungry and wounded is worse than being just hungry, and the odor of blood is a guaranteed deterrent to prey. With your knife in your favored hand, press its cutting edge into the wood by pushing against the blade's unsharpened spine with the opposite thumb.

For anchor stakes, use the same method to shave thin layers that extend progressively deeper, with each shaving reaching an equal distance. Every three or four layers, place the cutting edge across the top of the shavings, and press down hard with a rocking motion that cuts the shavings free at their inside end, leaving a flat, even bearing surface that will hold the pencil in place under force. Don't try to take too much wood at once, just thin shavings that are easy to shear with the knife's cutting edge. Continue until the anchor notches are at least one-half- inch deep, and clean and flat at their tops.

Pencil snares are arguably the most effective of spring snares.

The pencil's length determines how far apart the anchor stakes are set, and too wide is better than too narrow. The pencil should be straight, of equal diameter at either end, and strong enough to restrain the spring force being used. Carefully shave the upper ends

to give them flat surfaces that mate well against the flat upper ends of the anchor stake notches.

With notched anchor stakes, pencil, and cord at the ready, first tie a noose loop of roughly 8 inches in diameter—average for most small animals. Next, use the pencil length to determine how far apart to place anchor stakes, and drill—don't pound—them into the soil at either side of a likely animal trail; drilling them down with a hard, twisting motion is most effective. In

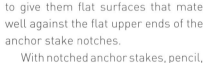

Pencil snares are effective in every environment that provides the materials to build them.

most instances stakes are anchored firmly enough at 3 inches. In snow they are best held in place by packing snow around their bases; pouring a few ounces of water onto the mounded snow helps to lock the stakes in ice.

With the noose held open to the desired diameter, tie the cord just above the slipknot to the pencil's center by wrapping the cord around the pencil twice, and tying it off with a square knot that will restrain a strong pull from above, without pulling against the noose suspended from the pencil's underside. Set the pencil into the anchor stake notches to how everything fits, and make adjustments as needed to noose diameter, height, stake height, and notch angles.

When everything fits, "cock" the trap by connecting it to a bent green sapling or over-head branch. If there is no suitable spring at the desired location, one can be created there by drilling a long, stout sapling into the ground. The spring needs only to be capable of exerting a strong upward pull against the pencil when it is bent over and held under force by the pencil in the anchor stake notches. When the pencil is cocked in place, open the noose and hold it open by hooking either side over blades of grass or tiny twigs. The noose's bottom should be suspended about 2 inches above ground to ensure that an animal passing between the anchor stakes in either direction pushes against it with legs or chest when its head passes through the noose.

## SNARE PLACEMENT

Snares are not as productive as movie writers might have us believe. Experienced fur trappers know that prey of every species will be intimately familiar with every facet of its domain, and will avoid noticeable changes made to a regularly used trail. Always keep that in mind when setting snares; when possible, use a snare cord whose color doesn't contrast against the surrounding terrain, and make as few disturbances to the environment as possible.

Game trails are the most likely places to set snares, but try not to leave scent from perspiration, chemicals, or your own urine within a hundred yards, and try not to leave any sign of having been there. Set as many snares as you can to maximize chances of success, then "run" them morning and evening to retrieve caught animals before they can be eaten by other predators or scavengers.

When it comes to survival, no technique is written in stone. Imagination is a potent design tool, and no method is wrong if it works. Available materials can vary greatly from one environment to another, or from season to season, and there is no right or wrong way to do anything; there are only methods that do or do not produce results. Practice the techniques described here to understand their principles, and to get hands-on experience, but do not be confounded when an environment doesn't provide the materials you've practiced using. Remember that you belong to the most adaptable species on this planet, and if any animal can figure out how to accomplish an objective, you can.

## FISHING FOR FOOD

With three-quarters of the earth underwater, seafood has been a mainstay of the human diet in every culture, and some type of edible fish is found in almost every permanent body of water. Under authentic survival conditions in almost any environment, fish are likely to be one of the most available and nutritious food sources. What you need is an arsenal of fishing techniques that yield maximum results with minimal effort and expenditure of time.

## FISHING KITS

There are as many fishing secrets as there are fishermen, but the most effective angling techniques all use manufactured equipment. Fundamental to a survival fishing kit is a spool of monofilament line; I prefer 10- to 20-pound test, because heavier lines work well for catching small or large fish, and the stronger weights can double as snare line for capturing small game and birds.

Hooks should be a mix of small- to medium-size, because small hooks can catch big fish, but big hooks are too large for smaller fish to take into their mouths. I prefer long-shank hooks because they're easier to grip when removing them from a caught

Where there is year-round water, there will probably be fish that can be caught —even by a small child using only a green branch with a line tied to its end. fish. Mixed hooks are sold inexpensively in the sporting goods aisles of department stores, often in their own secure containers. Hooks can also be safely transported in plastic pill bottles. Alternately, a number of hooks can be pressed against the sticky side of a length of vinyl or transparent tape, then covered with another strip of tape to keep them segregated, at the ready, and safer to handle.

Fishing weights should be of the "split-shot" variety in which fishing line is held between the connected halves when the shot is squeezed together. A variety of weights ensures that you'll have the right mass for a variety of waters and currents. Like hooks, these can be carried conveniently in a plastic bottle, or fixed between two strips of tape.

With these basics you have the means to fish anywhere, and all of the components can fit into a plastic freezer bag. But add to them as you see fit. For house, car, and especially boat fishing kits, it would not be overkill to have a well-provisioned tackle box and a rod-and-reel combo.

# HANDFISHING

In an almost humorous case of political irony, catching fish using nothing more than your own hands is illegal in many places—even some places where you'd be legally permitted to spear or net them. Nevertheless, handfishing is a common practice among backwoodsmen everywhere, and it's one of the more useful fishing techniques to have in your arsenal of survival skills because it requires no more than one working hand to put meat on the table.

Spawning fish that "run" seasonally in streams and rivers are ideal prey for handfishermen, because they will be plentiful, they will be preoccupied by reproduction instincts, and they are likely to be exhausted from their travels, especially farther upstream. Suckers, humpback salmon, and several

This bullhead (which in this position could break the fishing line it hangs from), is good eating by itself—tastes like chicken . . . really—but it might be more useful cut into strips and used to bait a dozen more hooks.

species of trout run in spring; pike spawn in early summer; and coho and chinook (king) salmon mate in the fall. Except for the largest of these, fish will likely scatter at your approach, hiding under sunken logs and undercut streambanks, where they instinctively feel protected.

Being a tactile technique, handfishing can be done day or night. The only restriction is that water must be shallow enough to reach the bottom with your hand, so shallow streams (where most fish spawn) are prime candidates for handfishing. The procedure is to simply lay your open hand flat, palm facing upward, against the stream bottom, then gently slide it into probable hiding spots. A hand sliding along the bottom will probably not disturb fish sheltering in these places, but avoid making quick or jerky motions that could cause prey to feel threatened. When you feel a fish's underside brush against your palm, close your hand hard around its body, driving your fingertips into its flesh. Do not hesitate or stop to look at what you've captured, because a wriggling fish is very tough to hang on to; immediately toss the caught fish onto the nearest bank, tossing it far enough ashore to be certain that it won't flop back into the water.

One caveat is that handfishing should only be attempted in streams or river sections that are shallow, fast-running, and (usually) gravel-bottomed. There are fish in sluggish, muck-bottom streams, but the undercuts where these hide are also home to turtles that lie in wait for fish, and it is possible that a finger could be mistaken for something edible by them.

## POLE FISHING

Fishing poles are actually clever devices. They enable an angler to elevate a baited hook away from the shore to reach fish hiding places, and to do that without exposing a silhouette or casting a shadow that might frighten off dinner. Fly fishermen use the amplified centrifugal force to flick baits far from their position, and modern rod-and-reel outfits exploit the same physics to cast baits many yards distant. A fishing pole greatly increases an angler's effective range, and his chances of success.

Fishing poles are simple to create from almost any environment that contains fish. Candidates are at least 5 feet long, ¼-inch in diameter at the tip, and at least an inch in diameter at the butt. It needs to be supple enough to transfer the vibrations of a nibbling fish to its holder's hand. It should also be springy enough to deny strong fish a solid pull that could break the line or the pole's tip, while at the same time tiring them quickly into submission. Good pole choices are found among the young dogwoods, willows, and other shrubs that populate most shorelines.

Pole fishing is a time-honored and effective means of catching the largest fish.

Slightly different needs apply to ice-fishing, where the classic image is of an angler kneeling next to a hole chopped through the ice of a frozen-over lake or pond, just far enough from the opening to avoid being seen from below. For this task a shorter pole is usually easier to manipulate.

To rig a makeshift pole, tie a length— usually 8 feet or more—of fishing line (6-pound test, minimum) or strong thread to the tip. Use a locking timber-hitch type slipknot or—even better—a natural protuberance to keep the line from sliding off the end. Tie a small hook to the free end of the line; smaller hooks can catch large fish better than large hooks will catch small fish, and long-shank hooks are easier to extract from a fish's mouth than shorter "trout" hooks. Weight the hook to sink to the bottom, or to hold in place against a current, with the needed number of split-shot sinkers.

Basic pole-fishing is simple: Swing or toss the baited hook to the preferred fishing spot, taking care not to place the hook where it can be snagged by and possibly lost among sunken trees and flotsam. Keep the fishing line taut, so that a tug on its end is clearly felt along the pole. A tug indicates that a fish has picked up the baited hook, and probably has it in its mouth. A sharp tug in return by the pole's tip may "set" the hook— that is, to drive its barbed point into the flesh of the fish's mouth; avoid yanking too hard, or you might pull the hook free before it becomes embedded.

When bottom-fishing, an occasional twitch of the pole end translates to a jump of the bait, which might stimulate the hunting instincts of an otherwise disinterested fish. The same applies to "jigging," a practice used for deeper holes in which a bait is held above the bottom and bounced up and down with upward flicks of the wrist.

When a fish is hooked, pull it in to shore. Small pan-size fish may be pulled directly from the water and swung onto shore. Larger, stronger fish are best pulled horizontally onto shore, not lifting them out of the water, because some species are notorious for breaking even heavy line with a sharp snap of their heads. Never let the line go slack when pulling in a fish, or it might escape using the same maneuver.

# FISHING FLOATS

Fishing floats, or "bobbers," have been used for as long as there have been fishing poles. The advantage of a bobber is that it holds the baited hook suspended in the water, in plain view of nearby fish, and it permits the bait to be adjusted shallower or deeper to accommodate species whose preferred hunting grounds are at differing depths.

In practice, a fishing float is simply a small, highly visible (to the angler) bit of anything that will remain on the water's surface while supporting the weight of a baited hook, and maybe a light sinker to keep the line straight and taut between them. Fishing line is held in place by friction, tightly enough to keep it in place, but loose enough for you to manually slide the bobber along it to make depth adjustments.

A bobber telegraphs activity at the hook below it by jiggling, traveling across the water, or submerging. Erratic behavior indicates that a fish is nibbling at the bait, and to have the bobber suddenly go scooting across the surface, or to disappear underwater, is a prompt to set the hook. Keep as little line slack between pole and float as possible, and set the hook with a long, smooth pull, giving a sharp tug when you feel the sudden resistance of a fish at the end.

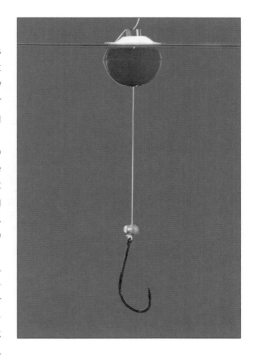

Fishing floats are available cheaply from tackle outlets, but there are numerous homespun alternatives that have proved equally effective as their manufactured counterparts. Laying the line parallel onto a capped pill bottle, then fixing it in place with a turn of vinyl tape around the bottle works very well, and is adjustable for depth by pulling the line in either direction.

Another time-honored fishing float is fashioned from a stick of dead, dry wood, about 1 inch in diameter and 6 inches long. Very carefully use a knife edge to split the stick lengthwise at its center, but no more than halfway from its end; do not try to force the knife edge through the stick, but rather rock it from side to side to wedge apart the two halves.

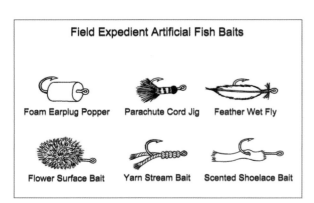

**Field Expedient Artificial Fish Baits**

Foam Earplug Popper   Parachute Cord Jig   Feather Wet Fly

Flower Surface Bait   Yarn Stream Bait   Scented Shoelace Bait

A few makeshift fishing lures.

When the split is finished, work the fishing line into the crack with a sawing motion, so that it is pinched firmly between the halves. Do not slide the fishing line more than halfway into the length of the crack, lest you cause the stick to split completely into two parts. With the line held snugly where you want it, toss the bait and bobber to a desired location and wait for a bite.

## THE TRIGGER LINE

The trigger line, taught to me as a boy by my mentor, Ojibwa Elder Amos Wasageshik, is one of the simplest and most effective methods of survival fishing,

The trigger line might be described as a spring snare for fish, and it works well enough to be outlawed in most places.

and one that almost anyone can make work for them right away. Part fishing pole, part spring snare, the trigger line can be set, then left unattended. When a fish takes the bait, the pole snaps free under force, setting its hook securely. Hooked fish remain tethered at the end of the line, alive but unable to escape until retrieved.

The mechanics of a trigger line are elementary; materials needed for a single set are one fishhook, one or two split-shot sinkers (depending on current), 10 feet of 10-pound test monofilament fishing line, a flexible green sapling, and a stout anchor stake fashioned from dead wood. Since more sets increases the volume of successes, a basic lightweight fishing kit for home or backpack should start with a 50-yard spool of fishing line, two dozen assorted split-shot sinkers, and 100 assorted fishhooks safely contained inside a capped plastic bottle.

The anchor stake, whose job it is to retain the springy pole, is best made from dry deadwood because it can be fashioned and notched more cleanly with a knife than green wood. A good candidate will average 10 inches long by 2 inches in diameter. Sharpen the end that will be pushed into the ground, then cut a restraining notch, similar to those used for the pencil snare, about halfway through one side, about 2 inches below the top end. Pushing downward with a hard twisting motion, drill the stake to a depth of about 6 inches into the soil at the edge of a stream or lake bank. The notch should always face downstream, in the direction of current flow, or away from shore when fishing ponds and lakes, because those are the directions a biting fish will probably "run" with the bait.

Next rig the pole, which should be made from a springy green sapling—common on most shorelines—about 3 feet long and with a base diameter of at least 1 inch. Tie on the fishing line about 2 inches from the tip at the pole's narrow end with a fisherman's slipknot, attach hook and sinkers, then firmly drill the butt end of the pole 6 inches into the ground about 2 feet inshore from the stake. Bend the vertical pole's upper, narrow end downward and wedge it into the anchor stake's restraining notch. The idea is to secure the pole under tension, but not so tightly that it can't snap free when the hook is tugged. Achieving a perfect fit may require whittling a flat surface onto the upward-facing side of the pole, deepening the restraining notch, or angling the upper flat surface of the notch to better accommodate the angle of the set pole.

When a satisfactory fit is achieved, bait the hook and toss it away from shore, making sure that there is as little slack in the line as possible. A fish tugging against the baited hook will pull the pole from its restraining notch, causing it to spring forcefully in a direction opposite the fish, and driving the hook's barbed point deep into the flesh of its mouth. The fish will remain there, tethered, until retrieved or released.

Some type of bait is always available where there are fish. Moist logs and rocks along shorelines can be rolled over to reveal earthworms, grubs are found in rotting stumps, and any insect that can be skewered onto a hook is bait. In summer or winter, freshwater clams can often be found close to shore, and chunks of clam flesh (which is so unpalatable as to be inedible to humans) have proved irresistible to most species of fish. And the first small fish landed can be cut up to bait several trigger lines, because fish eat other fish, even their own species.

Good fishing baits are often found in backpacks. A raisin on a hook has caught most freshwater species, while bits of summer sausage have proved attractive to pike and catfish. Surface-feeding trout have been caught on pieces of floating colored yarn tied onto a hook, while suckers, bullheads, and turtles have been caught on short lengths of shoelace saturated with animal fat—especially bacon grease.

Tips for making a trigger line more efficient include knowing what types of fish are likely to be caught where you are, and then setting the trap accordingly. Northern pike spawn up rivers in May, and their sharp teeth require that a steel leader be used; suckers spawn in the same time period, and they are more likely to pick up a baited hook that is weighted to sink to the bottom; bullheads and catfish forage close to the bottom and tend to tug gently against a hook; bass and brook trout hit a bait violently. Long-shank hooks are more easily removed from your catch's mouth, and smaller hooks can catch big fish, but large hooks will be stripped of bait by fish too small to swallow them.

Sharp, long, and with a spear point, this survival knife functions well as a weapon for fatally stabbing fish, and as a tool for cleaning them.

## KNIFE FISHING

Despite being almost universally banned by game laws, knife fishing has proved to be an effective, quiet method of putting larger fish like trout, salmon, and pike on the dinner table, especially during annual spawning runs. Spawning is hard, and exhausted fish caught up in the activity will often ignore a person who wades toward them slow and easy. The knife should be held low in a tight grip, point-forward and ready to stab forcefully enough to drive the blade in up to its hilt. The cutting edge should be held upward, because when the blade penetrates into the fish's body, ideally entering just below the spine and behind the gill, you should immediately raise the knife, as though trying to lift the fish out of the water. In most cases the struggling fish will cut itself free, falling back into the water, but too badly wounded to swim more than a few yards before turning belly-up.

## MEAT HUNTING

Should it become necessary to kill animals for food, squirrels are plentiful around the world, in cities and in rural areas.

At some point in a prolonged post-disaster scenario it might become necessary to rediscover our predatory natures. Humans have hunting instincts, science has proved that, and we are in fact the most efficient killers to ever walk the planet.

But we are also the only species afflicted with a conscience, and our acutely developed hunting instinct is balanced with the soulful knowledge that willfully ending a life is never to be taken lightly. No human worthy of the title enjoys killing, but meat is a natural and needed component of our species diet; and even if you don't believe that, the fact remains that animal flesh is a nutritious food, and eating it is preferable to starvation.

For some often contemplated reason, Homo sapiens alone lack most of the natural tools and sensory abilities that are critical to the survival of wild animals in a natural environment. Our night vision is weak, our hearing is poor, our sense of smell is negligible, and we have neither teeth nor claws adequate for attack or defense. We cannot pounce on a rabbit like a bobcat or run down a deer like wolves can, but we have a big, smart brain that can conceive of, and then construct, artificial weapons that more than compensate for what nature has denied us.

## HUNTING WEAPONS

The best hunting weapons are projectile types that enable a hunter to stand off and deliver mortal wounds in vital areas of a prey animal's body with the greatest attainable accuracy. A spear or sword is formidable in a fight, but rabbits and deer survive by being highly alert and running away fast at the first hint of danger. A human's best chance of turning these and most other wild animals into table fare is to strike from a distance with lethal force.

## BOW-AND-ARROW

Few kids don't make a bow–and–arrow by tying a cord between the ends of a bent, springy sapling and shooting straight sticks with pointed tips from it. The concept is simple enough for a child to understand, yet effective enough to have been the hunting and assault weapon of choice around the world for thousands of years. The ability to inflict serious to mortal wounds to prey or foes from distances well beyond the reach of spear and claw heralded a real turning point in the uniquely human quest for world domination.

The bow-and-arrow has been putting meat in the pot for millennia, and modern versions are more powerful and accurate than ever. (*Photo courtesy Blake Shelby, Precision Shooting Equipment*)

Enough children have pierced and killed small animals with their homemade bows and arrows to make spending a lot of time explaining the their construction a moot point—even an unfletched stick can fly straight enough for the few feet that often separates human hunters from prey. Good field-made bow staves can be fashioned from cedar, willow, or any springy sapling that flexes without breaking, and is roughly the same diameter—1 inch or more, depending

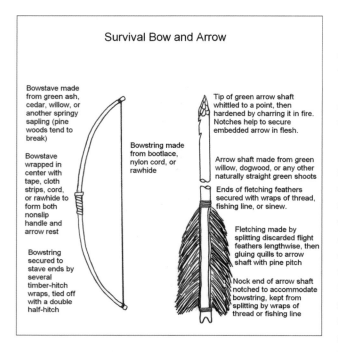

## Survival Bow and Arrow

Bowstave made from green ash, cedar, willow, or another springy sapling (pine woods tend to break)

Bowstave wrapped in center with tape, cloth strips, cord, or rawhide to form both nonslip handle and arrow rest

Bowstring secured to stave ends by several timber-hitch wraps, tied off with a double half-hitch

Bowstring made from bootlace, nylon cord, or rawhide

Tip of green arrow shaft whittled to a point, then hardened by charring it in fire. Notches help to secure embedded arrow in flesh.

Arrow shaft made from green willow, dogwood, or any other naturally straight green shoots

Ends of fletching feathers secured with wraps of thread, fishing line, or sinew.

Fletching made by splitting discarded flight feathers lengthwise, then gluing quills to arrow shaft with pine pitch

Nock end of arrow shaft notched to accommodate bowstring, kept from splitting by wraps of thread or fishing line

on the power desired—at both ends. Arrows can be any straight stick—many shrub and tree shoots are very straight—that is sharpened at the penetrating end, then hardened by charring in a fire. Bowstrings can be made from strips of animal hide, from shoelaces, or from the length of nylon cord that should be in every survival kit.

Better are manufactured bows made with modern materials and methods, and strung with stranded factory-made bowstrings. Traditional-style recurves and longbows are the simplest and most trouble-free. Because of their lower velocities and gentle acceleration stroke, they can shoot conventional cedar, aluminum, or carbon-fiber arrows, or you can make arrows for them right in the field in a pinch. Lacking sights, these are more difficult to master for technical shooters, but traditional bows are still a favorite among instinct-shooters at archery tournaments. With modern 4-blade hunting broadheads and a practiced archer, a bow of 50 pounds' draw is capable of taking deer-size game. Effective range is 30–40 yards.

More popular, more powerful, and more complex are the compound bows that have changed bowhuntbow hunting since the 1970s. These marvels of engineering employ wheel-cams that cause the force required to bend the bow to decrease as it is drawn to the ready position. The result is that less strength is needed to hold the bow at full draw, so it can be held in that position longer and with less fatigue to the shooter. Conversely, when the arrow is released, the cam system's power stroke becomes more forceful as the string drives forward toward its resting position. One downside is that this increased efficiency makes it unwise to use wooden arrows that are likely to splinter on release, possibly injuring the shooter; being restricted to aluminum or carbon-fiber arrows

means that in the long term, ammunition for a compound bow may be in short supply. The upside is that compound bows can be tricked out with precision sights, trigger releases, string silencers, kisser buttons, and an array of other performance-enhancing accessories. Effective range is 40–50 yards.

## CROSSBOWS

While a crossbow is not the long-range super weapon sometimes depicted in movies, it does have a place in the disaster-survival hunting arsenal. Despite draw weights of 150 pounds or more, studies have shown that a crossbow has essentially the same range and power as a compound bow of half its draw weight. The difference is that a crossbow's shorter bow, or "prod," releases with a shorter and more violent power stroke, resulting in approximately the same arrow velocity, but typically with a little

more yaw that detracts slightly from accuracy. Having a shorter arrow, or "quarrel," also means less mass, with less downrange inertia, and faster loss of velocity. Effective range for a 160-pound draw crossbow is 40–50 yards.

But crossbows also have a few advantages over long bows. Because the bow is held in the cocked position by its own mechanism, a crossbow hunter doesn't need to draw his bow, or hold it in the drawn position under tension until his target presents the perfect

shot. And because most crossbows are factory equipped with mounts for a telescopic sight, crossbow shooters can avail themselves of the same light-gathering advantages enjoyed by rifle hunters.

## AIR GUNS

When I stepped off the bus in Traverse City, Michigan, so many years ago, I carried a duffle duffel bag, a grant to attend Northwestern Michigan College, and a wallet with just $450 inside. I rented a room at a less than seedy hotel that had a kitchen, and stowed my gear. Then I walked to a nearby hardware store, where I spent $50

on a then state-of-the-art Crosman American Classic .177-caliber air pistol that could deliver a velocity of 600 feet per second with 10 pumps of its pneumatic forearm. I didn't know how long it would take me to find a job, but I had a good idea of how long it would be before I got hungry. As it turned out, I landed a good job in less than a month, but until then I roamed vacant buildings, shorelines, and tree-lined side streets with the Crosman tucked inside my emptied book backpack, in search of pigeons, squirrels, and occasionally a duck.

The modern hunting crossbow, although still a short-range weapon, is powerful and accurate to take most game out to 40 yards.

In practiced hands this Crosman pneumatic pistol has proved that modern air guns have evolved into true hunting weapons.

This .22 caliber air rifle is designed to take small game past 30 yards, with confirmed kills beyond 50 yards.

Driving a .177-caliber pellet at the speed of a .22 Long Rifle bullet, this Remington NPSS can take most small game out to 30 yards.

I still have that pistol, but it has been retired in favor of telescopic-sighted, break-barrel air rifles that cock and power- up in a single stroke, deliver bone-breaking energy past 25 yards, and boast the accuracy of a fine target rifle. Nitrogen-filled pistons enable the gun to deliver consistent compression and velocity when left charged for long periods, and especially in sub-freezing weather when conventional air guns lose enough power to be useless as hunting weapons. Quieter than any firearm, my .177-caliber Remington with synthetic digital-camouflage pistol-grip cheekpiece stock generates 1,200 feet per second, and is ideal for squirrel-size game. Its big brother, a .22-caliber Benjamin Trail NP All-Weather with black pistol-grip cheekpiece stock, is a veritable hammer, driving pellets at 950 fps, and with enough terminal force to take game larger than hares.

Adding to the value of either caliber as a survival weapon is the fact that power is derived from the gun itself, not from a cartridge. All you need are the "bullets." There will be no spent cartridges to reveal that anyone was there, no unnecessary weight to carry, and more than 1,000 shots can be carried in jacket pockets.

A caveat that should be observed with any type of rifle or pistol when hunting is to place shots precisely for fast kills. A wounded rabbit that runs into dense brush will certainly die, but it might not be found, and that would be a waste on multiple levels. A hunter's primary target should always be the head, and the usually instant death of a wound through the brain.

## THE ULTIMATE SURVIVAL FIREARM

There is no question that a modern firearm is the most effective personal killing machine yet invented, but if you could have a single firearm in a long-term survival situation, what would it be? This question has been a bone of contention for survival experts almost since guns were invented, and as long as there are two calibers in existence the argument will probably never end. Based on long experience—mine and others'—the best all-around choice is a light, fast-handling rifle or carbine chambered for the .22 Long Rifle caliber. The overriding factor in this choice is cartridge size, because without ammunition, all other pros or cons of any gun or caliber are meaningless. A standard "brick" of .22 LR cartridges weighs 4 pounds, and contains 500 rounds, packaged individually in boxes of 50 rounds each. Sealed in zip-lock bags with moisture-absorbing silica packets (purchased or scavenged from the packaging of other products), an entire brick can be carried in jacket pockets, or spread throughout your gear, and cartridges carried this way have remained functional for more than a decade.

Combat shooting legend Jeff Cooper once said that "The .22 Long Rifle is, for its size, the most lethal caliber in the world." Even so, the power of a .22 Long Rifle bullet tends to be very underestimated. A fairly typical Winchester T22 cartridge with 40-grain lead bullet has a velocity of 1,150 feet per second, and 117 foot-pounds of energy when it exits the muzzle. At 100 yards, that same bullet retains a velocity of 976 fps, with a respectable 85 foot-pounds of impact force. Loadings in the 1,150 fps range have proved to be the most accurate choice for sighting-in, casual target practice, and even competitive shooting. They are also the least expensive, but lack the "hydrostatic shock"—the ability to violently displace living tissue—to efficiently kill game larger than a tree squirrel. Even so, these bullets will consistently punch through four 4 inches of soft wood at 50 yards.

When the target is live prey, I load-up with one of the "hyper-velocity" Long Rifle cartridges that deliver souped-up to muzzle velocities in excess of 1,400 fps. These cartridges offer premium killing power with an almost explosive transfer of energy in live tissue. Proven performers include Remington's Yellowjacket (33-grain truncated hollow-point, 1,500 fps, 165 ft-lbs at the muzzle), and CCI's Velocitor (40-grain hollow-point, 1,435 fps, 183 ft-lbs at the muzzle).

When taking small game with a rifle, head shots are the order of the day to keep meat damage to a minimum, and to help ensure that every hit is fatal.

Benchrest trials using five types of ammunition, two rifles (a semi-automatic and a bolt-action), and two marksmen revealed that accuracy decreased slightly as velocity increased, but every loading tested easily placed five shots within 2 inches at 50 yards. Beyond 50 yards, all bullets were very susceptible to wind drift, and the conclusion was that a hunter should not take a shot past that range on a breezy day. Points of impact between different brands

Dubbed "The Squirrel Sniper" by those who know it, this custom Marlin Model 25 in .22 Long Rifle caliber is a good attempt at creating the ultimate survival firearm.

A telescopic sight is an advantage that no hunter should deny him- or herself.

varied only a few tenths of an inch at 50 yards, meaning that a hunter can sight-in with mid-velocity target cartridges, then switch to more lethal hunting ammunition with no need to re-zero his or her rifle sights.

Some shooters insist that the .22 Winchester Magnum Rimfire (WMR) is a better survival caliber, but .22 Mag ammo is not so common as .22 LR, cartridges are nearly twice as large, and it is triple the cost of hunting-class Long Rifle cartridges. Remington's .22 Magnum drives a 40-grain copper-plated bullet from the barrel at 1,910 fps, with 324 ft-lbs of energy, but its trajectory is actually less flat than the company's own Yellow jacket bullet out to 150 yards. When you compare effectiveness, price, cartridge size, and availability, the .22 Long Rifle is a better choice for long-term survival.

Long guns that shoot .22 LR ammunition tend to be lightweight and less expensive than other calibers, and virtually any of them will serve well as a survival rifle. More expensive factory-outfitted survival models have features like synthetic stocks, stainless-steel hardware, and weatherproof coatings that enable them to shrug off the elements. Budget-priced guns can be given almost the same weather resistance with a layer of spray paint. This simple procedure involves removing the barrel and action from the stock, and suspending the barreled action by a cord. Cover the ejector port and other openings into the gun's interior workings with masking tape, then spray the outer surfaces with several coats of black primer, allowing each coat to dry thoroughly before applying the next. I like to harden the dried primer with a layer of clear acrylic (floor wax). Repeat the process with the gun's stock, applying stripes of green and brown to the black as camouflage, if you wish. If the finished coating gets scraped off, paint applied to that area restores the gun's weatherproofing. In the decades since a few woodsmen dreamed up this homespun protective coating because there were no factory alternatives, it has protected dozens of "working" guns whose jobs include being exposed to sometimes harsh weather for days at a time.

In today's world, the primary sight on any survival rifle should be telescopic (I prefer to also have conventional "iron" sights as backup). Modern rifle scopes are rugged and weatherproof, and even a $40 bargain-basement model will serve well providing it has at least a 1-inch tube, an objective lens diameter of at least 32mm, and magnification factor no greater than 10x. Good candidates will have a nitrogen-filled body, JIS Class 6 waterproofing, and light-gathering metallic lens coatings (ideally phase-coated on both sides). Keep lenses covered whenever feasible, clean them gently with a soft, preferably moist, cloth, and never use saliva, as the enzymes in spit can damage lens coatings.

The ring-type scope mounts that make your gun and scope perform as a unit must be securely mounted, and all of the screws must be tight. Check the screws yourself, even if the scope was mounted by a gun dealer, because loose mounts are a major cause of erratic accuracy, and mounting screws are notorious for working loose. On my own survival rifles the scope mounts are solidly affixed to the gun's receiver with epoxy, which strengthens the attach points and makes changing scopes easier.

A large-bore handgun loaded with latest-generation expanding bullets is a good choice for hunting deer-size game.

## BRUSH PISTOLS

A foot of fresh powder blanketed the deep swamp where I crouched on snowshoes, concealed behind the snow-weighted branches of hemlock, spruce, and cedars. Thirty feet from me, two yearling whitetails were browsing those evergreens, hungry now that ground plants had been covered.

Like nature itself, I prefer not to take the finest breeding animals from a population. The still-healthy 100-pound siblings before me were precisely what I wanted for the freezer. I unholstered the Colt Lightweight Commander at my hip and, with a firm two-hand grip, slowly brought it to bear on the nearest deer. I could see twin trails of steam issuing from the deer's nostrils when it raised up to look around, but neither animal had detected my presence.

The Commander's subtle GI-issue iron sights squared on its target's left front shoulder. A gentle pull against its tuned trigger, and the short-barreled .45 ACP bucked against my palms, its normally deafening report muted by the snowbound forest. Almost simultaneously, a 230-grain Winchester SXT hollow point slammed with visible impact into my prey's left shoulder blade. The deer staggered sideways, then broke into the instinctive, blind death-run that hunters of the deep

When loaded with high-performance hunting ammunition, a large-caliber "combat" handgun has the fast-handling, hard-hitting traits that deer hunters look for in a "brush" gun.

83

swamp see only too often. The animal bolted across my path, unconsciously headed for a deadfall of giant poplars and spruces uprooted by the sometimes sometimes-vicious winds of Michigan's Straits—a place where retrieving its carcass would be an exhausting ordeal.

This was just the situation my Colt was designed to handle. The pistol tracked almost of its own accord, and I snapped off another round just before the deer leaped into that tangle of fallen trunks and limbs. My medicine (and my luck) was good that day; the second bullet penetrated both forelegs piercing the brisket, and driving a large hole through the heart. The deer somersaulted into a lifeless heap beneath a large cedar tree. My so-called combat pistol had just accounted for its second whitetail.

That success surprised some of my hunting buddies who still subscribed to that old myth about the .45 ACP being too inaccurate or too impotent to be an effective deer caliber, especially in an antiquated Colt M1911. But to experienced pistoleros, the assertion that "combat" autos (.45ACP, .40 S&W . . . ) are lethal to humans but not wild game has always been patently absurd.

The problem was that until recently the best bullets and propellents available for stubby, low-volume auto-pistol cartridges were dismal performers on live game; hunters aren't concerned with stopping power, they need killing power. For decades, only the .357, .41, and .44 Magnums generated enough velocity to expand a softnose hunting bullet, which meant that if you hunted deer-size game with a repeating handgun, it was probably a revolver.

That situation changed for the better in 1992, when Winchester bullet engineer Alan Corzine was working to create a bullet that would penetrate safety glass without fragmenting. To help anchor the heavy copper jacket, Corzine folded it over and crimped it into the bullet's large hollow-point cavity. The experiment failed, but when Corzine conducted expansion tests with that design against ballistic gelatin, the bullet's dynamics changed dramatically, with each of the six folded-over jacket anchors breaking free of its crimp to spread radially around the projectile's circumference, like petals on a daisy and leaving a wound channel nearly twice the bullet's original diameter. Against flesh, the failed design was devastating, setting a new standard for pistol bullet performance. A black polymer coating was applied to reduce bore friction, and the first of this new standard in hunting pistol bullets was dubbed Black Talon.

It's sinister-sounding name, black bullet, and tremendous lethality made the Black Talon easy prey for anti-gun propagandists, and it was outlawed for civilian use immediately. But the genie was out of the bottle; Winchester's even more powerful SXT was already in production in several calibers, but this cartridge's sporty name and copper-plated bullet were intentionally designed to be inoffensive. Remington built similar dynamics into a truncated bullet and called it Golden Saber.

This new breed of automatic pistol hunting bullets will not penetrate standard Kevlar body armor, because the dynamics of an expanding bullet engineered to transfer maximum kinetic force to its target are opposite those of so-called cop-killer bullets. Kevlar fabric absorbs a bullet's energy by spreading the force of impact over an area too strong to be penetrated. A pistol bullet meant to punch through it defeats that ability to absorb energy by being made from a hard material that doesn't flatten on impact, thus concentrating all of a projectile's force onto an area too small for the fabric to resist. The trade-off is that non-expanding bullets deliver little of the tissue displacement and hydraulic shock a hunter needs, zipping through flesh and leaving only a caliber-size wound.

Even with such lethal bullets, semi-auto pistol calibers are limited to hunting ranges of about 25 yards because their stubby designs tend to shed velocity quickly. The upside is that out to that range no shoulder-fired arm can match a combat pistol for rapid target acquisition, tracking fast-moving targets, and lightning-fast second shots.

Having taken 3 whitetails with it, I prefer the hard punch of a .230-grain .45 ACP, but I've been impressed with the performance of SXT cartridges in .40 Smith & Wesson. A 9mm will do the job in the hands of an expert marksman, but it's underpowered for deer-size game, even with the new bullets.

Semi-automatic handguns are not an ideal hunting or defense weapons for everyone. Pistol marksmanship is more difficult to learn, while greater accuracy is demanded because handguns do not deliver the range or killing power of rifles. But they are easier and lighter to carry than long arms, they can be brought to bear more quickly, and a pistol worn on the body is always at hand when it's needed.

## THE RANGER SLING

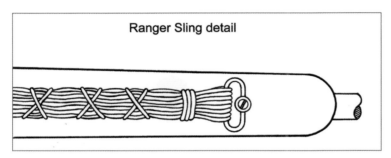

**Ranger Sling detail**

Among the gun gun-handling lessons I learned during child-hood—a few of them accompanied by a smack to the head to empha-size their importance—was the real value of a rifle sling. A properly slung long arm is a safe gun, because its barrel must always be pointed either upward or downward, and muzzle-down carry is always sound wisdom in falling rain or snow. "Getting into" a sling by wrapping it tautly around the forearm enhances a shooter's accuracy by steadying the barrel with an isometric force called dynamic tension, which is invaluable in situations that call for making long shots from an unsupported offhand position. And of course a sling is handy for just carrying the gun to which it's attached, leaving a hunter's hands free to negotiate tangled brush, or to drag a whitetail from the woods.

Not only is a Ranger Sling quiet and comfortable against the shoulder, it incorporates enough strong cord in its construction make it an invaluable asset under genuine survival conditions.

The problem is that conventional rifle slings have always been little more than a strap between forend and butt stock swivels, good for carrying and shooting the gun to which they're attached, but not much else. Attempts by manufacturers to increase utility by adding cartridge carriers, pouches, and other accouterments accoutrements to their slings have for the most part detracted from their usefulness by making them difficult to wrap around the forearm, cumbersome, and sometimes pendulously heavy.

The rifle carrier that has best served me personally for several decades is a simple homemade affair called the ranger sling, named after the elite military unit to which

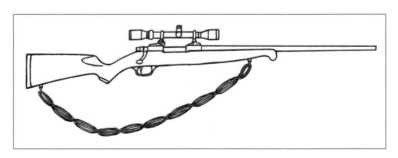

The Ranger Sling should be standard equipment for survival rifles.

its invention is credited. Comprised entirely of rope or cord—my own consists of 100 feet of 550-pound test parachute cord—the ranger sling is soft against the shoulder, the quietest of any sling I've used, and easy to get into for offhand shots.

In addition to working very well as a gun carrier, the ranger sling can have tremendous value as a ready source of strong cordage. I've taken lengths from my slings to replace broken bootlaces, to make a fish stringer, to lash together a shelter frame, and on a few occasions I've hung adult whitetails from a single strand of parachute cord and skinned them. Strap-type slings can't match a ranger sling in terms of versatility or usefulness, and "working" long arms adapted for use in places where civilization is far away are often carried by this design. So long as 4 feet of cord remain, a rifle, shotgun, or crossbow has a functional sling, but I've yet to noticeably deplete the first ranger sling I made, more than 30 years ago.

The first step in making a ranger sling is to measure it against both the firearm and user. Slip one end of the cord or rope you'll be using through the forend swivel of your unloaded gun (open the action), then tie that end off securely to the buttstock swivel. Pinch together the doubled cord from either side of the forend swivel to keep it from sliding freely, and shoulder the gun in barrel-up and barrel-down modes to get a fix on how long subsequent loops of cord will need to be, adjusting the length as needed.

I recommend allowing 3–4 inches of latitude when determining how long your ranger sling will be from swivel to swivel, because the finished project will be about 2 inches in diameter, and for those times when terrain or conditions dictate secure hands-free carry of a longarm across your back, with the sling running diagonally across your chest. The finished ranger sling is not adjustable, but not many hunters have need to adjust a sling once a comfortable all-around length has been determined.

When you've determined the desired length, cut this "master loop" free of the rest of the cord and tie it off securely to the forend swivel. The master loop never leaves the gun because it serves as the most fundamental means of carrying it, and because it serves as a gauge for applying a new ranger sling should you deplete the original's supply of cord.

Suspend your gun upside down by the master loop from a convenient, secure protrusion (I like doorknobs), again making absolutely certain that its chamber is empty, because you can't be too obsessive about gun safety. The gun's weight will pull the master loop taut. After freeing it of tangles along its entire length, tie one end of the remaining cord to either swivel, then run the opposite end through the opposite swivel. Pull the cord through until this first loop in the ranger sling is parallel to and identical to the master loop. Double the free end back through the opposite swivel, and add another identical loop over the doorknob.

And so on. This is the tedious part, threading consecutive loops back and forth between swivels until they've consumed 100 feet of cord. But be comforted by knowing that with every loop you add, the remaining cord grows shorter. When you've threaded all but 10 feet or so onto the gun, it's time to wrap up the project. Literally, because the final step in assembling a ranger sling is to bind together the strands of all those loops so they can't snag against brush. Start by winding the remaining cord around the massed loop strands in a wide spiral, with about 4 inches between each turn. When you've spiraled to the opposite swivel, thread the free end through the swivel and wind another spiral in the other direction. Repeat this spiral binding process until only enough cord remains to tie off securely to the nearest swivel. The final result should have a cablelike appearance, with no loose ends or loops sticking out.

You can also add to a ranger sling, as well as take from it. A short length of cord or light rope can be looped and spiraled over top of the existing sling. My favorite deer rifle's sling incorporates several types of cordage, from fishing fly line and nylon string to parachute cord, which adds greatly to its versatility in any environment.

While a completed ranger sling isn't repulsive, neither will it enhance the good looks of a favorite rifle or shotgun on the gun rack. A nice compromise between keeping your gun looking good in the den, yet functional in the field, is to make your sling using detachable spring-loaded swivels, preferably with screw-down locks to keep them fastened to your gun in rough country. This enables you to dress your finest rifle in a handworked leather sling for a day at the range, and quickly convert it to field readiness by changing over to the ranger sling.

## GUNSLINGING

While it is always a good idea to keep your gun in your hands, carried at port arms and ready, that just doesn't happen when a person actually has to carry a long arm everywhere he or she goes. The quandary, which has been studied in infantry troops, is that there is no comfortable way to carry a long gun on long marches, and it inevitably ends up slung over its owner's shoulder. In the conventional muzzle-up carry mode, a rifle is slow to get off the shoulder and into battery, and more than a few soldiers have become casualties before they could un-sling their guns. In a survival-hunting scenario, that same lack of speed translates into missed meals.

A good, simple compromise between the infantryman's need for speed and the fatigue that forces soldiers to carry guns as comfortably as possible is the "gunslinger" carry method that is attributed to the old Soviet Army army of Russia. In this method, a soldier carries his rifle muzzle-down, buttstock behind the shoulder opposite his trigger hand. By reaching straight down with the hand of the arm over which the rifle is slung, the soldier grasps the rifle's forend, swinging it forward and upward while turning his wrist inward to rotate the stock to a normal trigger-down firing position, and letting the sling strap fall smoothly from his shoulder. With his trigger hand, he then grabs the pistol grip of the stock and pulls the buttplate in snug to his shoulder, his opposite hand still gripping the stock's forend. A flip of the safety catch, a press of the trigger, and the soldier—or hunter—is in action. With a little practice, the transition between easy carry and ready to fire can be accomplished in under 4 seconds.

# SIGHT-IN YOUR OWN RIFLESCOPE

Calibrating a telescopic sight to make its point of aim agree with a bullet's point of impact at a specified distance is a fundamental component of marksmanship. Every shooter is obligated to know the procedure for sighting in his own gun before shooting at live targets, because a bullet that misses its mark can also be a dangerous thing.

Having a scoped rifle collimated, or bore-sighted, to bring its point of impact "on paper" helps, but it's only by happy coincidence that this procedure brings scope and gun to zero, where every bullet bull's-eyes its target at a preferred sighting range. Being preset for an established average, a collimator can't compensate for ballistic differences created by the variety of existing barrel lengths, propellants, or bullet weights.

Adjusting a rifle and scope to zero requires actually shooting holes into a target. The technique described here should enable anyone to mount a scope on a rifle, then to zero it without aid of a bore-sighter, and with only a half-dozen shots, or less. This procedure also allows shooters to zero a scoped rifle in the field, on almost any target from a standard paper bull's-eye to a cross of electrical tape stuck to a dead stump.

The first step is to eliminate any mechanical problems caused by movement between sight and gun. All screws used to fasten the scope base to the rifle receiver must be tight to ensure that no shifting can occur. Rings that hold the scope's tube must be fully seated onto their bases, and all screws between scope and rings must be snug (re-check them periodically). A loose mounting system guarantees that the rifle it wears won't put bullets where the crosshairs are, yet this is one of the most common causes of inaccuracy.

A mounted scope should be positioned so that a shooter can snap the stock to his shoulder and immediately see a clear, bright

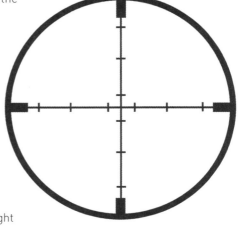

A precisely-sighted firearm can be a lifesaver under authentic survival conditions.

sight picture, without moving his head. The space between a shooter's eye and a scope's ocular lens that is required to see the clearest possible sight picture is known as "eye relief," and is typically engineered to be 4 inches. A properly positioned scope presents a clear, bright sight picture that fills the eyepiece from a comfortable shooting position, and doesn't whack a shooter's eyebrow during recoil.

One comment the owner of a scoped rifle is sure to hear from others who look through its sights is that his scope's crosshairs look "crooked." In a perfect world, crosshairs are exactly vertical and horizontal to a rifle's bore, and a rifle is never canted to left or right while sighting. In the real world, eyeballing crosshairs to the point at which a shooter thinks they look straightest is usually precise enough to keep groups inside 3 inches at an honest 200 yards.

If your bullets consistently land more left or right as you adjust the elevation turret upward—a phenomenon known as "stringing"—then the crosshairs may indeed be cocked to one side. Loosen the ring's retaining screws until you can gently twist the scope tube, and rotate it until its crosshairs look straight each time you pull the gun to your shoulder. To keep the crosshairs in that position, lightly tighten each ring retaining screw a quarter-turn at a time until they feel equally snug; this procedure is called "pattern torque tightening" by machinists who use it to ensure that all points of a mounted fixture remain level and stationary under pressure.

If your scope appears to be positioned correctly, but the sight picture looks blurry, the ocular lens—the lens you look through—probably needs to be focused. This problem can be corrected by loosening the ocular lens' knurled locking ring, located just forward of the ocular lens, and then turning the entire eyebell—usually clockwise—until the sight picture becomes clear. When you've reached a point of maximum clarity, fix the ocular lens in that position by turning the locking ring counterclockwise until it presses tightly against the eyebell.

Using the correct ammunition for your gun's scope setting is critical. A 220-grain bullet fired from a rifle that was zeroed using 150-grain bullets will impact lower on its target at a given range, and that disparity increases at longer ranges. Even the same weight and caliber of bullet from different manufacturers can have slightly different points of impact, depending on barrel length, type of action (i.e., bolt-action or semi-automatic), and bullet shape. Whenever possible, hunters should sight-in using the same make, weight, and type of ammunition that they intend to use in the field, and rifles should be re-zeroed following any change in bullet weights or brand.

Terrain is an often overlooked factor in the sighting process. Shooting downhill, for instance, will result in a point of impact slightly lower than it would be on level ground, because gravitational pull is greater, which causes trajectory rise to decrease. This is seldom a problem in the flat terrain of established target ranges, but it is something to be aware of when circumstances dictate that a rifle be zeroed in the field.

The right target can help to make the sighting process less challenging, particularly when working with a newly mounted scope. Shooting

Target
Front Sight
Rear Sight

Proper sight picture when using "iron" sights on a rifle or pistol.

soup cans is fun with a rifle that is already zeroed, but attempting to sight-in using a small target can be nearly impossible. A shooter needs to see where his bullets land, because bullet holes are the points of reference used to adjust point of impact. If you don't know where the last bullet hit, you can't determine how many clicks of the adjuster turret are needed to place the next shot on target, or even in which direction to make those adjustments. Large targets, especially those with 1-inch grids, are easiest to use, but a paper plate with a cross of contrasting vinyl tape in its center usually suffices in a pinch. Bits of masking tape can be used to cover bullet holes, or holes can be circled with a grease pencil, to extend the useable life of your targets.

Regardless of caliber, or the range at which you intend to ultimately zero your rifle, the first 3-shot group should be fired from 12 yards, and it should be fired with all the accuracy and precision a shooter can muster. The rifle's forend must be solidly, its barrel should touch nothing to avoid any possible deflection when it expands from internal pressure. Every shot should be aimed precisely at the target's bull's-eye, regardless of where bullets actually land. Never try to compensate for a bullet's point of impact by shifting your point of aim, and never shoot without a secure rest, because doing either makes sighting-in impossible.

Using the center of your initial group from 12 yards as a point of reference, the next step is to remove the scope's turret caps and adjust the windage and elevation knobs to bring the crosshairs into alignment with point of impact. Presuming a standard "1 click equals ¼-inch at 100 yards" (usually marked on the adjusters), crosshairs will move at a rate of 32 clicks per inch at 12 yards. If the group's center is 1 inch left of the bullseye and

1.5 inches low, anticipate turning the windage (side) turret 32 clicks right, and the elevation (top) turret 48 clicks upward.

Next, move back to 50 yards and fire another 3-shot group. Using the center of that group as a reference, adjust windage and elevation turrets at 8 clicks per inch. If the group center is 3 inches high and ½-inch to the right, adjust 24 clicks down and 4 clicks left.

The next, usually final group is fired from 100 yards, the optimum range for most deer hunters. Again, this 3-shot group should be fired with as much care and precision as its shooter can muster. At 100 yards, 4 clicks of the elevation or windage turrets equates to 1 inch of movement on a target. If your group's center is 1.5 inches high and 2 inches left of the bull's-eye, adjusting 6 clicks downward and 8 clicks right should place your bullets' point of impact directly on the bull's-eye.

While the above adjustments are ostensibly true for all scopes marked "1 click equals ¼-inch at 100 yards," do not expect that this will be exact for all telescopic sights, because all telescopic sights are not created equal. If your rifle wears a tactical scope that retails for $1,000, it should be expected to move the point of impact exactly ¼-inch per click at 100 yards. But if your gun is topped with a department department-store rifle scope that sold for $50, it cannot be expected to contain the same clockwork precision. An low-priced scope can get the job done very well once it has been sighted- in, but you may need to twist 5 or 6 clicks to equal 1 inch of movement on a target 100 yards distant.

## TELESCOPIC RIFLESCOPE SIGHTING CHART

**Yards to target clicks per inch 1 click equals**

| | | |
|---|---|---|
| 12.5 | 32 1/32" | (.031) |
| 25 | 16 1/16" | (.063) |
| 50 | 8 1/8" | (.125) |
| 100 | 4 1/4" | (.250) |
| 150 | 3 1/3" | (.333) |
| 200 | 2 1/2" | (.500) |
| 250 | 1.75 2/3" | (.666) |
| 300 | 1.50 3/4" | (.750) |
| 350 | 1.25 7/8" | (.875) |
| 400 | 1 1.0" | (1.00) |

Experienced marksmen recommend that scope adjustments be made using a process known as "there-and-back." With this technique, a shooter who determines that his scope needs, say, 8 clicks of adjustment will actually turn the turret 10 clicks in the desired direction, then back again 2 clicks. This practice helps to insure ensure that tiny adjustor gears inside the scope settle fully in place.

If you can't seem to change your bullets' point of impact, no matter how many clicks you adjust, it is possible that the crosshairs themselves are stuck in place—not uncommon with scopes that are stored for long periods. If you suspect this is the case, try rapping the scope tube lightly around its turrets with a soft tool (a rubber-handled jackknife works). Rapping the turret area gently is usually sufficient to free the mechanism.

Always keep scope lenses clean and free of abrasive sand or dust by wiping them with a soft, preferably damp cloth, like those used for camera lenses, and keep lenses capped when not in use. Never use saliva to clean them, as digestive enzymes in spit will erode the metallic coatings responsible for gathering and focusing ambient light onto a shooter's eye, resulting in a less vivid sight picture, especially in twilight.

## GROUP THERAPY

Find a hunter who seems to never miss his or her target, and you've probably found someone who spends considerable time shooting groups at a rifle or archery range. The purpose behind shooting groups is to make every nuance of sharpshooting an automatic function, independent of a jack-hammering heart and the flip-flopping stomach that afflicts everyone who sets his sights onto a live target. Veteran hunters often claim they cannot recall feeling the trigger, or even seeing the sights, when making what was ultimately a fine shot, because repitition had made doing those things conditioned responses, like automatically braking a car when you see a potential road hazard.

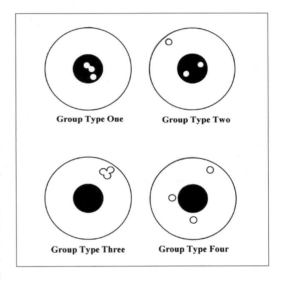

How far a shooter has gone toward achieving consistent precision is represented by the amount of area groups of 3 or—better—5 five shots encompass on a target (ammunition experts at CCI Corporation claim the ideal group size is 7 seven rounds). Plinking—shooting informally at cans and other impromptu targets—is great, but dedicated marksmen know that the secret to developing real proficiency lies in punching paper. The closer a shooter can get to driving every shot through the same hole, the more likely he will be to succeed at making a single flawless shot under less less-than than-perfect conditions.

Every shot fired into a group should be loosed from a steady platform, just as it should be if the target were a much much-needed meal. Long arms should be "benchrested" on sandbags if possible, although shooting across the hood of a truck, or even across a backpack, has often sufficed. Rifles should be rested on the stock forend only, never on the barrels, which must be free to expand from heat and pressure.

Handguns should be held with a firm two-handed grip, and the forearms rested on a stable surface. The objective is always to remove as much human variation from the firearm as possible, making it easier to predict where every shot will land because body motion has been mostly eliminated.

Shooting accurately "offhand"—without resting a rifle or pistol on a solid support—is a skill that every hunter should develop, but one that few savvy hunters employ if a tree branch is available. Plinking offhand at tennis balls in a vacant gravel pit is a lot of fun,

Shooting groups is one of the best analytical tools for improving a shooter's groups with any type of projectile weapon.

Shooting offhand — without using a solid rest to steady your aim—is a skill that should be practiced, but never used when sighting-in.

and already accomplished riflemen even shoot 100-yard groups from that position, but there are no instances in which using a rest won't improve accuracy.

Groups are also great analytical tools for diagnosing and identifying problems with your weapon—or your shooting skills. Like numbers, groups don't lie, and the grouping of bullet or arrow holes can provide a quantifiable, measurable means of determining how well shooter and weapon perform as a unit. Essentially there are four types of groups, all of which can have real value in determining where a shooter's inconsistencies lie:

## GROUP TYPE ONE:

A nearly ideal 3-shot group, with all points of impact tightly centered around the point of aim. This group indicates that sights are in proper alignment with a projectile's trajectory and point of impact at this range, and that the shooter was both steady and consistent. This is the kind of group that novices try to achieve and experts try to beat.

## GROUP TYPE TWO:

This group, with 2 two shots printing neatly together at the point of aim and 1 one straying widely apart from them, is what range regulars call a "flyer" group, with a "yanked" shot. Paired holes in the bull's-eye indicate that shooter and machine were in agreement most of the time, so the likely cause of a flyer is a flinch by the shooter. It is possible to have a wild variation in ammunition that causes a projectile to fly off-target, but this is very unlikely with even cheap ammo. The remedy is usually as simple as shooting another group or two to limber up the trigger finger. Like As with riding a bike, a practiced marksman never forgets the mechanics of sharpshooting, but in both instances he or she can anticipate being a little rusty after a long period without practice.

## GROUP TYPE THREE:

Nice tight grouping of all 3 shots, except not at the weapon's intended point of impact. This type of group suggests a marksman with real skill, even though no shots are in the black, and this is the only example in which a shooter is probably not at fault. Likely causes are sights that have been knocked hard enough to change their point of aim, or sometimes a change of ammunition weights and charges that result in different flight paths. The remedy is to adjust the sights so that point of aim agrees with point of impact.

## GROUP TYPE FOUR:

Shooting this type of group is a little embarrassing for veteran marksmen, even though everybody gets one now and then. All 3 shots scattered about the target indicates real inconsistency somewhere between human and machine. The most common cause is a flinch or other unsteadiness on the part of a shooter. Mechanical culprits can include loose scope mounts or, in some old military bolt-actions, a recoil lug inlet in the stock that has become enlarged enough by repeated firing to allow the action to shift on discharge.

Still, the reason for a scattered group lies with the shooter nearly all of the time, so before making sight adjustments, first fire a half-dozen groups to see if they don't shrink with practice.

Although the primary focus here has been on rifles and pistols, all of the above is pretty much generic to all hunting weapons. Archers, pistoleros, and riflemen who consistently hit what they shoot at are usually practiced group shooters. With good group analysis and regular range practice you'll know precisely what an arrow or bullet is going to do at a given range before you even fire, and that alone will help to make every shot as accurate as it can be.

## POT HUNTING

It was November in northern Michigan, and I was supposed to be deer hunting, but it seemed I'd brought the wrong gun today. The deer I did see were moving constantly, and those that weren't stayed in open fields, well beyond the range of a 170-grain 30–30 bullet.

In contrast, there seemed to be small game everywhere, and I carried a license to take them, too. I slung the empty-chamber Winchester muzzle-down across my back, and drew the Ruger .22 pistol at my hip. I went home that evening with a grouse, a gray squirrel, a cottontail, and a porcupine, all of which contributed to a pretty good wild game dinner.

This experience illustrates the origins of terms like "pot luck" and "pot shot," from an era when every rural schoolboy (and a few girls like Annie Oakley) learned sometimes-impressive marksmanship skills by shooting small game for the dinner table. Most started with a single-shot .22 rifle, sometimes a .410 shotgun, not because those guns are safer than large calibers, but to make sure that proper shooting skills became a conditioned response before introducing youngsters to a hard-kicking big-bore.

On the premise that a gun without ammo is just a poorly designed club, I still prefer the .22 lLong rifle Rifle as a survival caliber, particularly with hyper-velocity ammunition like Remington's hard-hitting Yellow Jacket. Game wardens generally concur that more deer are taken with a .22 rimfire than with any of the larger conventional "deer calibers," and forensic detectives recognize use of the .22 Long Rifle in a murder as one mark of a professional killer. In the real- world of meat hunting, size truly isn't all that important, but the ability to place a shot precisely where it is meant to land is critical.

Even so, one NRA study concluded that a typical sport hunter was most likely to get into trouble in the woods, and least likely to survive it; and the same study found that being armed actually contributed to both of those problems. Having a gun can induce an unfounded sense of security, which leads to a reduced sense of caution, and the most common manifestation of that is simply getting lost in the woods. Compound being lost in a harsh environment with inefficient conventional sport-hunting techniques that are derived from a sense of fair play, and burn more calories than they net, and being well armed is no guarantee that you'll eat.

If your goal is to shoot dinner, follow the same philosophy that generations of successful afterschool hunters used: Small game is more plentiful than big game, usually easier to get close to, and easier to kill. Schoolboy pride and an ammunition budget made many kids into efficient hunters and deadly marksmen (American traits that shone in both world wars), and a large portion of the meat in an average rural family's diet came from a mix of smaller game animals, few of which were not considered fair game if their flesh was even moderately palatable.

As this ruffed grouse demonstrates, pot-luck is an effective means of getting meat for dinner.

The best thing about pot hunting, especially in a genuine survival situation where success may be critical, is that it requires no hunting skill. Whether you've just survived a light plane crash in the northern Rockies or a mega-hurricane in South Carolina, you will probably see the most wildlife simply by walking through wooded areas at an unhurried pace, preferably alone, but quietly in any case. As experienced birdwatchers know, a remarkable percentage of wild animals seem reluctant to flee at the easy approach of a single person, and hikers can often get within a few feet of them.

Pot hunting by definition means that most of a hunter's encounters with game will come as a surprise, so you have to be always ready to shoot as you walk, because prey animals can often tell from body language that you are in predatory mode. The gun must be in your hands, at the ready, but always pointed in a safe direction—the most holy rule of gun safety. Never touch the trigger of any firearm unless you mean to pull it, and keep the safety engaged until that time, but be prepared to mount the stock to your shoulder and snap the safety to fire position as soon as you see a game animal. A telescopic sight, set to low magnification (to provide the widest view), makes the job easier, because you have a clearer sight picture and a single sight—the crosshair—to place on a target. With practice, you'll find that this process becomes automatic and fast, as well as safe.

In one comprehensive study, all brands of .22 Long Rifle ammo consistently held 5-shot groups within a 2-inch diameter at 50 yards. At 100 yards group diameters remained under 4 inches, with a 3.5-inch drop from the 50-yard "zero" setting. Standard high-velocity 1,150 feet-per-second ammo can punch through 4 inches of pine at 50 yards. Hyper-velocity, 1,500 fps, ammunition blasts through 6 inches of pine and delivers explosive results against live tissue—to put it bluntly, a hyper-velocity CCI Stinger or Remington Yellow Jacket bullet will consistently gut rabbits out to 50 yards.

The problem with being stranded in a wilderness is that there is no one around to help; the upside is that local game is less likely to flee at the first sight or scent of a human, because they probably haven't been hunted much. As you get closer to civilization, game will probably be more wary and tougher to draw a bead on, but in untrampled untrammelled wilderness—the kind of places most people want to get out of in normal times— some short-lived species might just stare, having never seen a human before. Refrain from actually going after any animal; stalking is a high-intensity exercise that burns more calories than it nets, especially against prey that is alert to your presence.

In recent years there has been a gradual shading of any armed civilian as suspicious, at least. In normal times, the decision to carry a gun is made for you by local regulations prohibiting the carry of firearms. But in places where, or times when, help might be a day away, and being armed might in fact save one's life, local laws often require no more than possession of a small-game license to be armed in any season. Sliding a rifle into your kayak might draw stares, and a long arm strapped onto a backpack will certainly be questioned, but being politically correct and unarmed is no help if your canoe has been hulled on a rock, or if you turn an ankle. Let your own good sense dictate whether or not a survival gun is needed.

## SQUIRREL HUNTING

Squirrels have an honored place in history. The importance these prolific rodents have had in the early development of America is reflected in the way that highly accurate muzzleloading rifles of .45 caliber or less were once known as "squirrel guns." In the vast

Squirrels are found around the world, in the city and in the country, and all of them are edible.

forests of the New World, tree squirrels were a plentiful year-round source of meat, and squirrel stew was regular fare.

The squirrel family is a broad one, including everything from marmots to chipmunks, but traditional hunters are concerned primarily with tree squirrels of the genus Sciurus, particularly the fox squirrel (*S. carolinensis*) and the gray squirrel (*S. niger*). This family also includes the half-pound red squirrel, although that species has never been popular with hunters because of its small size. Nonetheless, all squirrels are edible and nutritious (although most are lacking in fat), and some species of them are found almost everywhere in the world, which makes squirrels the most important game in a real-world survival scenario.

Adult fox squirrels weigh up to 2.5 pounds at maturity, making them the largest tree squirrels, while grays, which may be either gray or black, weigh up to 1.5 pounds. Both species generally cover the eastern half of the United States, and they share similar habits, mating seasons, and food preferences.

One difference between them is type of forest preferred by each color. Gray squirrels that are black tend to live among oaks and maples whose bark color approximates their fur color. Gray squirrels that are gray prefer gray-barked trees, like beech. Fox squirrels generally include pines in their chosen territories, and their grizzled rusty-red coats are all but invisible against the dead needles of a wind-broken branch. Few animals are better at hiding in plain sight than a tree squirrel.

Food preferences and behaviorisms are largely the same among tree squirrels. Acorns, winged maple samaras, pine cones, and other nuts are prized for their nutritional content, and the forest floor beneath these trees will often be littered with nut-bearing twigs that have been nipped free by a foraging squirrel's sharp incisors. The typical procedure is for a squirrel to cut free a dozen or so fruited twigs from their parent branches, simply letting them fall to earth, before descending to harvest and cache the nuts.

Gray and fox squirrels cache supplies of winter food in hollow trees and rock crevices, but most of the nuts gathered are buried individually in small, shallow holes near the parent tree. Hunting lore claims that squirrels remember each acorn or hickory nut they bury, but the truth is that a squirrel's nose is among the keenest in the animal world. A hungry gray or fox squirrel can detect the scent of a buried nut through more than 6 inches of hardpack snow, then burrow down to retrieve it, leaving body-diameter diagonal tunnels whose entrances are marked by a small spray of excavated dirt. They never do seem to find all of the nuts they've buried, which guarantees a regularly replenished crop of young trees to replace those lost to age or weather.

In spite of acute olfactory senses, good eyesight, and an elevated habitat that affords advantageous use of both, there are chinks in old bushytail's armor. Among the most profitable is a short attention span that traditional hunters exploit by just sitting quietly for about 15 minutes after shooting and retrieving one of their number. Whether it's forgetfulness or simply a drive to continue with daily life, squirrels that melted into the trees at the first hint of danger seem to ignore a source of fear if it also ignores them. I've taken more than a half-dozen squirrels without changing location using this time-honored method.

Personally, I prefer simply to walk along remote two-tracks and wooded hiking trails until an opportunity presents itself, a technique someone once dubbed "stroll-hunting." Freshly cut nut-bearing twig ends lying about on the ground tell of harvest work in nearby trees, and are a sure sign that squirrels are among their branches. Tunnel-like excavations under fallen leaves, sometimes with a spray of fresh soil at their openings, identify nut caches that their owner won't venture far from on penalty of losing claimed territory to another squirrel.

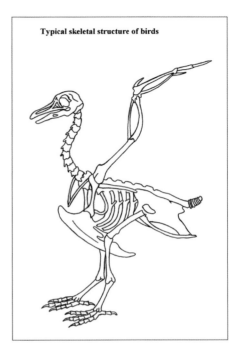

**Typical skeletal structure of birds**

Skeletal structure of a typical bird, showing breastplate that becomes extremely sharp when cut.

Listen too for barks, sharp chirps, and chattering from the surrounding woods. The most successful squirrel hunters have a knack for identifying, then locating, their prey by using the sounds it makes. They've learned to recognize the hollow, chirping "bark" of a rutting male as it sits atop a branch proclaiming its dominance and availability. They know that a frantic monkey-like chattering from high in the canopy will probably reveal a pair of adult squirrels fighting over possession of a tree.

The alarm call of both fox and gray squirrels is a rapid "kuk-kuk-kuk" that most folks can imitate by sucking tongue against molars to produce a low-pitched clucking sound. A staccato clucking denotes a high level of alarm that will send every squirrel within 50 yards into hiding for the next quarter-hour or longer. If a predator passes by without incident, its leaving will probably be announced by a slower "kuk . . . kuk . . . kuk" that diminishes in frequency as the predator gets farther away, eventually ceasing when the danger is gone.

In fact, the squirrels' own alarm system can be turned against them. Stalking a white-tail is easy compared to sneaking up undetected on a dozen sharp-eyed, keen-nosed bushytails in elevated positions, so I don't even try to be stealthy. Instead, I just walk casually along until a squirrel raises the alarm, noting mentally from which tree the call seemed to emanate, but continuing on past that spot until the alarm call diminishes to an "all clear." Then I stop, hunker down, and wait quietly for the squirrels to resume their activities.

It really isn't the squirrel's fault for telling its brethren that the coast is clear, because in nature there are few predators capable of catching a squirrel that see them coming. A hunter who raises the alarm can use it to first identify an area of squirrel activity, then lull the populace into a false sense of security by seeming to withdraw to a distance where the animals instinctively feel safe. The advantage for a hunter is that this distance is usually within the effective range of a rifle or shotgun.

The focus of most sitting hunters is on catching forgetful squirrels who return to foraging or mating, but in places where squirrels have been hunted hard enough to teach them that a human within sight poses a danger, all activity may cease so long as a hunter is present. Cold, windy days can also inhibit foraging activities and make squirrels keep to the trees, where there's less danger of a predator using noise and air currents to mask its attack.

One optical tool that I have always carried religiously when squirrel hunting is a mini-binocular in the 10x28mm range. These start at under $50 in most sporting goods outlets, and their value for spotting hidden squirrels is hard to overstate. Not only does a good binocular magnify its sight picture to reveal anomalies not apparent from farther away, it gathers in light to make the picture appear brighter than it actually is, and greatly reduces backlight glare that can help to obscure hiding squirrels.

## PREPARING GAME

When you have a dead carcass in hand, the next step is to render it into food. In every case, be it fish, bird, reptile, or mammal, that means removing entrails. If an animal is cooked with its organs still inside, stomach and intestine contents, bladder and other fluids may foul the meat around them and make it inedible, even poisonous. In the case of some fur-bearing mammals, it is especially necessary to remove dark spots around the hind knees, the anus, and above the tail, because these mark the location of musky scent glands whose skunk-like secretions can also make the flesh surrounding them unpalatable.

The first step, regardless of species, is to make a shallow incision through the belly skin and the muscles beneath it from the anus to the breastbone. For all but the thinnest-skinned species (rabbits, bullfrogs . . . ) you will need a cutting instrument for this task, preferably a knife, but even a sharp rock or a door key will do. Do not cut through the breastbone of a bird, because the edges of this plate-like bone are razor-sharp when cut, and try not to perforate organs, although that will likely be impossible. Spilled stomach and intestinal contents have a terrible smell, but if they are washed, or even wiped off with grass, they do no harm to the meat or its taste when cooked. Neither does urine from the bladder harm the meat.

Cooking a cleaned fish over fire.

When you reach into the abdominal cavity to pull out the entrails, begin pulling from the trachea, or as close to it as possible. Every animal's innards are attached at the throat and anus, and must be cut (or yanked hard) free from those points. Organs are also held in place on all species by a thin, tough membrane at the ribs and along the spine; in fish, birds, and smaller animals, innards can be pulled free of these membrane anchors without aid of a knife.

No animal must be skinned, but mammals and birds smell awful when their hair or feathers are burning away, and it's easier to slice the skin from ankle/wrist joints to the abdominal incision, then peel hide away from the meat beneath; excepting some tough-skinned species like catfish and sharks, fish do not need to be skinned, or even to have their scales removed, as the skin of a cooked fish generally slides off of the meat. For birds, I find that skinning them is a lot faster and less messy than plucking a carcass free of feathers.

Skinning is more pulling and peeling than knifework, whether the game is a raccoon or an elk. Find a loose edge of skin over firm muscle, then drive a forefinger between hide and meat, and pull the skin away. When enough skin is loosened, grab it in a fist and pull hard. Use your knife only to cut the hide away from problem spots that refuse to pull free.

An alternate method that many squirrel hunters use is "back-skinning," which begins with a continuous slice through the skin from the base of the tail, along the spine, to the base of the skull. Simply peel the skin away from either side of this cut, working it over

the head, and down the legs to the feet. Sever the feet at the ankles, base of the tail, and at the neck. Then make an incision from anus to breast and pull out the entrails. The back-skinning method is fast and easy to master for most small game, and it works well for deer-size game, too.

Large animals require that meat be removed from their limbs and bodies in chunks. There really is no wrong way to take these hunks of flesh from the bones they cover, and conventional meat-cutting methods are not necessary. Rabbit-size game can be quartered for stew or roasting by chopping the hind quarters from the spine, then hacking them in half at their crotch, through the pelvis bone, and slicing the floating shoulders from the muscles that connect scapula to shoulder. If you lack cooking pots, squirrel-size animals and fish are most easily spitted in one piece; a green stick run through the anus and out of the neck enables a squirrel or muskrat to be cooked over hot coals; fish are most easily bent into a U, then skewered through both sides and cooked over a fire.

# Shelter

## THE NEED FOR SHELTER

**S**helter-building is an essential part of human existence. That we still have an instinct for it is demonstrated by toddlers who crawl inside cardboard boxes and kids who make tents out of blankets, or by the fun a group of children have while building a "fort" from old lumber. Lacking natural protections from the elements, we humans are born with a primal desire to be sheltered. Few people today have been subjected to conditions that demanded they build a shelter for their immediate survival, and the fundamentals of shelter construction have not had real value in most normal lives in a long time.

Even if we take it for granted, nothing is more fundamental to human survival than shelter from the elements; among mammals, only our species is in peril from simple naked exposure to the outdoors, and you need not be in a snowy north woods to "freeze" to death. At 40 degrees Fahrenheit, with a wind of 25 miles per hour, the cooling effect is the same as it would be at an ambient temperature of about 10 degrees. Throw in a soaking rain that can lower felt temperatures by 20 degrees, even under windless conditions, and the result can kill an unprotected person in only a few hours. Lower the temperature of the toughest man's internal organs by only 5 degrees, and he will be on the verge of death, and probably in a coma. Ambient temperatures lower than the human body's 98.6-degree norm robs warmth from skin, and the rate of heat loss, without wind or rain, can be life threatening in temperatures as high as 50 degrees.

Put a shelter into the equation, and survival under the worst conditions becomes a lot more likely. A roof negates the cooling effects of precipitation, walls defeat chilling winds, and the enclosure as a whole helps to contain radiated body heat by creating what is essentially a bubble of motionless air that hinders the loss of precious body heat to the outside. An effective shelter is much like a spacecraft or submarine in that it creates a habitable space in the midst of an uninhabitable environment.

In times past, every homesteader and trapper was obligated to build a home using only materials provided by the environment.

## SHELTER-IN-PLACE

If the threat is radioactive, chemical, or biological, FEMA recommends that citizens in the affected zones shelter in place. With this sound strategy, people in the high-density population areas that are most likely to be targets of a "dirty" bomb exploit the numerous material and psychological advantages of facing danger from familiar territory.

A dirty bomb employs high explosives—potentially even a homespun potassium-nitrate "fertilizer" bomb—to disperse chemical, radioactive, or biological toxins through the air over broad distances, most probably from an elevated position upwind of the target area. Chemical toxins are probably least effective as terror weapons in open places because even nerve gases tend to spread fast in open air, and are quickly diluted beyond effectiveness—these weapons are most horrific in enclosed spaces, like high-rises and subway tunnels. Biological pathogens are more dangerous, but unless a germ or virus gets past a victim's immune system to establish a foothold—thereby making her or him contagious— most will die within forty-eight hours. Radioactive elements like plutonium or uranium-235 are most dangerous, because affected particles attached to dust motes remain deadly in small doses practically forever. In any of these instances, a gauge

of the toxicity level of outside air will likely be the presence of dead birds, pets, and insects.

Sheltering in place essentially means turning wherever you might be into an impenetrable fortress against whatever dangers are in the air. FEMA recommends sealing any potential drafts that could bring in air from the outside with duct tape. Clear polypropylene plastic sheets, like those used to cover lumber in rainy weather, can be precut from continuous rolls for each window and labeled. When needed, they are placed over the windows indicated by their label, and duct-taped around their edges to prohibit any outside air from reaching inside.

Duct tape will safely seal cracks.

Duct tape seals all cracks in doors, while plastic sheeting is duct-taped over the ventilation openings found in most attics and sometimes in foundations. It is important that all manner of ventilation be turned off, including furnaces and air conditioners.

Even more convenient are prepackaged window-seal kits that are designed to serve as temporary storm windows. These typically employ a frame of double-sided tape around a window casing over which a clear plastic membrane is stretched and held in place by the sticky upper surface of the tape. Costs average about $2 per window, and the convenience of having all individual components in a single, ready-to-use package makes it well worth the price. Pre-cut window seal kits are a handy part of every shelter-in-place survival kit.

FEMA recommends sheltering in place in a single room to keep preparation time to a minimum. That room should be one adjoining the bathroom. It should also be as elevated as possible, because even the lightest contaminants are subject to gravity and will become most concentrated at ground level. Be certain to break out sufficient water from your stores for drinking and flushing (1.6 gallons/6 liters per flush) before sealing the room. Tap water may be contaminated with toxins, so do not turn on a faucet or you risk being trapped in an enclosed space with the very pathogen you're trying to avoid. An exception

would be if you were at ground zero and have been contaminated directly; then, according to FEMA, "decontamination is needed within minutes of exposure to minimize health consequences," and using a shower is the lesser of available evils.

Other good advice from FEMA includes using extreme caution when helping others who have

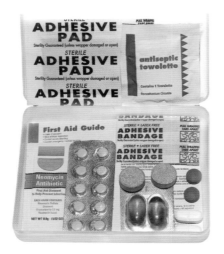

been exposed to chemical agents. Remove all clothing and other contaminated items that are in contact with the body. Contaminated clothing that would normally be removed over the head should be cut off to avoid contact with the eyes, nose, and mouth. Seal contaminated clothing and other items into a plastic garbage bag. Decontaminate hands using soap and water. Remove eyeglasses or contact lenses. Put glasses in a pan of household bleach to decontaminate them, and then rinse and dry. Flush eyes with water, and wash face and hair before thoroughly rinsing with water. Blot—do not swab or scrub—with a cloth soaked in soapy water and rinse with clear water.

Bring other survival supplies into the room that is to be sealed, like sleeping bags, food that can be eaten from a can or is self-heating, toilet tissue, and plastic garbage bags for isolating empty food containers and other organic waste. Coffee drinkers should have instant coffee to help ward off the headaches of caffeine withdrawal, and don't forget a first-aid kit and any prescription medications.

Sheltering in place is likely to be a highly stressful experience. A quality battery or dynamo (crank) powered AM/FM/shortwave receiver helps to reduce the frustration of not knowing what is happening outside; shortwave has been especially useful for gathering news from foreign countries when a media blackout has been imposed. A deck of cards or a multiplayer board game like Monopoly provides an outlet for emotions. Novels and comic books serve as a temporary escape from unpleasant reality. LED lights and lamps help to keep the nights from being so unnerving, and extra batteries help to keep them operating. Candles and oil lamps are not recommended for shelter-in-place situations because they remove oxygen from an environment that is sealed off from the outside world.

Being sealed into a small space carries its own hazards. There is no escape for moisture, and within a day or so your shelter-in-place will become a damp, steamy interior jungle. A dehumidifier is suggested for as long as there is electricity, because most houses contain

A quality AM/FM/shortwave radio receiver provides improved peace of mind when you can't go outside.

some form of spores that will mature and thrive, possibly creating respiratory or other problems.

Air will also become a problem after a few days, and the more people there are breathing it, the quicker it will become so. It has been surmised that house plants can help by converting exhaled carbon dioxide into breathable oxygen, but there is no data available. What is known is that the typical home-cum-shelter can contain no more than two or three days of breathable air before carbon dioxide levels rise to the point of causing life-threatening hypoxia.

Should a shelter-in-place become uninhabitable, it may become necessary to leave the affected area. This means exposing yourself to an environment that could still be hazardous, and the best direction to travel is always upwind of ground zero. Most dangerous would be breathing whatever residual toxins might still be present and attached to windborne dust, pollen, or spores. A good defense against airborne contaminants is an N95-class respirator mask approved by the National Institute of Occupational Safety and Health (NIOSH, www.niosh.gov). Rated to remove 95 percent of particulates from the air that gets to its wearer's lungs, N95 respirators vary from simple surgical-type masks priced at less than $15 to molded rubber masks with one-way exhalation valves and replaceable filter canisters for about $70.

Long-lived LED lamps and lights are must-have items for shelter-in-place survival kits.

## MANUFACTURED SHELTERS

Every traveling survival kit should incorporate a portable ready-made shelter, whether that kit is a backpack, kayak, or the trunk of a car. For these outfits, the shelter will be a tent, defined here as a portable, collapsible fabric shelter that is rainproof, stable enough to resist strong winds, and strong enough to remain standing under several inches of snow.

Most tents today are comprised of a large, rainproof sack that is held erect by the tension of two or more flexible poles that are bent over and attached to the upper tent sack, then anchored into grommets or pockets at the tent's ground-level corners. By crossing the poles, their opposing tension can form a "free-standing" dome that needs no stakes

A simple N95 respirator removes 95 percent of airborne particles before they reach its wearer's lungs. A more sophisticated N95 respirator features one-way exhalation valve and dual replaceable filter canisters.

Weighing-in at around 3–4 pounds each, single-person bivouac shelters are ideal for the emergency evacuation backpack.

or guy lines to remain erect; this design is sometimes used for smaller tents, but is most often seen in larger models designed to sleep two or more people.

Smaller, low-profile single-person bivouac shelters, or bivys, often use shorter poles to form half-hoops at either end of a small tent sack with just enough of a roof to inhibit claustrophobia and to provide a valuable dead-air space between an occupant and the outside world. With an average weight of 3–4 pounds and stuff-sacked dimensions about the same as a loaf of bread, bivys have become standard issue for Canadian soldiers, survival-minded daypackers, deer hunters, and hikers who like having the means to quickly escape cold wind and rain. Some bivys are freestanding, and these are the best choices for set-up on rock, deep snow, or other terrain where driving tent stakes into the ground is not feasible. The smallest and lightest bivys are usually not free-standing, and need to be staked or tied off to anchor points to remain erect; this type is my usual choice, but in winter I affix cords to trees instead of staking them.

One important mark of a quality tent or bivouac shelter is the presence of taped seams in the rain fly. These are identified as flat strips of waterproofed fabric, usually the same material as the rain fly, covering seam joints where the rain fly was sewn together. Taped seams are more expensive on the manufacturing end, but they virtually guarantee a waterproof roof, and their presence usually indicates a quality product.

The floor of your tent or bivy should be a "bathtub" design, consisting of a single piece of waterproof material extending several inches up the walls on all sides. My old camping buddy Phil learned the value of that feature when he pitched his North Face tent in a driving rain late one night. He awoke early the next morning to the feel of water rushing under his body. He

This ultra light freestanding bivouac shelter is one example of how modern tents can create a bubble of survivability in a hostile environment.

had pitched his tent in a natural runoff, which the previous night's downpour had turned into a flowing stream. We kid him about trying to make a waterbed out of his tent, but the important thing is that he and his bedroll stayed dry.

All doors and windows must be covered with fine-mesh "no-see-um" netting to keep out the hordes of biting insects that conspire to torment campers, rob them of sleep, and generally make

The tents and bivy shelters of today are lightweight, compact, and easy to erect under adverse conditions. Having one of them in hostile weather might literally save your life.

the wilderness experience less than pleasant. The bug-proof doors should be double-zippered and separate from the tent main door to allow free air circulation on warm nights without fear of intrusion by mosquitoes, ticks, chiggers, and other annoying, perhaps poisonous pests.

Likewise, all entrances in the tent's rain fly, which usually serves as its outer skin, should open and close from inside and out with heavy-duty, preferably YKK-brand, zippers. An overhanging awning strip should surround the closure all around to keep water from seeping through the closed zipper teeth, and zippers should operate easily, without snagging or binding. Bear in mind that these zippers may be expected to function in rain, sleet, sand, or snow, and they are not permitted to fail, so give the zippers in any tent you're considering for purchase a few good pulls to help ensure they're up to the task, and unlikely to snag at an inopportune time.

Poles are literally the backbone of any tent; without them, even the best tent becomes just a rainproof bag. To make them short enough for transport, the poles break down into roughly foot-long sections with male and female fittings at either end of each section, with sections held together by elastic "shock-cord" through their centers. When unfolded, pole sections fit together to form a long pole, itself held together by tension from the shock-cord. And these longer poles form the framework of the tent.

The least expensive and least durable tent poles are made from fiberglass sections with metal tubes crimped to one end to accommodate the unadorned end of the next section. The danger is that fiberglass tends to crack, or even break under repeated flexing, but with proper, gentle use, these poles will endure several years of frequent camping trips.

Best, lightest, and most expensive as far as tent poles are concerned are models made from tubular aluminum; aluminum tent poles are exceptionally strong, and where they're offered as an option, the difference in weight is as much as a pound, or about half the weight of fiberglass poles.

Whichever type of tent pole you have, always be gentle with the shock-corded ends. Tent manufacturers claim almost unanimously that snapping pole sections together under the tension of their shock-cord is the biggest cause of split fiberglass poles and deformation of mating ends, so it pays to treat them gently.

When you return to civilization, don't just toss the stuff-sacked tent into a corner until the next outing. Even a budget tent deserves good care, and the lower its price, the more care it is likely to need. The first step is to un-sack and spread the tent to make certain that it's completely dry, because even synthetics can mildew and eventually rot in a closed, damp space. Be sure to empty the tent sack of dirt, rocks, or abrasive sand that can wear it from the inside before packing it back into its sack.

Never launder any part of your tent in a washing machine, no matter how dirty it gets, because that can damage polyurethane interior coatings, and destroy its waterproofing more effectively than any abuse. Instead, set up the tent and wash it gently with a soft cloth and clear, soapless water. After the erected tent has dried thoroughly, reweatherproof its rain fly with a silicone-base spray-on waterproofing agent like NikWax's TX-Direct or Camp Dry, available for about $10 at most sporting goods outlets.

When storing a tent in its stuff sack, I prefer to spread the tent sack, more durable floor facing down, and roll the stakes and tent pegs (usually contained in their own smaller stuff sack) loosely inside. Then I slide the roll into the tent's stuff sack and store it in a dry place, preferably inside a snap-lid plastic tote box. When needed, the tent is ready to strap onto your grab-and-go backpack, and when you slide it from its stuff sack, just grab the loose end of the roll and give it a flick of the wrist to lay out the tent, poles on top, ready for pitching.

## DEBRIS SHELTER

This is the only type of shelter I teach in my basic 3-day wilderness survival course, because it is versatile, adaptable, and almost universally buildable in any terrain that affords even the shrubbiest vegetation. The moniker debris shelter alludes to a type of shelter that is constructed all or mostly from whatever materials are provided by its occupants' surroundings. No two debris shelters are exactly alike, and construction materials can vary broadly, depending on what the surrounding terrain has to offer a creative builder. The beauty of a debris shelter is that, once you have a grasp of its basics, it can be constructed

A debris shelter takes its name from a versatile design that permits it to be constructed of whatever debris might be found in any environment.

from virtually any terrain—even snowbound forest—so a creative eye is beneficial when scouting for building materials.

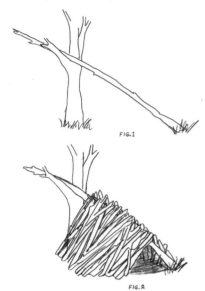

FIG.1

FIG.2

The most important component for all debris-type shelters is a main support, a stout pole 8 to 10 feet long, 3 or more inches in diameter at the base. Suitable candidates can often be found standing upright, but dead, because some trees do not live to maturity. Ideal choices will stand more than a dozen feet tall, dry enough to snap off when you push hard against them, but solid and unrotted throughout. Bridge the thinnest end of the pole across a solid object, and heel-stomp or chop it to length; a suitably long main support should be at least 2 inches in diameter at its narrow end.

Elevate the thick end of the main support by wedging it into the limb crotch of a standing tree, into a rock crack, or onto an X-frame of two lashed-together and crossed saplings—whatever solid support will hold it at least 3 feet above the ground. It is important that the narrow end of the pole be the one against the earth, because if it should give under the weight of snow, for example, only a few inches at the low end are likely to break, and the entire shelter will not come crashing down.

At this point, install the sleeping pallet on the ground directly below and parallel to the main support. This critical part of any emergency shelter serves to keep a sleeper's body from making direct contact with the earth, which will absorb body heat faster than it can be generated, even in summer. In woodlands, the usual configuration is a platform formed by placing relatively straight, body-length, dead saplings and limbs on the ground, alongside one another, until a rough bed, about 2 feet wide, takes shape. Minimal diameter of each pallet member should be 2 inches to ensure adequate insulation.

The shelter's triangular walls are constructed by leaning lengths of branches at an angle between main support and ground from either side. The amount of floor space is determined by how far apart the wall supports are set, but smaller interior space

Once you've established the dimensions of your shelter, install the sleeping pallet, while there is still room to do that from the outside.

retains body heat better. Place a few "framing" sticks against the main support to set the shelter's internal dimensions, and add more layers of dead sticks to that skeleton. Set the placement and size of the triangle-shaped door at the high end on the shelter's leeward side, faced away from prevailing winds (some prefer to set it at the open, highest, end, but this forces feet-first entry).

Although held in place only by friction and weight, every wall stick added increases overall strength. Note that shorter sticks can be used at the lower foot end of the shelter, and it doesn't matter if a wall stick extends beyond the main support—in fact, having wall sticks cross in an "X" above the main support provides a place to hang wet clothing and frequently needed gear. Add branches to the wall, including the head-end, until only the inverted-V doorway is left uncovered and gaps of less than 2 inches exist between the sticks.

The next step is to seal the frame to keep air inside the shelter as motionless as possible, impervious to howling winds outside, and able to shrug off rainstorms of less than biblical proportions. In many places, bracken ferns are an ideal roof covering until winter snows bury them, but so are layers of wet, compressed leaves peeled from the forest floor or clumps of sphagnum moss pulled from the ground in a cedar swamp. The objective is to seal the shelter frame sufficiently to block out daylight—and rain. Almost any material that will cover an area of the frame is suitable. Remember to shingle the roof, beginning at the bottom with a row of overlapping cover material, with each ascending row overlapping the one below, to ensure that rain runs off.

Alternately, a quicker, slightly more skeletal frame can be erected, and simply draped with a tarp or a plastic painter's drop cloth. In winter, the frame can be sealed with packed snow to form a solid shell that retains body heat more efficiently than a double-wall tent.

Adding a frame of dead sticks onto the main support.

A completed debris shelter covered with an insulating roof of bracken ferns that have been applied shingle-fashion (from the bottom upward) to help shed rain.

Sealing a shelter's walls against the outside can be done with a variety of available materials, from mud and grass to damp leaves to snow.

A debris shelter roofed with spruce boughs

Whatever roofing material you use, add another layer of spaced-apart poles over it to hold everything in place should a wind come up.

A debris shelter can be made small and in a hurry, or it can be made large enough for even several people to live in comfortably.

When no daylight penetrates the roof, add a thick layer of dry foliage—dead leaves, ferns, grass—to the sleeping pallet inside, to soften protuberances, and add insulation. Dry foliage can also serve as a blanket, trapping radiated body heat with surprising effectiveness. In a pinch, green foliage will suffice better than no padding, but the moisture in green vegetation means that it is constantly cooling as it dries, and some—like pine boughs—exude glue-like sap for days after being cut. The goal is to create an effective shield between your body and the cooling effects of earth and air. Whatever material you use to accomplish that, a good rule of thumb is to use more than you think you'll need.

As mentioned, doorway placement should always be away from prevailing winds—preferably, the shelter site will itself be isolated from wind. The doorway can be closed to minimize heat-stealing air flow by pulling a layer of dead branches over it from the inside, with a ground sheet, with slabs of wood pulled from the outer shells of rotting stumps, or with sheets of birch bark stripped from fallen trees.

You might opt to leave the doorway uncovered, with a small fire outside, about 5 feet in front of the opening, far enough to avoid burning the combustible (never forget that) shelter, but close enough to radiate warmth to its interior. A "reflector" wall of deadwood, snow, or anything else that can be stacked densely to a height of at least 2 feet helps to bounce radiated heat back toward the shelter opening, and blocks ground winds.

In most environments, a single-occupant debris hut can be built solo, and with no tools, in well under 3 hours. Despite their ease of construction, some debris shelters have withstood heavy winter snows for more than 10 years; the design is functional anywhere it can be built, and a few have literally served as home to adventurers for months at a time. Subzero windchills and driven precipitation have no effect inside its walls, and solid construction promotes a greater sense of security than collapsible fabric shelters. If you had to, you could live in—and build onto—this shelter for years.

## WEARABLE SHELTER

Another version of the shelter-in-place philosophy might be simply defined as dressing correctly for whatever weather you might be facing. Whether it's a light windbreaker on a breezy day or a self-contained spacesuit on the moon, we humans have a demonstrated ability to create facsimiles of the insulation, armor, and other protections that nature provides for wild species around the world.

The principles of why a layered cold-weather outfit is so effective can't be explained in the 30-second public-service commercials that air frequently in snow country. An efficiently layered outfit is a system, and how efficiently that system retains warmth has everything to do with the type of garments worn, the materials used in them, and the sequence in which layers are arranged. Keeping warm is not rocket science, but it is a science, and everyone who wants to actually enjoy snow country should be familiar with the thermodynamics of layering with today's high-efficiency synthetic fabrics.

There are essentially 3 layers in a cold-weather outfit: A base layer (long underwear) is first, worn in direct contact with the skin, followed by an intermediate layer (which may be two or three layers), and finally, a tough, weatherproof outer shell. Each of these layers performs a specific function that is different from, yet complements, the others, and each component needs to be easily removable to facilitate mixing and matching layers in changing weather conditions.

Most important, I believe, is the base layer, or "long johns." This layer captures an atmosphere of warmed, motionless "dead-air" over its wearer's skin to retain body heat. Yet it must breathe well enough to allow swift dissipation of perspiration vapors, and at the same time absorb as little moisture as possible. Cotton in any amount is a bad choice, because it sucks up and holds moisture (like a towel), displacing insulating dead air with cooling wetness, and it dries slowly, subjecting its wearer to constant cooling from evaporation.

Wool, the traditional base layer fabric, still ranks high as an all-weather insulator, but most find it uncomfortably itchy. More skin-friendly synthetic insulators, like Duofold's ThermaStat and Medalist's very warm X-Static, are as good as wool at dissipating moisture while retaining body heat. Base layer sets (top and bottoms) made from synthetics or wool retail for around $40.

For the legs, I find that densely-woven nylon six-pocket overpants ($30) worn over base-layer bottoms are equal to most cold weather. In double-digit subzero temps I add a second base-layer bottom sized large enough to fit loosely over the first. Wool works well here, shielded from the skin by a softer synthetic layer. If your budget allows, uninsulated six-pocket Gore-Tex overpants (about $80) are great for sledding in any weather. For snowmobile camping, with mixed physical activities and exposure to cold for several days, I like German army surplus double-wall heavyweight wool trousers.

The intermediate layer, which might actually be two or even three layers, depending on activity levels and temperature, is worn over the base layer. Its job is to further inhibit loss of body heat from the base layer by providing additional layers of warmed air, while also conducting moisture vapors outward. Here is where that scratchy wool knit sweater becomes useful (I periodically pick up a half-dozen new-condition "camping sweaters" from resale shops for about $3 each).

Covering the base and intermediate layers is an uninsulated windproof and waterproof jacket shell, preferably with a detachable hood. The shell is unlined because the layers beneath provide insulation; the shell only prevents trapped body heat from being whisked away by wind. That function is important: a snowmobiler riding 35 mph on a calm 20-degree day is facing a windchill of minus 20. Combine that constant chill with driving sleet, snow, or rain, and a weatherproof shell jacket ($80 and up) could be considered a survival item.

The traditional one- or two-piece insulated "snowmobile suit" is not recommended even for winter wear because these bulky outfits don't allow insulation to be added or removed to maintain a comfortable level of warmth. Insulated coveralls are too warm for even short hikes into the woods and basically offer the choice of too warm or too cold, because

A windproof hooded parka shell is essential to an effective layered outfit in any season.

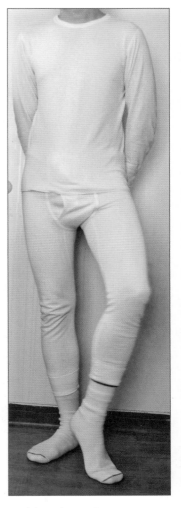

A base layer—long underwear made from wool or a skin-friendly synthetic fabric—is the first step in creating a layered clothing system that can keep you comfortable in any weather.

they are either on or off. Most hold several pounds of water when saturated, and lower-end models are not rainproof.

Socks are a critical component of any cold-weather outfit, because keeping the feet from feeling clammy is no less important than it is for any other part of the body. Socks, too, are a system, with a lightweight, slippery liner sock of non-absorbent material, covered by a thicker insulated outersock. Liner socks cost about $6 a pair at outfitter stores, but department store acrylic dress socks are cheaper, and perform as well. Outersocks (I like the SmartWool brand), retail for about $10 per pair, but most give years of service. Once again, cotton in any amount is bad; cotton socks can make feet feel cold in the best boots, while a good sock system gets the most warmth from an inadequate boot. Avoid the mistake of pulling on additional socks, as these can constrict circulation through the feet and actually make them cold.

Quality footwear is a must-have for any survival kit, even in the inner city. Sneakers and loafers aren't adequate for the gritty existence of life in survival mode, especially if circumstances demand hiking over long distances. Mid-calf hiking boots provide the support to protect ankle joints on rough terrain and rubble, aggressive lug soles to prevent slips, armor to shield delicate feet from sharp debris, and enough support to travel many miles a day with minimal fatigue. Better models incorporate micro-fabric waterproof booties to keep feet drier and warmer, and vent panels help feet to stay cooler in hot weather. Good boots can be purchased for under $100 (models change fast—watch for closeouts), and adequate boots can be found in department stores for less than half that.

Proper boots are especially important in snow country, where feet are subjected to sometimes viciously cold windchills and are constantly in contact with snow.

A liner-and-outer sock system is comfortable, dryer, and warmer than any single sock.

If your survival strategy dictates traveling on foot, a stout, comfortable hiking boot can be vitally important.

Rugged gloves are essential armor when daily life gets gritty.

This ladies' winter pac boot is equal to any cold on earth.

Wherever there is snow on the ground you'll be well served by a full-blown pac-boot, with ankle-high uppers, removable liners, and a comfort rating of at least minus-40 Fahrenheit. Prices for insulated pac boots (it pays to stick with name brands like LaCrosse and Rocky) begin at about $80.

Handwear is also critical, because fingers are vulnerable to cold and to injuries. In warm weather, rugged cowhide gloves protect hands from lacerations and blisters, and retail for about $15. In winter, mittens are theoretically warmer than gloves, but most outdoor enthusiasts prefer to have their fingers free to operate independently. Insulations like Thinsulate and ComforTemp, encased in weatherproof shells, make gloves at least as warm as mittens, even in wet, windy conditions. In very cold weather, I wear a light knit acrylic liner under the main glove; these are available from the childrens' section big box stores for about $1 per pair. Good winter gloves, with gauntlet-length wrists, retail for around $40 a pair.

A warm hat is frequently overlooked by snowmobilers, because riders normally wear a helmet. Remove your helmet at a trail stop, however, and you might be wishing for a warm cover. This is where that detachable jacket shell hood comes in. In my shell's hip pocket resides an inexpensive ski mask made from acrylic yarn, available for under $5 at most department stores. In bitterly cold temperatures the ski mask can be worn fully down, even under a helmet, to protect the frostbite-prone nose and cheekbones, or rolled up to cover just the ears and head. There are fancier hats, but a knit ski mask and windproof parka hood have proved comfortable in windchills of minus 60 degrees Fahrenheit.

Because the layers in a cold-weather clothing system are removed and added as needed, a place to stash clothing is essential. Some machines have enough storage space to suffice, but a comfortable fanny pack or day pack, kept fastened to the machine under normal conditions, is great for that job, with room to spare for dry socks, munchies, and a few survival items.

Put all of these together and you have an effective, lightweight outfit that adjusts to keep you warm, dry, and comfortable in virtually any conditions, from freezing rain and sleet to a subzero blizzard. Our forefathers could only have wished for such an immunity to cold when the phrase, "you'll catch your death of pneumonia" had a more ominous tone than it does today.

# WEATHER

The sky was filled with thick, rolling black clouds that swept across the heavens at a disturbing pace as I hurried back to camp. Already the woods had become dark enough to strain my eyes, even though it was still early evening, and the moisture content of the surrounding air was perceptible on my cheeks. Lightning flickered through darkening skies, accompanied by thunderclaps so loud that some caused brief moments of disorientation. I could see a wall of heavy rain coming my way over the darkening northern Michigan hills, and I figured it would be best not to get caught in this one.

I made camp about a half hour before the first marble-size raindrops splattered hard onto the forest floor. By then I'd built and banked my fire against the coming deluge and was rolled snugly inside a sturdy lean-to shelter. Rain began falling in sheets, punctuated regularly with a deafening crescendo of thunder and blinding lightning flashes that nevertheless induced a feeling of deep contentment. I fell asleep.

I hadn't been asleep more than a few minutes when an ear-splitting crash mixed with the sounds of splintering wood popped my eyes wide open—just in time to be blinded by a brilliant flash of white light. Spots danced before me as a ghostly blue haze of electricity made the hairs on my forearms and head stand erect. I knew without looking that a very large tree had fallen much too close to where I lay, wide awake and entirely frightened for the next several hours. I finally fell asleep again sometime before dawn.

I awoke the following morning to clear skies and sunshine so golden that it made me wonder if the previous night hadn't been just a dream. It hadn't. There, not 50 feet behind my shelter, lay a century-old beech tree, its massive trunk twisted and splintered by inconceivable power. I was awed, but mostly I was happy that it hadn't fallen on me.

I dug out my 7-transistor AM radio to see if there would be news about the previous night's weather. It seemed fitting that the first sounds to come from its tinny speaker was Maureen McGovern singing "There's Got to Be a Morning After," the theme song of the then newly released movie *The Poseidon Adventure*.

Weather is the most dangerous threat any of us are likely to face in the woods, and it must never be ignored. As the story above illustrates, lightning is always a potential

danger in stormy skies, but it represents just one of many atmospheric hazards that need guarding against.

## IDENTIFYING APPROACHING WEATHER

Weather reports from local radio stations are a woodsman's first and best line of defense, despite inaccuracies, because radar and satellite imaging can detect the approach of storm fronts days before they arrive. Always check the extended forecast for your target area prior to leaving civilization, and try to catch a local weather report every day on your pack radio. Meteorologists are more often right than wrong these days, and when they do err its usually on the side of harmlessness.

Surprisingly accurate short-term forecasts can be obtained from reading changes in the local environment. The tiny brown pismire ant, whose circular mounds are found along virtually every dirt road, gravel shoulder, and sidewalk crack in North America, will work diligently to close up these mounds when rain is coming. With fair weather on the horizon, the ants' mounds are flattened disks of contrasting sand against the earth, their entrance holes left wide open to facilitate ventilation and constant ant traffic. Changes in humidity and barometric pressure warn the insects of impending rain, and workers rush to close nest entrances more tightly against flooding with chimneys of cemented sand that often resemble tiny termite mounds. Occasionally the ants will cry wolf and no rain will fall, but they're never wrong about conditions being favorable for a good shower, and the taller their chimneys, the more likely it is that you're in for a deluge.

Fish behavior can also be an indicator of approaching rain. As air becomes heavier from increased humidity, flying insects hover just inches above the surface of lakes and streams, within reach of trout, bass, and other fish that rise up to eat them with sometimes impressive airborne leaps. Bugs also fly close to water at sunset, attracted by its residual heat, but fish feeding on the surface during the day are a sign that rain is likely.

Birds that feed on flying bugs, like swallows, sparrows, and starlings, take advantage of the calm, heavy air that precedes a rainstorm for the same reason. Their sometimes frenzied

feeding, with aerobatics that would put an F-16 to shame, is another sure sign that rain is on the horizon.

To an observant woodsman, the air itself can tell of approaching weather fronts. Probably everyone has heard of the proverbial calm before the storm, even if they haven't actually seen it in person. When birds, cicadas, squirrels, and other normally vocal critters stop their serenades during the day, it's because they've stopped mating, feeding, and feuding to seek cover against approaching weather. In most instances, the air will be dead still and the sky overcast, but I've also been surprised by a sudden stillness in the forest on sunny days, usually just minutes before a violent thunderstorm hit.

Be aware too, that all animals and most insects tend to go silent in the middle of especially hot summer days. Again, this is because they've sought out a cool hole or burrow to sleep away the day's worst heat. In either case a hiker or backpacker is well advised to follow the animals' example.

Clouds offer another option for determining what kind of weather a hiker can expect in the near future. Moving fronts are preceded by winds and clouds moving away from the oncoming weather, and their direction is a good indicator of what type of weather to expect. In probably most places around the world, winds from the north of northwest indicate a cold front moving, while southerly winds bring warm air. High, thin cirrus or "horsetail" clouds denote cold air; white cotton-ball clouds accompany warm temperatures and fair

skies; dirty gray or black cotton-ball clouds mean you should keep shelter close at hand.

Be alert, too, for storm clouds that are moving in a different, opposite, direction from prevailing winds on the ground, because these may indicate the clashing temperature fronts that can create tornadoes.

# AVOIDING WEATHER PROBLEMS

Once you've identified approaching weather, the next step is to avoid potential hazards it might bring. The most common weather problem for campers is water in the form of rain. A good rule of thumb for folks who must be out in the rain is to subtract 20 degrees Fahrenheit from the actual temperature, then dress accordingly.

Rain also has a strong influence on where a camp should be placed. If there are hills in an area, be alert for and avoid ravines between them that might serve as natural runoffs. This may be particularly important in high rock country, where a hard rain spread over several square miles of nonabsorbent stone can quickly accumulate into a raging flash flood. A high spot within a small, isolated (not part of a runoff) valley is your best choice in the woods, where most rain is absorbed by spongy humus. In rock country, pick a place well to one side and at least 20 feet above suspected drainages.

# LIGHTNING

As the anecdote at the start of this chapter illustrates, lightning is also a real concern to people on foot in the great outdoors. The old truism about never taking shelter under a tree during an electrical storm has no meaning in a forest—which is actually one of the safer places to be—but tall trees that extend above the canopy and other high points are to be avoided. Any object projecting above its surroundings, including your body, is a potential lightning rod. Open fields and rocky outcrops are good places to stay away from when the sky starts rumbling.

# TORNADOES

As anyone who's lived in tornado or hurricane country can testify, wind is sometimes nature's more frightening force. In the timber country where I grew up, loggers with long life lines were constantly alert for widowmakers—large dead branches and treetops that break off, frequently for no apparent reason, and come crashing earthward with the force of whatever weight they carry. Injuries from widowmakers are actually quite rare, but it wasn't long ago that a 15-year-old boy canoeing Michigan's Au Sable River with his family was killed when a large white birch came apart and crashed down onto his head. Old woodsmen get that way by never disregarding the possibility that a tree will fall in the forest.

In most cases dense lowland forests, like dry swamps, are the safest places to escape Old Man Wind. Air currents that reach them are diminished by surrounding higher ground,

and a thick mass of evergreens further diffuses even strong winds to a mere breeze. In these externally quiet places the real force of a wind is evident in the swaying of tall trees that stand above the surrounding canopy, and these are the very trees a camper should give a wide berth. Trees whose topmost branches receive the full brunt of strong winds routinely snap off, and when the winds reach 50 mph tall trees of any genus can be pushed hard enough to snap off several yards above the ground, bringing perhaps several tons smashing downward. Be especially mindful around large birches, poplars, and aspens, all brittle trees that share a tendency to drop large dead branches.

The upside is that widowmakers are never silent, but the location of a sudden cracking noise overhead might not be immediately apparent. Never stop to look upward, but run to the nearest large tree and wrap your arms tightly around its trunk; this is one instance where being a tree hugger can literally save your life. There, protected by a shield of heavy live branches that grows stronger nearer the ground, you're virtually untouchable by falling wood of any size, even if it falls from the tree you're holding.

Tornadoes are the most frightening and powerful of winds, and in recent years we've seen only too clearly how they can form almost anywhere a warm front collides with a cooler air mass. Flat, open terrain is most conductive to twister formation, but I've experienced three tornadoes in the tall timbered hills of northern Michigan, and the only good thing I can report about any of them was that no one present was injured.

Thick forest offers little protection from the destructive power of a tornado, and nowhere is that power more apparent than in places where twisters have laid miles of strong trees over at crazy angles, brushing them aside like windblown grass. I've noted, however, that cyclones in a woods always follow the path of least resistance, just as they do in open country, and standing timber helps channel this energy more predictably. that means two-tracks and seasonal roads are likely tornado routes, as are riverbeds, valleys, railroad grades, and lakeshores—anyplace that offers a clear avenue for wind to flow. Obviously, these places are to be avoided if you suspect a tornado will form in the area. This almost always means abandoning your vehicle to seek safer cover. If you can pull your car of truck into a nearby narrow valley between two tall hills, this will greatly increase its chances of survival. But such refuges aren't always available, and you're best advised to leave your vehicle in any case.

As always, local weather broadcasts are your best source for up-to-the-minute news about tornadoes, but don't ignore changes in your surroundings that could mean a twister is coming your way. Again, sudden dead silence in the woods, often accompanied by a perceptible clamminess in the air, is always a good indication that rough weather is on the horizon. A warm rain that suddenly turns cold, sometimes bringing sleet or hail, means you're right on the front where a twister might form, and if that rain suddenly goes from vertical to horizontal behind a driving wind, seek shelter immediately.

Most tornadoes occur in the afternoon, when the earth is cooling, but if you hear the trademark freight-train roar at any time of day put at least 200 yards between yourself and likely tornado avenues as quickly as possible. Never try to ride it out inside a building unless it has a basement or cellar, and don't make the obviously foolish but still common mistake of zipping yourself into a tent. Better to lie flat on the ground than to be contained inside anything that catches the wind.

The best strategy for surviving a tornado is to get below the surrounding terrain in a depression too small to be settled into by the microbursts (mini twisters) that always surround a funnel cloud. Large culverts at stream crossings are good places to take shelter, but these may be in short supply. In the woods seek out a small, preferably deep, holly large enough to accommodate your body and lie flat, facedown, hands locked behind your head until the winds pass. Being in a depression means winds pass over you, while trees snapped off or toppled by them will fall across instead of onto your prone body.

# SNOW

Snow can be very dangerous to hikers but while there have been numerous cases of death by exposure, this shouldn't be a concern for modern backpackers who know where they're going and equip themselves accordingly. Of greater concern are subtler and less obvious dangers posed not by the cold, but by the soft, fluffy powder itself.

In places where winter is a season, the worst danger comes from hardpack—a compacted layer of normally permanent snow that covers the ground till spring. This hardpack layer can exceed 4 feet in depth on the level and consist of more than 200 inches of actual snowfall. Fresh powder falls onto this in accumulations that may exceed a foot; these are compacted by their own weight and the warming effect of weak winter sunshine.

# SHELTER

In sunless temperatures of 20 degrees Fahrenheit or less, hardpack is usually a pleasure to walk over, because its frozen upper crust is hard as rock. But let a few of bleak midwinter sunlight hit that crust and it will turn brittle, too weak to support a human's weight, yet solid enough to force you to step down hard with every forward step. This bone-jarring experience can run a trained athlete to exhaustion within a few hundred yards, and it has killed more than a few hunters. A solution I was forced to find one winter during an unseasonable warm spell was, as I noted previously, to pack out to the nearest road during the wee subzero hours of morning, before the rising sun softened the crust too much to support my weight.

The solution, which I recommend for anyone who snomobiles, hikes, or hunts in snow country, is to wear a pair of quality snowshoes whenever venturing out onto hardpack. Skiers who stick to groomed trails are usually exempt from this rule, but backcountry snowmobilers should always be equipped to hike over long distances. In fresh powder a snowmobile trail can be as tough to walk on as the surrounding snow, crusted just enough to make step an effort. Throw a track or blow a piston even a couple of miles from civilization under such conditions and you're very much stranded without a pair of snowshoes.

In mountain country you also have to be alert for avalanches, which can bring hundreds of tons of snow sliding downward with sufficient force to wash away buildings and vehicles before settling to layers that might exceed 20 feet. A rule of thumb is that any grade 30 degrees or more above level has the potential for a snow slide in mountain country. (Brunton's 8.4 prismatic compass has a clinometer needle for reading grade angles.) Wooded hills are generally exempt from this rule, because so many trees block the way on even steeper slopes, but if several tons of snow gets a start above the tree line, building mass and momentum as it descends, a forest below won't stop it.

The best idea is to give potential avalanche areas a wide berth whenever possible. When this isn't possible, look for places where rippled, rounded layers of snow lying at the bottom of a hill indicate a recent avalanche; these places usually offer safe crossing until the peaks above become snow-heavy again. Be especially wary during or immediately after a heavy snow. Always try to walk on the shaded side of hills to avoid the possibility that sunshine will loosen a slide above you. The same applies in a valley, where either side might pose a danger. If the terrain permits, I recommend trekking 100 yards or so up to the shaded side to completely avoid a slide from the opposite, sunny side.

Loose rocks also pose a year-round danger in many places, frequently blocking mountain roads when they avalanche and sometimes bashing unlucky motorists. Beware of all places where loose rock, especially shale, overhangs your trail, and go well around them, even if this means leaving established hiking trails. If you can hear loose stones skittering downward from the force of wind alone, take it as a red-hot danger signal and adjust your course accordingly.

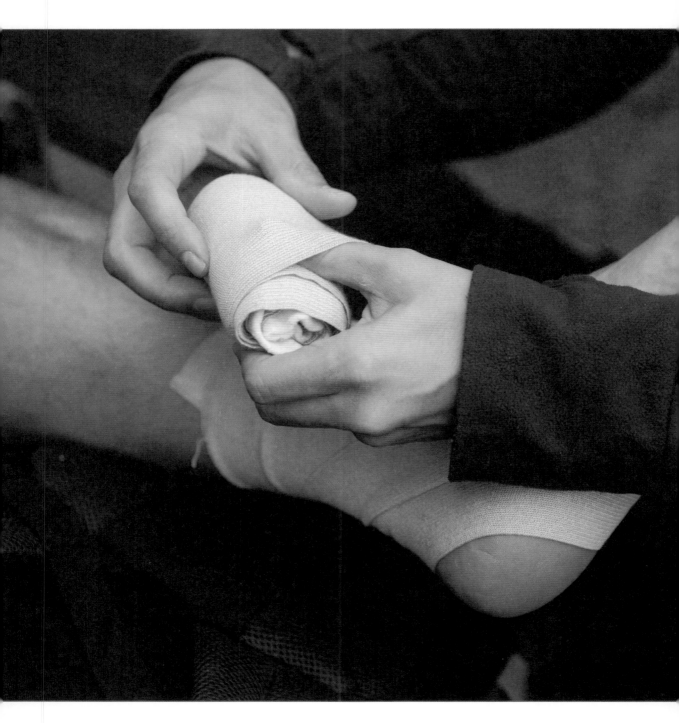

# Medicine

**M**edical troubles are a given in the aftermath of a disaster. To cover every contingency would require numerous medical degrees, and legalities prohibit dispensing medical advice here. Instead, medical information presented in this chapter is anecdotal, from actual experiences, and from practicing paramedics, those everyday heroes who make a profession of saving lives in hostile environments.

## FIRST-AID KITS

When working paramedics need a "jump kit" medical bag for their personal vehicles, they don't take an off-the-shelf outfit. There are too many times when a tool is indispensable in one environment, but deadweight in another. A prepacked first-aid kit that adequately addresses every contingency is a chimera, so Emergency Medical Services personnel build and streamline their lifesaver field kits to accommodate the environments in which they operate. Air-activated heating pads (www.heatmax.com) are good for treating shock in any season, but especially valuable for treating hypothermia in cold weather.

However basic or comprehensive a medical outfit might be, it has to share the traits of being as lightweight and compact as possible, with pockets and other dividers for segregating hemorrhage, pain killer, and other sub-kits into easily accessible niches. And it needs to be convenient and comfortable to carry, so that it is never left behind.

Injuries and emergency first-aid are anticipated outcomes in any type of disaster.

Injuries are a feature of every disaster, and it might be invaluable to have some background in emergency first-aid.

Most versatile for families or groups who might need to relocate to a more friendly locale is the daypack first-aid kit. Originally designed for short-term hikers, daypacks have evolved to suit urban residents as well, and the numerous pockets in the latest generation of "street" packs can form the foundation of a very sophisticated emergency medical outfit. Secure pockets for PDAs, laptops, cell-phones, and MP3 players are readily converted to hold bandages, pills, heat packs, water bottles, and medical tools, while the latest in ergonomic suspension development allows the loaded pack to be carried all day with minimal fatigue.

## HEALTH MAINTENANCE

Doctors are unanimous in their opinion that people with strong, adaptable immune systems are less likely to become ill and quicker to shake off whatever infirmities might get a foothold. In every plague there have been people whose resistance to infection has made them immune to whatever pathogens were causing the epidemic. Little is in fact understood about the adaptability of the human immune system, but it has been demonstrated many times that our own bodies possess an innate capability to fight off viruses, bacteria, parasites, and even to kill cancerous growths. No antibiotic has ever matched that ability, so it pays to keep your immune system operating at peak efficiency.

## MULTIVITAMINS

Multivitamin tablets are part of any long-term survival medical kit. At least some necessary nutrients are bound to be lacking in a post-

A paramedic's emergency medical, or "jump," kit (top), is owner-assembled to maximize the number of advanced field medical procedures it can enable an EMS professional to perform, but the Coleman Base Camp first-aid kit ($15) is a good choice for the car or house disaster-survival kit.

disaster diet, and multivitamins help to guarantee that your body will receive a recommended dose of most nutrients every day.

Although a good multivitamin can turn a rough meal from nature into a balanced diet, it must be absorbed through the digestive tract. People whose job it is to empty portable latrines and campground outhouses report that a large percentage of vitamin pills pass through the colon nearly intact. Some brands claim to have overcome this problem, but even their absorption can be maximized by thoroughly chewing each pill, then washing it down with plenty of water. (Note that chewing is not recommended for prescribed pills, especially those that are designed to be time-released).

## ANALGESICS

Pain killers are a must-have component for every first-aid kit. Pain warns us that we are injured, keeps us from increasing damage to injured areas, and keeps us alert in what might be a situation that demands it, but it can also rob victims of restful sleep and inhibit clear thinking.

Over-the-counter analgesics that should be in every first-aid kit include ibuprofen (Motrin), which diminishes pain, fever, and swelling. The standard 200-milligram tablets can be "stacked" to 1,000 mg to increase potency. Naproxin sodium (Advil) also reduces

Inside the jump-kit and Coleman Base Camp first-aid kits. The simplest first-aid kit is nothing more than an assortment of (for example) Band-Aids, safety tape, triple antibiotic ointment, a half-dozen ibuprofen, and a QuikClot bandage in a ziplock freezer bag that is carried in a jacket or thigh pocket. Another option that has proved itself for carry in automobiles is the camera bag-type shoulder satchel, whose compartments are further subdivided by individual foot care, cold remedy, hemorrhage, and other specialized kits in ziplock bags.

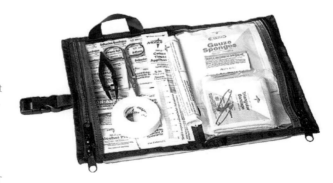

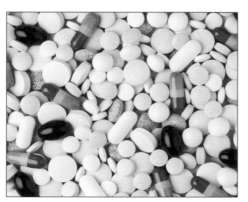

pain, swelling, and fever, with twice the potency per milligram as ibuprofen, but should not be stacked. Both of these pain killers are in the family of NSAIDs—Non-Steroidal Anti-Inflammatory Drugs.

Acetaminophen (Tylenol-brand) is a less-effective pain killer than the NSAIDs, but it also reduces fever and is gentler on the digestive system. Acetaminophen mixes well with other drugs, and is a common ingredient in cough and cold medicines; it is sometimes used in conjunction with aspirin and caffeine to combat migraine headaches (Exedrin). My doctor tells me not to mix acetaminophen with ibuprofen or naproxen sodium, as these cancel out one another.

Acetylsalicylic acid, or Aspirin (Bayer) is a synthetic form of the mild NSAID—salicylic acid—that is found in the bark of willow trees, and is still used as medicinal tea today. In addition to being a pain killer, anti-inflammatory, and fever-reducer (antipyretic), aspirin is an antithrombotic, which inhibits the platelets that form blood clots. Aspirin is also an effective blood

Designed primarily to accommodate all the electronic gadgets and gizmos that have become part of many urban lifestyles, the multipocket versatility of "street" backpacks makes them close to ideal for use as basic or advanced field medical kits.

thinner, and 81-mg "childrens'" tablets are often prescribed to be taken at the onset of a suspected heart attack or stroke.

It is never a good idea to use analgesics of any kind to overcome pain enough to go on. Pain is a warning to stop, to let your body recover from an injury. To take a pain killer so you can stand to walk on an injured knee, for example, could cripple you for life.

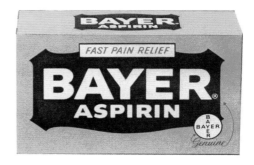

## ANTIHISTAMINES

Benadryl (Diphenhydramine hydrochloride) is best known as an antihistamine for reducing allergic symptoms caused by insect stings and bites, limiting the effect of rashes from poison ivy and other irritants, and combating respiratory anaphylaxis.

Diphenhydramine HCl (found in Benadryl) has also been called the "poor man's atropine," because like the more potent atropine, epinephrine, and Adrenalin, Benadryl helps to reduce the respiratory fluid secretions and distress brought on by exposure to nerve gases (including high levels of the nerve agents

Over-the-counter pain killers can be invaluable in the wreckage of a disaster with mass casualties.

found in insecticides). No dosage data has been established for this purpose, so it is recommended that victims not exceed the dosage recommended on the package.

## LACERATIONS

Cuts to the skin are among the most common injuries during and after a disaster. Knives and axes may become tools of daily life, jagged rubble can tear skin, and torn metal can slice through clothing. Left untreated in a less-than-sterile environment, small cuts can become infected overnight. And if that infection isn't checked, septicemia can set in, followed by gangrene, which may then swiftly kill the wounded area (necrosis), making amputation or surgery necessary, or even kill its victim if the infection becomes systemic.

A basic cut kit consists of a tube of triple antibiotic ointment, three or more four-by-four gauze bandages, several alcohol prep pads, and at least one roll of gauze "Safety Tape" (http://generalbandages.com), which sticks only to itself and holds even when wet. After cleaning the wound, I wrap several turns of tape around either side of the cut, gently pushing the edges almost together. Skin edges should be left slightly apart to permit serum (fluid) drainage as the injury closes from inside. If bleeding persists, tape a pressure bandage large enough to more than cover the wound directly on top to apply blood-stopping downward pressure. After eight hours, I unwind the tape, clean the wound—which has usually stopped bleeding—and apply a looser bandage of safety tape to protect the injury from contamination and bumps.

## SUTURES

Larger wounds—a gash to the ankle, for example—have been effectively closed by "butterfly sutures." These sticky tape strips adhere tightly to skin and replace stitches for many wound-closure applications, but they might not hold in place unless the wound is immobilized for at least three days. Even after that, do not stress the wound more than is absolutely necessary, and cease activities if you feel a sting from the sutures, lest you tear it open again.

Having known a man who nearly lost his leg after stitching a wound closed with needleland thread, I am wary of using sutures in the field. But veteran

A recent emergency medical tool that has become invaluable to field medics is the clotting pad; the one shown is also impregnated with silver to ward off infection when help is a long time coming.

Pain, fever, diarrhea, vomiting—all of these and more are to be expected in the aftermath of disaster, and being able to effectively address those medical issues is good for both the victim and the caregiver.

paramedics insist that suturing is necessary for large wounds, especially those that are torn in different directions and require that skin be stretched back together from the outer edges toward the middle. Sterile stitch-suture kits are available from medical supply outlets for about $6.

## HEMOSTATIC DRESSINGS

The latest in antihemorrhaging agents is a bandage impregnated with clotting agents like Zeolite, Chitosan, and Kaolin, which cause blood to clot on contact. Best known under the brand name "QuikClot," these bandages can seal even arterial bleeds that would otherwise be fatal in just minutes, and they have more than proved themselves in combat. Recently made available in several configurations to the general public, these bandages are a must-have for the survival first-aid kit. For information online, visit: http://quikclot.com

### GENERIC FIRST-AID KIT ITEMS

Following is a list of necessary items for a general-purpose first-aid kit. Thanks to veteran paramedic Cheanne Chellis for her assistance in compiling this list.

1 or more pairs of nitrile gloves
1 tube antibiotic ointment
1 roll 1-inch-wide safety tape
   Butterfly sutures, assorted sizes
1 sterile suture kit
1 bottle ibuprofen (or Naproxin sodium) tablets
1 package glucose tablets (for hypoglycemia))
1 bottle aspirin
1 bottle multivitamins
10 MSR Micropur MP1 water purification tabs
10 Benadryl (diphenhydramine) antihistamine
   capsules
10 Loperamide hydrochloride anti-diarrhea caplets

1 1-liter water bottle
1 tube liquid hand soap
6 alcohol prep pads
1 pair EMS shears
1 thermometer with protective case
1 locking forceps
1 pair toenail clippers
1 pair tweezers
1 small pair scissors
1 toothbrush
1 QuikClot antimicrobial hemostatic pack, 50 mg
1 package sewing needles, assorted sizes
1 small flashlight or headlamp

## REFERENCES:

*Be Red Cross Ready Safety Series Volume 4: A Family Guide to First-Aid and Emergency Preparedness* (http://www.redcrossstore.org)

*Be Red Cross First-Aid and Emergency Preparedness Quick-Reference Guide*

** If you take prescription medications, consult your doctor about having an emergency supply of those on hand.

## MEDICAL DEHYDRATION

Different than just being thirsty, medical dehydration is brought on by challenges to your body from outside influences. Most common is diarrhea, which is essentially an attempt by your body to flush out toxins and infection, but can be brought on by numerous causes. Some viruses and bacteria can wreak havoc on a digestive tract, and parasites are guaranteed to send a victim's lower intestine into turmoil. So can foods that are too rich, too coarse, or spoiled. Diarrhea is not an illness, but a symptom of an illness.

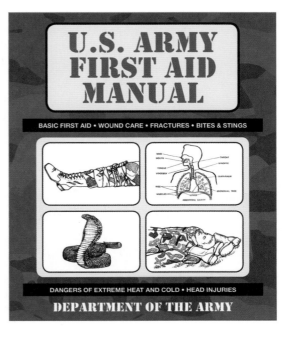

Vomiting is another symptom of some other medical problem. It too can be brought on by viruses, microbes, parasites, and bad food. Vomiting is also common during times of high stress, and upset stomachs are a normal circumstance in post-disaster conditions.

Although vomiting and diarrhea are not primary illnesses, they can be a hazard in themselves—sometimes becoming even more life-threatening than the original ailment. The problem is dehydration, because the attempted bodily purging that manifests itself as either vomiting or diarrhea saps water from tissues for the flushing process. If either is prolonged, loss of fluids needed to operate other metabolic functions can result in a multitude of troubles, like loss of electrolytes—especially potassium—that control heart rhythm. Combine the chronic expulsion of vital moisture with the added complications of fever and infection, and either of these symptoms can be fatal within just 2 or 3 days.

This U.S. Army First Aid Manual is a timeless source of advice and information about hardcore survival medicine.

If proper medical attention is not available, the treatment is to "push" fluids into the victim. Clear water helps to flush affected tracts, but replacement of electrolytes with sport drinks like Gatorade is best. Lacking these, it is important to replace lost saline and calories with 1 teaspoon of table salt and 1 tablespoon of sugar per gallon of water—these measures cannot be exact for everyone in every case, but are good rules of thumb. Like-wise for the amount of water a victim drinks, but the need to urinate should be frequent, and urine should be clear and well diluted, not dark or with a pungent odor.

Although vomiting and diarrhea are symptoms of a greater illness, they can become serious impediments in themselves. It's hard to travel when your bowels are misbehaving, and it's tough to be stealthy if you're retching. It could become necessary to treat nausea

with Dramamine or a stout tea of wintergreen, spear-mint, or peppermint leaves to diminish nausea. Diar-rhea can be quelled with loperamide HCl (Immodium AD), and I've seen good results from a sweet-smelling tea of shaved blackberry roots, made strong enough to be rose-colored in a cup.

## WILDERNESS DENTISTRY

Dental problems are a part of everyone's life, and if the services that make life civilized are disrupted, a lost filling can become a bona fide medical emergency. While I cannot legally tell anyone what to do about that, I can relate to you how I have dealt with more than one bad tooth when there was no dentist available.

In one instance I'd been in a wilderness for two months when my left bottom molar split in two while eating. Within days the broken molar began to ache from its roots. The pain was tolerable with an assist from ibuprofen at bedtime, but then the gum became inflamed and sore to the touch, and the aching became bone-deep and constant. I continued to chew with the

Dental problems will happen, and when they occur at a time when normal commerce and services are disrupted for even a few days, they can become life-threatening unless dealt with.

broken tooth, hoping to loosen it from its moorings, and kept it brushed clean, but after a few days my jaw began to swell from an infection at the molar's roots.

Having almost died from an abscessed tooth as a child, I determined that most crit-ical was preventing pressure from building under the molar, which could cause trapped poisons to be forced into my bloodstream. I began by localizing the infection with a wash-cloth soaked in hot water, itself folded into a watertight plastic bag, then wrapped inside a dry towel. I held the makeshift heat pack against my jaw, directly on top of the infected molar, where it created an artificial fever to bring the poison to a head.

When the applied heat had caused a blister to form on the outside of my gum, making the skin there taut, I took a large carpet needle from my sewing kit and felt around for the most swollen spot. I didn't sterilize the needle, although I should have, because I reckoned it couldn't carry anything worse than the germs that were already there. Except for my too-small Star Flash signal mirror, I didn't have a reflecting surface, and that meant the whole operation had be done by feel alone.

Predictably, the highest point of the induced gum boil was directly over a root, and that seemed a good place to lance the infection. I steeled myself, then shoved the carpet needle directly into that spot, perpendicular to the gum. Tears welled in my eyes as I drove the needle inward until its tip scraped solidly against a root. I wiggled the needle in a circular motion, widening the point-of-entry, and felt the electric shock of a pus sac bursting from around still-living nerve. I felt an immediate sensation of relief as pressure was released from that painful area.

With thumb and forefinger, I squeezed the infected gum around the hole I'd lanced, forcing trapped toxins to exit under pressure. After each hard squeeze I wiped away copious amounts of yellowish pus with tissue paper, which reduced the swelling considerably. When the tissue came away bloody, I figured the infection had been purged—for now. I hadn't cured the problem, but I had prevented the molar from becoming more than an uncomfortable distraction for a while at least.

The hard part still awaited me. The abscess had killed the tooth, and the flesh socket surrounding it would keep infecting, trying to push the now-foreign object out of itself, for as long as the molar was there. I had no choice but to extract the tooth.

Dentistry isn't a contingency that is usually addressed by survival lore, and the topic is in fact mostly avoided in any company. I didn't have dental tools, so I'd have to make do with my cabin-building tools. I took the big lineman's pliers from my tool bag and sterilized its jaws with alcohol pads. I snapped its disinfected jaws together a few times; surely no dentist would approve, but they would have to do.

By feel alone I managed to lock the pliers' jaws around the molar. Tooth enamel is hard, and the knurled jaws slipped a few times before I found a grip strong enough to twist against. I squeezed the pliers' handles hard as I rocked and twisted the molar in its steel jaws. The pain was literally blinding as my eardrums registered the cracking sounds of living flesh ripping from bone. My vision narrowed to a dark tunnel dancing

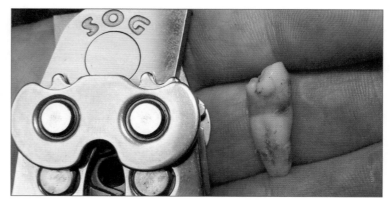

This premolar (not the molar of the author's story) became abscessed in the deep woods and had to be extracted without pain killers using a SOG multitool.

with bright spots, and I channeled the energy of this powerful stimulus to twist the pliers even harder.

The molar came free with an almost subdued crunching sound, and suddenly I was holding the dead tooth before me. The good news was that I'd extracted the roots cleanly on one side; the bad news was that the other two roots were still there, broken off below the gum line. I rinsed my mouth with salt water and spat blood until the hemorrhaging

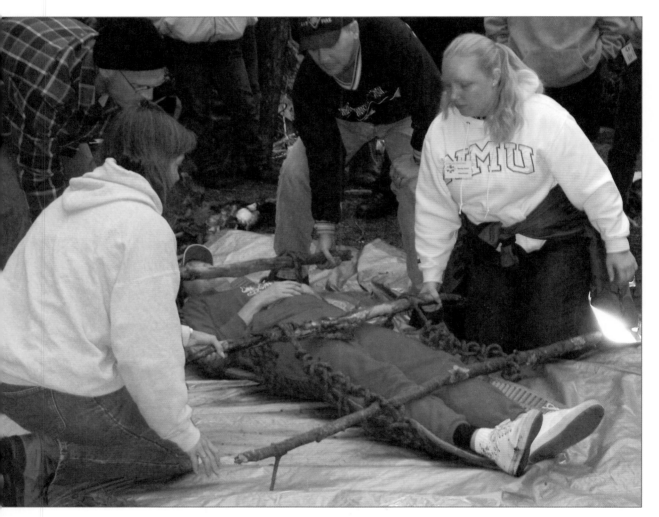

These paramedics are training to use materials at hand to evacuate a disabled victim over rugged terrain.

stopped. I could feel the remainder of the tooth still embedded in its socket, where I couldn't get at it with tools.

The dead root wasn't a great danger to my health, but it was an irritation. The gum healed around what had now become a sliver of foreign material, and there was an occasional jolt of pain when I was chewing. If I ignored the pain, I'd awaken the next morning with the gum around it feeling tender and swollen. It wasn't over yet; the root had to be extracted too.

This was my first experience with home dental extractions, and I really didn't know how to proceed. I honed my Spyderco folding knife to shaving sharpness and prepared to perform oral surgery on myself. I laid the tip of its blade against the outer gum, directly over where the dead root lay trapped, and pushed the cutting edge inward through the soft tissue until it stopped against the root. I could only guess what was happening as I operated by feel alone, but I felt the gum separate from around the embedded root.

Blood was flowing, and I spat bright red several times as I felt for a grip with the pliers, but the pain was negligible—probably due to endorphins. When a corner of the pliers closed securely onto the broken root from above and below, I squeezed the pliers' handles hard and twisted. A flash of pain formed the center of my vision as the root tore from its moorings, coming free in the jaws of my pliers.

Like an iceberg, the extracted root was larger than it had seemed, measuring roughly half an inch square by a quarter-inch thick. I rinsed my mouth with salt water to help stanch the bleeding, happy at having that annoying chunk of bone gone, but concerned that the incision might not heal correctly. A dentist would have stitched the cut gum together, but I doubted I could perform that operation, so I left it to heal on its own.

The incision and empty socket healed quickly and without secondary infection. I brushed the healing gum when I brushed my teeth, to remove particles of food and to toughen it, and in 2 weeks it had healed enough to chew on that side.

Again, none of this is presented as advice, only as an anecdotal report of how one man dealt with a problem molar. Whether you will have to deal with a similar dilemma will probably depend on the period and severity of privation you must endure, but I believe that relief from dental problems can be a topic worth addressing when constructing a first-aid kit.

## TRIAGE

Disasters are defined by large numbers of casualties. People being burned jumped to their deaths from the World Trade Center; bloated corpses floated along flooded city streets after Hurricane Katrina; rotting bodies had to be hauled away and buried unceremoniously in mass graves after the Haitian earthquake, and for days the moans of crushed, dying victims could be heard from under the rubble of collapsed buildings.

Public services are sure to be stretched beyond capacity following any type of mass-casualty disaster, and first aid may need to become rudimentary as medical supplies run low.

Survivors of all of these disasters were thirsty, in shock, in mourning, and in need of assistance themselves.

Nothing about a natural or man-made disaster is a good life experience, and you won't want to be around one any longer than you have to unless you are a trained search-and-rescue professional. Few natural disasters take us by surprise these days, and while newscasts tend to focus on the bravado of future victims who refuse to comply with orders to evacuate, most people are responsible enough to withdraw to safety with their loved ones. As paramedic Cheanne Chellis observed, people who are not medical professionals rarely have the training needed to effectively assist in a mass-casualty situation, and there is nothing good to be gained from being present if you don't have to be. The best strategy for someone who is caught in the aftermath of a disaster is leave for a safer, less hostile area immediately.

# Security and Defense

**W**hen the grand old city of New Orleans was hammered by Hurricane Katrina, even the most ardent believer in doomsday had to be surprised at how swiftly that nexus of cultures disintegrated into lawless anarchy. Within a week the remains of the city saw a scourge of roving predators and looters, and average citizens who had not heeded the official order to evacuate found themselves fearing to be on the street. One of the most haunting sights was an Associated Press photo showing a pair of toddlers playing innocently on a sidewalk in the shadow of a decaying corpse in a wheelchair.

It is a fact that hard times make hard people, both mentally and physically. And while adversity brings out the best in some people, it makes others purely mean. If you are reading this book, it's a fair bet that you wouldn't want to be one of those who can survive only by preying on others. This author's recommendation is that you the survivor should avoid making contact with the marauders who inevitably coalesce into gangs after any disaster that causes an interruption of goods and services. Combat is the antithesis of survival, and you gain nothing by engaging hoodlums in any kind of conflict.

Even so, there might come a time when it becomes necessary to defend one's self or loved ones, and should that frightening situation come to pass, it pays to be sure that you'll have the upper hand. That doesn't necessarily imply the use of lethal force, just an ability to swiftly and surely blast assailants with enough physical and mental anguish to derail an attack while you escape.

# PERSONAL DEFENSE

There might come a time when it's necessary to defend oneself or loved ones, when you cannot reason with an aggressor or walk away. Should that come to pass it will be reassuring to have the upper hand. That doesn't necessarily imply the use of lethal force, or even firearms, just an ability to swiftly and surely blast assailants with enough physical and mental anguish to derail an attack while you find safety.

## NON-LETHAL DEFENSE

Real-life hand-to-hand fighting doesn't resemble the ballet-like choreography seen in martial-arts movies. It is dirty, painful, and exhausting, and frequently leaves the winner seriously injured. One Shotokan instructor advised, "Run away. If you can't run away, hurt your assailants until you can run away."

To summarize Master Bruce Lee's secret, practice with kicks and punches trains the body to accurately deliver blows, while the key to fighting an actual opponent lies in not having a plan, but rather anticipating and responding to the opponent's actions. Beyond that, avoid getting hit, and hit as hard as you can against sensitive areas—like the groin, the short ribs along the bottom of the ribcage, the collar bone, the eyes, the knees... Wherever it would hurt to be hit on your own body is a target on your opponent's body.

## CHEMICAL DEFENSES

Aerosol bad-guy repellants have been on the market for a long time, and that fact alone is proof of their value to average citizens. One of the latest and most improved versions of a pepper-spray blaster is the Tiger Light (http://www.tigerlight.net), which claims a 96% effectiveness at stopping assailants in their tracks. At night, the Tiger Light masquerades as a bright LED flashlight, but should someone bent on evil spring from hiding, a flip of the wrist turns the unit into a weapon that can envelope a half-dozen assailants in a dense cloud of burning, choking capsicum spray before they can close their eyes or hold their breaths. The unit's heavy metal body, held against the palm by a padded strap, is a bludgeoning weapon by itself.

Meaner versions of pepper gas that once caused a media uproar are the aerosol oven cleaners that have been referred to as "poor-girl's mace." The caustic lyes contained in oven cleaners burn skin on contact, causing ulcerated sores unless washed off immediately. They can also cause permanent damage to the eyes.

## STRIKING WEAPONS

From China to Galilee to the Sherwood Forest of Little John and Robin Hood, staves

and walking sticks have served as effective weapons for defense and offense. The end of a 5-foot walking stick being swung with intent is traveling about 90 miles per hour—the speed of a Major League fastball—and one blow from it can break bones, even kill.

A more effective version of the staff is the lance, a long, stout, sharply-pointed spear —preferably with a dagger-type spear point for stabbing and slashing. Not meant to be thrown, a lance extends the distance to which its owner can inflict wounds, and with a spearhead increases the severity of those wounds. A preferred weapon of the Spartans, the power of a long spear is still demonstrated in the way African lions will actually withdraw at the approach of Masai tribesmen carrying their traditional long spears and shields.

The ko-budo-nunchaku is an ancient Japanese rice-threshing tool that proved dangerous enough as a weapon to be quickly outlawed throughout the United States in the 1970s. Known colloquially—even on television—as "Numchuks," the nunchaku is essentially just a pair of equal-size wooden billy-clubs, each about 18 inches long, that are joined securely to one another at one end with about 6 inches of tough rope or chain. When swung from one end so that the free end strikes a target, the impact force transferred to the target is magnified beyond what a single club would generate; and when the blow is delivered using heavy-weight "combat sticks," a single strike is often enough to render an assailant harmless with perhaps multiple broken bones and internal injuries. In the hands of an expert, the nunchaku's flexible design is deadly fast, able to change direction fluidly, to strike with lethal energy in one place, then again in another so fast that

it can't be seen. But the beauty of this weapon is that it can be used effectively by someone with no training at all.

## EDGED WEAPONS

When I was a boy, and in a few years throughout my adulthood, my family and I raised pigs. In autumn I'd herd a selected 260-pound hog into the kill-chute, where I'd shoot it through the top center of its skull with a .45 ACP. The pig always collapsed instantly, but then it needed to be "bled" to drain as much blood as possible from its tissues before its heart stopped beating, otherwise there would be objectionable blood clots throughout the meat. And this had to be done within approximately 5 seconds of the gunshot, before the pig went into the mindless but violent after-death kicking convulsions that are a trademark of hog-killing. I'd safety the Colt and lay it down, draw a long, narrow-blade knife, drop to one knee and drive it almost to the hilt into the carcass's neck, just above the sternum. Then I'd draw the inserted blade's cutting edge across the neck, making an incision 6 inches deep by 10 inches long, and cutting through the top of the pig's heart. Some farmers skipped the shooting step altogether, "sticking" 200-pound hogs with a quick slash that left them walking around for the next 2 or 3 minutes before falling over dead from blood loss.

As the above is meant to illustrate, knives and swords are fearsome close-quarters weapons, capable of inflicting a mortal wound with every strike. What this pig-sticking story did not describe is how awful a weapon a knife can be. When my shaving-sharp blade's tip drew across a hog's heart, it severed the tissue almost effortlessly, opening a huge, fatal gash that allowed all of the pressurized blood in the animal's venous and arterial systems to literally spurt outward in a great red gush that washed over my hand up to the wrist. A rinse bucket close by enabled me to quickly wash off my hand and knife, because blood can make a knife handle dangerously slippery—something to be aware of in selecting a personal-defense knife. Police officers are instructed to draw their sidearms at the sight of a knife, and to shoot a knife-wielding suspect who closes to within 10 feet of them, because within its reach, a knife can inflict more severe wounds than a pistol.

## TACTICAL FOLDING KNIVES

In today's world, the dirk has been down-sized to become the "tactical" folder, a locking-blade folding knife that usually clips to the inside of a hip pocket, where it is secure, but easy to draw. Tactical folders typically have blades of at least 3 inches, with sharply

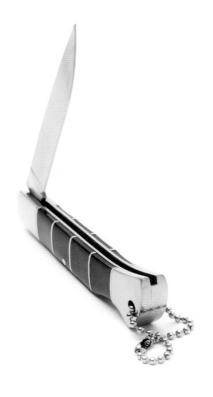

pointed tips. They are designed for fast deployment, and most now have legal "opening-assist" mechanisms that push the blade into battery as soon as the user pushes against its opening stud, hole, or lever. On most days these close-quarters combat folders are relegated to opening mail, but they can be a formidable defensive weapon when danger steps from the shadows.

A tactical folder is designed to effectively slash and stab. Based on fatalities due to knife wounds, stabbing is the major cause of death, largely because those wounds penetrate deeply enough to pierce vital organs. The point of a tactical folder is pointed, with a false edge opposite the cutting edge at the tip of its blade to enable easier penetration through heavy clothing—even Kevlar vests. Some have an inch or 2 of serrations at the beginning of their cutting edges, adjacent to the "choil" (the unsharpened portion of blade between where the cutting edge begins and the knife's handle). The serrations help when cutting through thick rubberized fabrics (tires), thick plastics, and wet hemp rope, but also shred their way through heavy ballistic nylon and most fabrics.

A tactical folder needs to be rugged, strongly made and assembled to open, handle, and close smoothly enough for its operation to become a habit. It must have a secure lock to keep the blade from closing over its user's fingers. It must have an ergonomically-contoured handle that provides a sure grip in all hand positions, even when slippery, and won't allow a user's hand to slide onto the blade. It should also be unobtrusive in carry mode, comfortable for its owner, and not strikingly colored, or positioned to attract attention.

## FIXED-BLADE FIGHTING KNIVES

Even though he has designed one or two folding combat knives, martial arts master James Williams (www.bugei.com), himself one of the most dangerous close-quarter fighters in the world, openly admits that a fixed-blade knife is always a preferred combat knife. The strength of a one-piece blade with a full-length hilt (handle) incorporated into its design is much greater than with a two-part knife, and it's ready for action as soon as it is drawn. A good combat fixed-blade knife can be used to pry with from any direction, and except for the very tip of sharply-pointed designs, it should be unbreakable under maximum hand pressure.

When electronics warfare expert Lt. Colonel Iceal Hambleton was shot down by a missile over Vietnam in 1972, he survived for a week while evading enemy patrols who badly wanted the knowledge he possessed, all the while making his way to a safe extraction point. When Hambleton was attacked by a machete-wielding farmer while raiding the man's hooch for food, the 53-year-old Hambleton overpowered his assailant and killed him with the 5-inch blade of his issue USAF Survival Knife.

Most knife-fighting experts consider 5 inches to be on the short side for fixed-blade combat knife, even though most admit that 4 inches is sufficient to quickly end a human's life. Larger knives with longer blades are most preferred, because the object is always to get the pointy end into the other guy before he does the same to you, and longer reach is better. The real deciding factor is how comfortable a person is with his or her knife; if a knife feels comfortable in your hand, able to be used, manipulated, and switched between grip positions without fear of cutting yourself, it's probably a good choice for you. A larger knife is no advantage to a person who doesn't wield it easily.

## DIRKS

Aside from ceremony and open warfare, full-size swords with blades the length of a person's leg were not common everyday wear; they were just too cumbersome for normal activities—like sitting in a chair—and long blades were impeded and entangled in the confines of most buildings. But going about unarmed is unwise during lawless times, and that problem was nicely remedied by the dirk, a heavy shortsword that can slash through bone or stab through a ribcage with equal ease, and do either in the blink of an eye.

Combine those properties with modern manufacturing technologies and today's greatly homogenized and precisely hardened alloys, and you have the finest fighting blades in the history of mankind, available at prices nearly anyone can afford. Even in untrained hands, a dirk can sever bones and tendons with a single clumsy blow, or it open wide an abdominal cavity; in expert hands it can cleanly decapitate an enemy. In normal times, the carry of a dirk, even openly, may be considered a felony, but that in itself is a good indication of just how effective this shortsword can be in a no-holds-barred street fight.

# ESCAPE AND EVASION

Whether you should relocate before or after a disaster, or hunker down and wait it out can depend on a number of variables. Most authorities agree that heavily populated areas will not be good places to stay after a disaster like the recent Haitian earthquake that left unidentified corpses piled like cordwood on the sidewalks of Port-au-Prince. The world recoiled at the sight of nameless thousands being plowed into mass graves by bulldozers, but the health hazards posed by so many decaying bodies made them an immediate threat to those who survived.

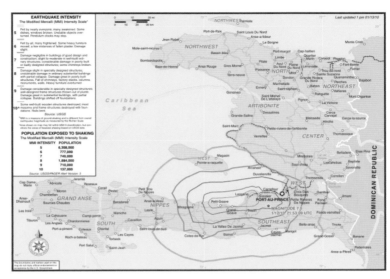

In urban areas there may be little point in attempting to drive out of a city because, as in the movies, all avenues are likely to be blocked by the cars of people who have already tried it. A motorcycle or scooter might get through, but probably the best wheeled escape vehicle is a bicycle. Bicycles today can be tricked out to carry a tent, sleeping bag, and other equipment strapped to their frames, but a bug-out bike is probably best kept as light as possible for carrying past obstacles, while survival gear is carried in a small pack on the rider's back.

# BUGGING-OUT

If you must relocate to escape the effects of falling volcanic ash, windborne radiation, or to find a more hospitable place to live, use information from the preceding chapters to outfit yourself as functionally as possible before embarking.

Emphasis should be placed on water, water purification, and water carriers, with drinking needs estimated at one to two gallons per adult per day, depending on exertion levels. Food needs should be assessed using the FDA's 2,000-calories-per-day recommended daily diet as a minimum, and foods carried in your traveling backpack should be dry and lightweight.

Survival gear for an on-foot egress from inhospitable areas is mostly the same as it would be for navigating any wilderness: a map of the country being traveled, a good compass (satellites may be out of commission), warm bedroll, lightweight bivy shelter, first-aid, food, water, and the means to obtain more food and water. Canadian bush pilots carry backpacks loaded with back-country provisions because if reaching safety after surviving a crash entails walking long distances—and in Canada it probably will—a backpack loaded with no more than a third of its bearer's weight is the best method of hauling survival gear.

Bugging-out of a devastated area after a disaster is unlike crossing a less hostile wilderness, because a post-disaster scenario will entail keeping your head down, moving furtively, seeing other survivors before they see you, and avoiding contact until you can positively identify whether or not those others are friends or foes. You believe you have something to live for and a future worth rebuilding; they may not share your optimism.

There is little good about the process of survival, which by definition means that a person is being subject to conditions that have a potential to be fatal unless something is done to at least moderate the dangers they pose. Anticipate that your own disaster-survival experience will be heartbreaking, with injured people you cannot mend, sickly people you cannot heal, and thirsty people you might not be able to provide with water without taking it from your own family. There is sometimes a fine line between what has been termed "lifeboat survival" and the noble traits that constitute humanity. I believe there are no right or wrong answers for such dilemmas: there are only survivors and otherwise, and survivors must live with the choices they make.

## THE BUG-OUT BAG

The surest means of escaping a post-disaster city will usually be on foot, which means that your home survival system will include what has recently become known as a bug-out bag. Once called a "grab-and-go" backpack, the bug-out bag is a survival kit that can be snatched up and carried away at a moment's notice.

In real life, possible needs for a grab-and-go survival kit are generally less than adventurous, but no less critical. A family that awakens to find its house on fire, or flooded, or about to be flattened by a powerful twister may have time to grab one item before fleeing into a chill night. That one thing should be a large, easily carried survival kit packed with as many potentially lifesaving tools as it can hold.

## BUILDING A BUG-OUT BAG

No survival kit can provide for every contingency in every environment, but some items are generic to all conditions. Most fundamental are water, shelter, warmth, and food, either in the form of the provisions themselves or tools for obtaining those necessities. Which of those needs is most important depends entirely on the situation—in the desert, water may be critical; in a northern Ontario winter, it will be warmth—so use as much foresight as possible to predict the conditions your bug-out kit will be called upon to address.

Begin with the container into which your tools will be placed. This grab-and-go survival kit needs to be easily transportable, preferably wearable—that pretty much narrows the options to a backpack. The all-purpose survival backpack has a carry capacity of at least 2,000 inches, a full, padded suspension that includes waist belt and sternum strap to help make the loaded pack a part of your body, and as many secure pockets and pouches as you can find, to accommodate segregating gear into individual kits that can be easily found in the dark. A good day-and-a-half backpack, as this size is generally known, can be had for under $100, fully outfitted with the necessities of survival in all environments for around $400, and weighs in at an all-day carry weight of under 20 pounds.

## PERSONAL SURVIVAL KITS

The grab-and-go backpack shouldn't be the only layer of protection a person has against unpleasant surprises. A favorite jacket can be transformed into a rudimentary survival kit, and many outdoor knives made today include cargo pouches on their sheaths. A parka shell in hurricane country can easily carry a working-size folding knife, a butane lighter and tinder in a ziplock bag, compass and map, AA flashlight, cord, granola bars . . . and still have room to spare. Think of your disaster preparedness system in terms of levels: A belt knife kit will keep you breathing under almost any circumstances; an outfitted parka shell kit allows a few more comforts; the bug-out bag has all you'll need to weather a disaster in relative comfort.

The following lists include some of the best survival tools on the market today. Products mentioned by name should be viewed as examples of acceptable quality only, because some manufacturers discontinue models as fast as they introduce new ones. None of the survival kit contents listed here are absolute, and they should be added to or subtracted from as needed to match different situations. Some items are duplicated in larger and more capable kits, because, as NASA already knows, it pays to have some redundancy in an environment where small problems can have large consequences.

## BELT KNIFE SURVIVAL KIT:
- Knife, strong, sharp: Schrade EXTREME BT01, Ontario Knife RAT-7
- Sheath: Secure snap-down retainer, thigh tie-down, large cargo pouch
- Compass, pocket: Silva Type 7, Brunton 11HNL
- Fire Starter: Ultimate Survival Technologies Strike Force or Sparkie

## POCKET SURVIVAL KIT:
- Compass: Coleman 3-in-1 compass/whistle/match case, Brunton 11HNL with whistle
- Map: Trail or topographical, preferably laminated with clear contact paper
- Folding Knife, pocket-clip, open-assist: Columbia River Natural, Schrade
- Fire Starter: Butane lighter, UST Sparkie, waxed cotton-string "fire wicks"
- First-Aid Kit (in ziplock bag): Roll of 1-inch Safety Tape, tube of triple antibiotic ointment
- Space Blanket or disposable painter's drop cloth

## SURVIVAL PARKA SHELL (INCLUDES ALL OF THE ABOVE):
- Parka Shell, hooded, many pockets, waterproof, ventilated: Columbia Titanium
- Orienteering Compass: Brunton SightMaster, Brunton 8099 Eclipse
- Folding Multi-Function Tool: Gerber Multi-Tool, Buck BuckTool, Leatherman
- Fire Starter: Butane lighter, Strike Force flint-and-steel, tinder
- Cord: At least 15 feet of military-issue parachute cord
- Gloves, leather shell: Wells Lamont
- Fishing Kit (in pill bottle): Hooks, sinkers, at least 20 feet of strong fishing line
- Snacks: High-carb, 1,000 calories, for fending off hypoglycemia
- Water Bladder: One-liter, MSR Platypus
- Water Purification Tabs: Katadyn MicroPur MP-1
- Flashlight: Gerber OMNIVORE, Coleman AXIS AAA LED headlamp
- Signal Mirror, lightweight, with sighting hole: UST Star Flash

## SURVIVAL DAY PACK, ALL-DAY CARRY (INCLUDES ALL OF THE ABOVE):

- Daypack, many pockets, padded, adjustable harness: Exponent Otero, Kelty Bison (camouflage)
- Compass: Brunton 8099, Brunton SightMaster
- Map: Detailed area map, topographical preferred
- GPS (optional, secondary to compass)
- Heavy Machete (strapped onto pack): Ontario Knife SP-8, Kershaw OUTCAST
- Shelter, bivy-type, compact: Exponent Kraz X1, Integral Designs Mega Sola
- Water Filter: Katadyn Vario, MSR WaterWorks II
- Water Bladder: MSR Platypus 2-liter
- Sleeping Bag, ultralight mummy, synthetic-fill, rated about 20 degrees: Exponent Canyon
- Sleeping Pad: Therm-A-Rest Pro-Lite 3 (inflatable), Therm-A-Rest Z-Lite (closed-cell foam)
- First-Aid Kit: Packed in its own kit, comprehensive—dysentery, pain, bleeding, allergies, sprains . . .
- Fire Starters: Butane lighter, matches, waxed-cotton "fire wicks," military Trioxane tabs
- Cord: GI 550-pound parachute cord, 50 feet or more
- Cord: Nylon packaging string, 50-yard spool
- Socks, synthetic-knit, padded: SmartWool, Wigwam
- Radio Receiver, AM-FM-SW: Kaito KA1102
- Cook Set, lightweight, designed for boiling: European military surplus cook pot set, MSR Titanium Mini-Cookset
- Cup, metal, about one pint: Coleman Peak 1, MSR Titan titanium cup
- Spoon, teaspoon with metal handle bent backward into a hook, for snagging hot handles from fire
- Food, nonperishable, 6,000 calories (three days) per person: Granola bars, rice, raisins, chocolate . . .
- Spear Head, Frog, three-tined, carried with points safely embedded in foam, etc.
- Slingshot, folding, latex-tubing, wrist brace: Wham-O Wrist Rocket

## OPTIONAL ITEMS FOR THE SURVIVAL KIT

How important an item might be to survival depends on conditions. If you suffer a dizzy spell from hypoglycemia, getting blood sugars back to operating levels is imperative. In a cold rain, making fire may save your life. In desert, water becomes critical. Since you can't predict what item might have lifesaving value, it pays to prepare for as many contingencies as you can. Presuming a person knows roughly where on earth he or she will be, should a situation come up that requires survival techniques, that person can prepare to live indefinitely with whatever conditions might be found there.

# SHARPENING KNIVES AND EDGED TOOLS

My grandpa used to say that he knew only six people who could properly sharpen a knife, and that he'd taught the skill to three of them. He probably wasn't exaggerating by much; the science of making knives sharp hasn't been part of the average person's life since a fixed-blade sheath knife was part almost every American's daily work attire. A rugged knife is the original multi-tool, enabling its owner to cut, chop, whittle, skin, butcher, drill, and it could be a prudent sidearm in the days when there was more wilderness than people. As the need to use a knife tapered off, so did the need—and then the ability—to sharpen them back to working condition.

Honing a knife—or lawnmower blade, axe, or scythe—to shaving sharpness demands first knowing why a sharp edge is sharp. The key to sharpness lies in bringing both sides of a blade to meet at a very pointed and highly polished apex. A dull blade is one that has had that very pointed joining of its two sides worn off, which basically translates to driving a broader surface area into a material being cut, and requiring more downward force to sever a given material. Restoring, then polishing an edge to its original (or sharper) bevel is accomplished by removing sub-microns of blade material until the sharpest and most-pointed meeting of the two sides has been achieved.

The original knife and tool sharpener is a dense, abrasive sandstone, and it served people who relied on their blades well into the twentieth century.

The traditional re-sharpener is a stone, coarse enough to abrade a few molecules at a time from a blade when the two are rubbed against one another. If you can keep the angle between knife and stone constant while smoothly grinding the sides of a blade to terminate in a keen point from handle to blade tip, you can achieve an edge that requires care in handling. By polishing that even bevel against a harder honing surface—like the traditional Arkansas oilstone—to make it mirror-smooth, even an axe can be honed to hair-shaving sharpness.

I believe you can forget all you might have heard about keeping a blade at a specific angle to a honing surface. Most American and European blades have cutting edges ground to 20 degrees, while Asian knives are historically angled to 15 degrees, but that really doesn't matter, because gauging precise angles by eye alone is virtually impossible. The secret of an expert honesman is a learned ability to "feel" the edge as it slides against a honing surface. If it slips, catches, or slides jerkily as you grind the blade against it, then there is not a broad enough or flat enough surface against the stone to create an even bevel that drags smoothly. A skilled knife sharpener

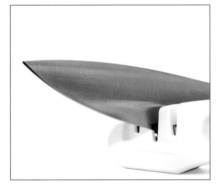

This inexpensive Chef's Choice manual sharpener has three blade guides with pre-angled diamond hones at their bottoms to sharpen and smooth the edge of virtually any knife to skinning sharpness.

In actual trials, Smith's Edge Pro manual knife sharpener enabled men and women who had no skill with conventional honing stones to apply hair-shaving edges to a broad range of blade styles.

can restore his or her knife's cutting edge in the dark, just by feeling how smoothly the blade the blade drags. Angle doesn't matter—old skinners sometimes increase the angle it their knives' edges to create a steeper point where the sides meet, which increases the amount of wear needed to make it dull (but makes it more prone chipping when used for chopping).

There is no wrong way to create the sharp bevel of a keen edge. The classic honing motion is to begin at the choil, where the sharpened edge ends, just ahead of the handle. Move the blade in a circular motion that grinds it against the honing surface at a narrow angle, as though you were trying to slice a very thin layer from the hone. As you rotate the blade in even-size circles, draw the knife back from handle to tip to grind an even cutting edge with a needle-sharp point. As the circling blade rounds the "belly" that leads to its point, raise the handle to increase the honing angle as cutting angle changes.

It's usually easier to sharpen a knife by grinding its edge against a hone, but some blade metals like D2 tool steel and beta-titanium tend to roll off to one side when they meet at a thin point. These metals get sharpest by honing with the edge, with most friction applied away from the cutting edge. All edges can be sharpened by honing with their cutting edges, but they must first have an evenly-beveled cutting edge.

To save time when sharpening a very dull knife, I use a coarse aluminum-oxide "stone" (it's actually man-made), available at most hardware and department stores for around $10. A larger stone, 3 inches by at least 6 inches, provides a safer and more efficient grinding surface. I wet the stone with water (never put any type of oil on an aluminum-oxide hone or it may be ruined forever, its porous surface clogged by non-abrasive varnish), and then grind a blade hard against it in a back-and-forth motion, toward the edge then away from it. This motion permit's a forceful push against the hone that maximizes the amount of metal ground off, and quickly "sets" its edge. I repeat the back-and-forth motion up and down both sides of the blade until the beveled cutting edges are even on either side, and the blade feels sharp, but rough. It doesn't matter if the bevels are a little rough, so long as they are even, because a finer hone can polish a rough edge better than it can create a new one.

A keen edge drags against a thumb dragged crosswise over it—never run your thumb lengthwise with the edge, because a sharp blade literally splits skin with only slight pressure. Finally, you can "strop" a good edge to hair-shaving sharpness by polishing it with the edge against a wide leather belt or strap to stand it up and create a surgically-sharp blade.

## SHARPENING TOOLS

Many attempts have been made to create a sharpening tool that enables anyone to put a shaving edge on a knife, but only recently have a few succeeded at making almost everyone nearly as good at sharpening knives as the best honemasters. The latest generation manual sharpeners are typically pull-through designs, with two V-shaped notches comprised of two intersecting blades that form each notch;

An improvement on a time-honored method, Smith's Diamond Tri-Hone Sharpening system can put surgical edges on knives and scissors for many years.

the carbide side mills nice, even bevels onto the dullest straight-edge knives, while the ceramic side does a bang-up job of polishing straight- or serrated-blade knives to a keenness that might raise your eyebrows.

Using the latest sharpeners is endearingly simple: Place the blade being sharpened in the appropriate notch, starting at the choil, and draw the knife backward smoothly toward its tip. Light downward pressure is best, especially in the aggressive carbide notch; if the blade chatters and catches as you pull it through, ease up on the pressure being applied. Try to keep the blade at right angles to the sharpener to ensure even cutting on either side, and raise the handle upward as you round the blade's belly, toward the point. Notch blades are ambidextrous to accommodate left- or right-handed users, and blades are reversible to extend their lives. Blades can also be replaced when (if) they wear out. Replacement carbide or ceramic blades are available, but the originals are likely to last several years with regular use.

If you prefer the control and versatility of traditional honing stones, it's hard to go wrong with a simple round (knife) or rectangular (axe) aluminum-oxide honing stone, double-sided with coarse and medium grits, and priced at about $10 to start. About twice as expensive are crystalline diamond-impregnated hones. Some hones are rods, which can sharpen strap-cutter and gut hooks, some are flat like conventional honing stones; all are touted to last forever.

Smith's Diamond Tri-Hone Sharpening System is an example of how sharpening tools have improved in recent decades. The Tri-Hone's 2.5"x8" Coarse (325-grit) and Medium (750-grit) diamond stones, and a Fine (800-1,000-grit) Arkansas oilstone mounted onto a rotating triangular spindle make it simple to take a knife from completely dull to razor-sharp with one convenient tool. An advantage of the Tri-Hone design over conventional honing stones or ceramic-rod sharpeners is that it offers superior stability and angle control—critical for tough, hard-to-sharpen steels like ATS-34 or D2. The Tri-Hone's stand holds whichever stone is used 5 inches above the surface it rests on, the ideal height for a kitchen table or counter top. Rubber feet help to keep the unit from sliding as blade is worked against stone. TDiamond Tri-Hone is priced at $99.99.

For field sharpening there are now pocket-size sharpening tools that are ideal for anglers and hunters who might dull their knives in places where the bulk and weight of conventional sharpeners is inconvenient or prohibitive. Two of the easiest to use and most effective go-everywhere sharpeners are Lansky's Quick-Fix and Smith's Pocket Pal. The Quick-Fix uses two notched guides with a coarse carbide bevel-cutter on one side of a large easy-to-grip tab, and ceramic polishing blades in the other notch. The Quick-Fix retails for $6.

Smith's Pocket Pal uses coarse carbide and 600-grit ceramic blades set into V-shaped notches to quickly repair dulled or damaged cutting edges, then polish them to deer-skinning sharpness. The blades are reversible and replaceable, but it's not likely most of us will ever need to replace them. Adding to the sharpener's usefulness is a 2-inch long, 400-grit tapered rod, set jackknife-fashion into the opposite side, for sharpening straight or serrated edges. The Pocket Pal retails for $10.

# THE ULTIMATE SURVIVAL BOAT

For centuries the best-known boat for getting away from it all was a canoe. Conventional V-bottom rowboats draw too much water to get over half-submerged logs and mud flats. A canoe, the pickup truck of frontier trappers, is top-heavy and unstable, especially when lightly loaded, and real skill is needed to keep it upright in a whitewater rapids. A flat-bottom riverboat, or john boat, is stable and it has a shallow draft, but its handling is sluggish, and so is its speed over water.

Then along came the plastic, then fiberglass, and now carbon-fiber kayaks, and exploring the back-country by water became dramatically easier. If the canoe is a pickup truck, a kayak is a mid-engine sports car. Easily the fastest muscle-powered boat, a kayak can cover more miles in less time, which can be important to part-time adventurers who have to be back to work by Monday.

These qualities make the kayak a fun high-performance boat, but it has a practical side as well. An ability to negotiate shallow, twisting waterways, submerged logs, and rock-strewn rapids turns the craft into an angler's dream. Isolated holes that are beyond the reach of conventional fishing boats are easily within a kayaker's grasp, as are the unmolested lunker-size fish that inhabit them. Waterfowl hunters can also benefit, slipping silently into marshy shallows where ducks and geese wouldn't expect them, then retrieving downed birds without the assistance of a dog.

Unlike a sports car, a typical kayak in the 12- to 14-foot lengths preferred by backcountry paddlers has plenty of trunk space. Most will carry their operator plus at least 100 pounds of gear stashed in watertight deck storage hatches and behind the seat. Backpackers who are used to counting ounces and sacrificing comfort to keep gear weight down will rejoice at the cornucopia of luxuries that can be fitted into a kayak. Kayakers can carry extra camp stove fuel, a radio, night-vision and camera equipment, and much more that is denied to their sweaty weight-conscious terrestrial counterparts.

Or you may opt to outfit your kayak as a hardcore survival system, with modern lightweight high-efficiency camping gear that turns it into a "bug-out" boat. The ease with which a kayak's double-blade paddle causes it to slice through water means you don't have to be an athlete to cover 15 miles in a day, even upstream and fully laden with supplies. Handling performance and watertight integrity enable a kayak to tackle stormy seas that would be too rough for a canoe or rowboat (always wear a Personal Flotation Device). Rugged polyethylene hulls make the boats nearly indestructible, and built-in flotation keeps a kayak on the surface no matter what. Accessories like a deck compass, bilge pump, watertight deck and dry bags, and a "leash" that keeps your paddle attached to the boat further enhance a kayak's seaworthiness in country where self reliance is a necessity. We middle-aged outdoorsmen can also

A kayak is also the most maneuverable personal watercraft. Unlike a canoe, a kayak paddler is seated amidships, with legs extended and most of his weight actually below the waterline. This gives the boat a low center of gravity, like a racing car, which provides excellent stability, and causes the kayak to pivot from its center, rather the turning from the stern. Covered decks fore and aft keep water out of the boat, and watertight integrity can be made complete with an optional "spray skirt" that seals the cockpit from its rim to the paddler's waist. Fully outfitted, a kayak is the only boat that can roll 360 degrees (an "Eskimo roll"). Olympic and whitewater kayakers exploit their boats' handling performance to the max, tipping them literally onto their sides to hang turns as tightly as possible, much the same as a road motorcycle.

appreciate that a 14-foot kayak weighs about 15 pounds less than a canoe of the same length.

Don't take my word for it; rent or borrow a kayak and see for yourself why kayaks have been outselling canoes more than three to one since 2001. With a blend of proven Inuit design, high-strength but lightweight materials, and computer-aided engineering, today's kayak just may be the ultimate backcountry survival vehicle.

Whether you're on a lonely mountaintop road or in a cul-de-sac in a subdivision, a fallen tree can be a trap if you don't have the tools to remove it.

## LUMBERJACKING 101

American trees are under assault; some pests, like the jackpine budworm, are native, while many harmful insects and fungi have arrived from other states—even other continents–as a result of human commerce. The introduction of alien parasites has devastated whole forests, and it isn't a question of whether a dead tree will fall, but of when, and in which direction. During stormy weather, weakened wind-felled trees can block roads, knock down power lines, strand travelers and cut off entire communities for days at a time. Being most likely to fall in the direction of least resistance (open areas), wind-felled trees seem attracted to yards and driveways, and the damage a falling 2-ton tree can inflict on a building or vehicle is impressive.

A few resort property owners have hired local talent, sometimes learning the hard way that not every resident of the big woods is an accomplished lumberjack. Many fell problem trees themselves, and some do the job well, but there has been tale or two of woe from those who flattened the very possessions they were trying to protect.

The secret to dropping a tree where you want it to land is to make sure that it has no alternative, particularly when the trunk is next to a structure that cannot be moved, and especially if the tree is already leaning in an undesired direction. That means anchoring the tree under force in the direction it needs to fall, which requires a simple winching outfit. Basic components include a quality "come-along" hand winch (about $70), 50 feet of climbing rope ($50), and

Putting down a tall, heavy tree right where it needs to go demands a few simple lumberjacking tools, like these telescoping scaling ladders.

10-plus feet of vinyl-coated cable ($20) or nylon tow strap ($15), all of them rated to work under loads of no less than 2 tons. You'll also need a way to attach the pulling outfit at least 10 feet high on the trunk (higher is better because it provides more leverage); a step-ladder can suffice, but many deer hunters already have more portable, and safer, tree-scaling ladders.

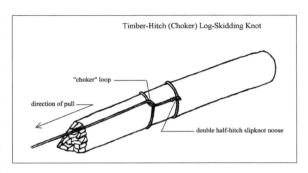

The "choker" knot used by lumberjacks to haul smooth-sided logs through a forest: a slipknot noose locked in place by a half-hitch.

Most critical is to be absolutely certain that every component is in top condition, because a 10-pound winch that snaps free under tons of force can break any body part it hits. Besides being certain that every component is rated for the job, it pays to be compulsive about frayed ropes and straps, broken cable wires, and anything that looks worn. Work gloves, eye protection, and even a hard hat are always good ideas, because some mistakes can be made only once.

While direction of fall is dictated by safety, a falling tree's path to the ground should be as free of obstructions as possible; a half-fallen tree suspended from the branches of another standing tree can be extraordinarily dangerous. The potential for a "widow-maker" is much less with a ton or so of force helping to pull the tree down, but a clear path to the earth is essential. In most instances, hangers can be freed by shifting the winch's anchor point to one side, using the rope already tied around its trunk, and pulling the stuck tree loose from a safe distance.

How the winching components are connected is important: Try to keep the anchor tree directly in line with your desired impact site, and farther away than the tree being felled is tall. The anchor cable or strap is looped down low on the trunk of an anchor tree, and the loose end hooked to the cabled end of the winch. Release the come-along's locking pawls to allow the reel to turn freely, and extend the cable to its full length by pulling the winch away from the anchor.

Pull the climbing rope—already tied ten feet up the trunk of the tree being felled with a "choker" timber-hitch—through the fixed hook at the winch's opposite end, and tie it off as tautly as you can. Some knot work is required, so it helps to bone-up on the basics (the Boy Scout Handbook is a great start). Knots that are winched against can pull very tightly, and tying them with a doubled rope makes them easier to untie. With the anchored winch tied off as tautly as you can get it (the winch should be suspended in air), take up the remaining slack with the come-along, but do not pull hard against the tree yet. Do be sure that your ladder is out of the way at this point.

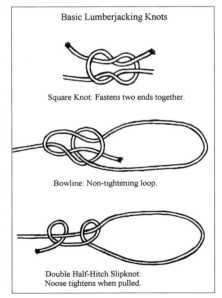

Three of the most useful lumberjacking knots.

Tying off the winch that will pre-load a tall tree's direction of fall to ensure that it impacts precisely where it was meant to go.

Cutting the felling notch

Making the final felling cut after the felling wedge has been removed from the opposite side.

Next, chainsaw a felling wedge from the trunk facing the place you want the tree to land. Like a right triangle, the flat bottom of the wedge is made by cutting horizontally into the trunk to a depth of slightly less than half its diameter. Do not cut more than halfway through the trunk as this can cause the tree's mass to shift and pinch your chainsaw bar like a vise. The second cut angles downward at roughly 45 degrees to meet the first cut at the trunk's center. When the wedge is free, push it off to one side, knocking it loose with an axe if you need to. Next, winch the lines tight between notched tree and anchor, just until the top branches of the notched tree move when you pull the winch handle.

Stepping away as a 2-ton tree heads for earth.

The final, felling cut is made from the opposite side, angling downward from about 6 inches above the apex of the wedge notch; this creates a step to help prevent the tree from falling in any direction except forward. Begin by making certain that all tripping hazards are removed from the surrounding area before making this cut, because you'll want to step back several feet from the falling tree's butt. Depending on how it lands (steep hills are especially dangerous), trunks have bounced 10 feet into the air, sometimes coming to rest many feet from

Everything about lumberjacking is hard, heavy, or sharp.

their stumps, so it pays to be farther away than you think is necessary. Normally, a tree will give plenty of warning as it begins to fall, cracking and creaking as it slowly leans toward the winch. At the first sign of a lean, disengage your chainsaw and begin moving away, because the tree is falling. Resist the urge to rush backward; remember that you have a running chainsaw in your hands, and that it will take several seconds for the tree to fall.

Being cushioned by branches, no winch has yet suffered from being under a falling tree, and a typical outfit can pull down dozens of trees before any components need replacement. Besides a chainsawing kit, other lumberjacking necessities include a good single-bit axe ($15), with a flat back that can be used as a sledge. A pruning-type handsaw (about $15) is handy for de-limbing trunks where a chainsaw is too clumsy, or might kick back. And it never hurts to have an extra strap or cable, in case the nearest anchor point is far away.

The jackpine budworm, emerald ash borer, gypsy moth, and a growing roster of other native and alien timber pests have shown that they are with us to stay. Probably none will wipe out the woods they feed on, but many of them kill large trees, which are then guaranteed to fall over at an unpredictable time in an unforeseeable direction. The same trouble occurs with fast-growing, short-lived trees, like aspen, cottonwood, and birches. As long as humans and trees live together, and in places where use of large machines is prohibited, there will be a need for old-fashioned lumberjacking. If possible, hire a repu-table (and insured) professional to fell problem trees. If that isn't feasible, never attempt to fell any tree without help, and approach the task with slightly-obsessive forethought and caution. Never cut any tree within touching distance of a power line; that is always one for the pros. As one old-timer put it, "Everything about lumberjackin' is hard, heavy, or sharp, and that's all you really need to know."

## CUTTING WOOD WITH AN AXE

Cutting wood with an axe has a method. Nothing about it is easy, but there is definitely an easier way and a hard way. Begin with your master (strongest) hand gripping the axe handle about halfway up, knuckles pointed in the same direction as the blade's cutting edge. The other, weaker, hand grasps the lower end of the axe handle, where it flares outward into a "toe" that helps to prevent the hand from slipping off of the end.

With hands positioned on the axe's handle, cock the head back over your right shoulder (if you're right-handed) like a baseball bat. With the axe's cutting edge angled slightly inward (the desired angle changes), swing the

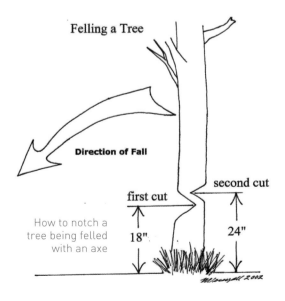

**Felling a Tree**

**Direction of Fall**

first cut

second cut

How to notch a tree being felled with an axe

18"

24"

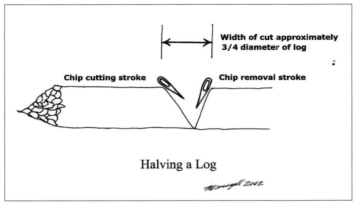

Width of cut approximately
3/4 diameter of log

Chip cutting stroke     Chip removal stroke

Halving a Log

*Cutting through a
downed log with
an axe.*

head from your shoulder toward the log to be cut. Apply power to the axe handle with your master hand, driving the head in a smooth arc while the weak hand anchors the toe of the axe handle with a firm grip. As the axe head draws closer to its target, allow your master hand to slide easily down its handle, stopping when it reaches the opposite hand. The objective is to allow the heavy steel head to accelerate smoothly and steadily toward the point of impact, so that the cutting edge is driven home not by the force of your muscle, but from the energy of the axe head's own inertia.

When the cutting edge drives into wood and stops, give the axe handle a hard twist, either upward or downward, whichever direction best splits the largest shingle of wood of wood from the main body. On the next hit, come in at the opposite inward angle, cutting (ideally) the layer of wood you've split free of the log in a single large chip. Tricks include saving yourself work by starting your cutting notch extra wide, so it doesn't need to be widened because the notch became too narrow before you'd chopped through the log.

When chopping down a standing tree, first determine the direction in which you want it to fall, and tie the trunk off if possible (as described above), to help ensure that it can only fall in that direction. The next step is to "set" the felling notch; the first stroke makes a cut that is perpendicular to the trunk, about 2 feet above the earth; this sets the bottom of the cutting notch. The second stroke is applied downward at a 45 to 50-degree angle, at a distance above the first cut that equals roughly two-thirds the diameter of the trunk being cut. This width insures that there will be sufficient room to remove chips as the notch becomes narrower toward the trunk's center. A hard outward twist of the embedded axe's handle helps to loosen both its head and large chunks of wood.

When the initial notch, which faces the direction of the intended fall, has been opened to a depth that equals about two-thirds of the trunk's diameter, the axe wielder moves to the opposite side, away from the direction of the fall, and cuts the felling notch. This second notch is centered about 6 inches above the apex of the first, creating a ledge of sorts that prevents the tree from falling backward. This keeps you opposite the direction in which the tree will fall. I should take no more than a few good chops before the trunk cracks and begins to lean. Step back a dozen feet at this point, because it is not unheard of for butt ends to bounce ten feet into the air when a large tree impacts the ground.

Chopping a downed tree in two is a bit different than felling it, because there may be no getting around to cut from the opposite side. The initial cuts need to be nearly as wide as the log is thick to keep the V-shaped notch from coming to a point before the length has been severed. Unlike a felling cut, in which the bottom of the notch is kept generally perpendicular to the trunk, both cuts are angled inward from the opposite sides to remove as much wood as possible per swing.

## CLEARING THE ROAD

The hunting party had become trapped in a mountaintop lodge when high winds and heavy snow literally flattened large tracts of mature pine forest. When fair weather returned, the group found its road back to civilization impassable to vehicles, and nearly so to a man on foot. Even armed with chainsaws, the stranded hunters, and the rescue party that was coming up the mountain toward them, found the going slow and the manual labor prohibitively exhausting. In the end, it took the mechanical muscle of log-skidders and bulldozers to break a trail through the toppled tree trunks.

This incident illustrates a problem that has afflicted many a backcountry camper. Roads leading into the most remote and interesting places are by nature unpaved two-tracks, usually bordered by trees, and occasionally leading through places where it would be surprising to see another person. Frequently in such places, high winds will weaken the root system of a large tree enough for it to be uprooted and topple over, or sometimes a top will snap off, and if the place they land is across the road that leads out, even a relatively small spruce or aspen can stop the gnarliest 4x4.

Downed trees and branches are a feature of many natural disasters, and it could be imperative to have a means of clearing streets and roads.

Storm-downed trees can strand you whether you're in the forest or the suburbs.

Pocket-size and able to tear through even tough-knotted jackpine, Ultimate Survival Technologies' SaberCut manual chainsaw has earned a place in disaster survival kits.

If you've already humped a full pack a half-dozen miles getting back to your vehicle, finding its only route to a paved road blocked by a couple of tons of green wood can be downright depressing. The logistics of safely cutting through a 24-inch diameter poplar trunk at both sides of the road, dropping a 2-ton log that's suspended a foot off the ground from either end by roots and branches, then moving that log out of the way requires tools not generally found in the backs of highway vehicles.

A chainsaw is great for this job, but the machine, its 2-stroke gas, bar oil, chain sharpener, bar wrench, spark plug wrench, and tensioning screwdriver are items most folks who aren't lumberjacks don't habitually carry in their vehicles. If you know your road may lead into a place so distant that you'll rely on driving to get back, it's not a bad idea to have a chainsawing outfit.

Even more dependable and convenient to carry are hand tools, and the first and most reliable mainstay of any lumberjacking chore has always been the axe. A bit of practice is needed to achieve accuracy and skill swinging an axe, but no tree trunk, branch, or root is too thick to be halved by this chopping tool.

Most versatile and usually easiest to master among axe designs is the single edge Collins-type axe, with a 3.5-pound head (5-pound heads are available), and a flat side opposite the cutting edge that works well as a heavy hammer. Available with hickory or fiberglass handles, a good axe can be found at most hardware stores for under $20, but its real value at a backcountry roadblock can make it priceless.

Next in line in terms of importance is an efficient handsaw, because springy smaller trunks and branches that bounce under an axe blow are often parted most safely with a saw. The old traditional bowsaw can still be found in the boxes of rural pickup trucks everywhere, but modern manufacturing technology has created toothed cutting edges that surpass anything a lumberjack of old had available. This increase in cutting efficiently is due in large part to continuously improving steel alloys and hardening processes, but better tools also enabled creation of a very sharp opposing-teeth design that literally shreds wet or dry wood fibers. Known by names like "Razortooth," and available in blade sizes ranging from Corona's 18-inch pruning saw to Gerber's folding backpack saws, even Stanley's "Sharktooth" carpenter-style saw has proved able to zip through 12-inch green logs with surprising ease. Retail for any of these averages around $20, depending on blade length, which again belies the value that a good saw might have in the boondocks.

Most portable is the SaberCut manual chainsaw from Ultimate Survival Technologies (www.ultimate survival.com). Weighing in at 6 ounces with its ballistic-nylon belt case, this unit is essentially the cutting chain of a motorized chainsaw, but with nylon strap handles that loop over a user's wrists. Its 24-inch chain cuts and clears accumulated sawdust in both directions, without twisting or binding, and my own field trials prove that it will handle hard woods like maple and oak. Cutting teeth require little maintenance beyond occasional lubrication and sharpening with a standard chain saw blade sharpener. This tool has become a permanent part of my backwoods driving and ATV survival kits. At this time the SaberCut retails for $30.

After separating a fallen tree into pieces, you'll need to move those sections out of the road, and if the fallen tree is a large one, even a four-foot section of trunk can weigh hundreds of pounds. For this, you'll need a good come-a-long hand winch rated to exert at least two tons of pulling force (about $50), a 12" steel extension cable ($12), and at least fifty feet of quality three-quarter-inch nylon marine rope (under $20). With 4,000 pounds of mechanical muscle, a secure anchor point (sometimes your own vehicle), and 12 feet of pull, a lone camper has the power to drag all but the heaviest trees out of the way, and also the option of exerting that force from the side opposite his vehicle.

Conveniently contained in a duffle bag, along with leather work gloves and safety goggles, all of these tools take up surprisingly little space in even a small car's trunk. With this winching outfit, knowledge of a few basic knots (square knot, half-hitches, timber hitch, and bowline), and a modicum of ingenuity, virtually no passenger vehicle cannot be pulled out of a snowy ditch, muddy washout, or loose sand, which only adds to its potential value as a permanent part of the two-tracker's survival kit.

It doesn't take a large tree lying across a road to stop even rugged 4x4 trucks; if you can't remove the tree, you might be stranded for a long time before someone else does.

Although my own experience has been mostly limited to clearing truck-wide passages through wind-felled timber, it seems likely that a few tree removal tools might also prove handy for urban residents. Every year, tornadoes, hurricanes, and ice storms topple or break apart large trees in residential neighborhoods, separating people who live there from medical and other critical services until the way has been cleared. Most folks already know that they should never even approach a downed power line, but nearly any tree or branch that isn't lying against high voltage can be moved out of the street.

With a total cost of less than $120, and taking up less space than a spare tire, a good winching outfit is hard to overrate when big trees block a road you need to take. Whether in the suburbs or a vast wilderness, it beats standing there feeling helpless.

# GETTING UNSTUCK

You're bouncing slowly along a remote 2-track road, enjoying the serenity of a vast wilderness, when suddenly one front tire falls into the grassed-over hole left by a log skidder during the wet season. You slip the transmission to 4-low and try to back up, but even before you press the accelerator, you know your vehicle's weight is setting on the undercarriage, not the tires. Afraid of digging yourself in deeper, you get out to survey

No land vehicle is immune to getting stuck, and in some environments spending a night stranded on the road can be downright dangerous.

the problem, confirming that the front end is "high-centered," and neither front tire is getting traction.

Your cell-phone can't get a signal out here. It's a 10-mile hike to the nearest paved road, 20 miles to the nearest town, and the woods will be dark in an hour. With sunset, a surprising coolness settles into the forest, forcing you to cover your bare goose-pimpled arms with a jacket, as well as to protect your torso from hordes of whining mosquitoes that fill the air from sunset to dawn. Judging from previous tire tracks, you aren't likely to meet with anyone else on this stretch of truck trail for days, maybe weeks. That cold feeling in your belly is more than an evening chill.

Any vehicle can get stuck; the question is, can you get it unstuck and back underway?

Generations of two-trackers can relate to the trials of getting waylaid by a stuck vehicle far from home. It can happen to anybody, and it will happen to every boondocker sooner or later. Where I live, anyone who claims to have never been stuck in snow, sand, or mud is either under sixteen years of age or lying. The pertinent question is, how long will you sit there, immobilized in an environment that will probably be less than comfortable?

Just as motocross and mountain bikes are equipped differently than their paved-road counterparts, so too does a backcountry 4x4 require accessories not normally found in highway vehicles. For these, a two-track vehicle extrication outfit is essential. Basic components include a manual come-along winch, a pair of tow straps, a single-blade axe, and a long-handled pointed shovel. The come-along, attached by cables between a stuck vehicle and a solid anchor point, provides up to 3 tons of pulling muscle from any direction. The axe and shovel are invaluable tools for manipulating the environment to better suit your needs; dead, broken sticks wedged under a tire help to increase traction in mud, a shovelful of sand is great for ice, and sometimes getting unstuck from deep snow is as simple as knocking down the hard-pack under your vehicle's chassis.

The price of a quality cable-type come-along, rated to pull two tons, averages about $70; nylon tow straps rated to match cost about $15 each; a shovel is around $12; a single-bit Collins axe, with a flat back that can serve as a hammer, retails for about $15. I also carry one-hundred feet of 2-ton braided climbing rope—about $45—to extend the reach of the winch, and to secure the vehicle from rolling backward while I reset the come-along. For less than $175, you can have the means to pull your car or truck out of almost any place it gets stuck, to drag wind-felled trees from across roads, or to help others to get unstuck. The winch and straps fit neatly into a large gym bag. The

Getting stuck is a contingency that should be prepared for in vehicle-carried disaster survival kits across the board.

169

entire outfit takes up little space, so it can always be handy in the trunk of the smallest car for dragging wind-felled trees and debris from suburban and city streets after a storm.

Before using your winching outfit in a genuine situation, familiarize yourself with its workings, especially how to back-off tension from the come-along. Determine where the winching points on your vehicle are beforehand, and never pull directly against the bumper of any car or truck. Be certain that all components are in good working condition, because having any part of the outfit suddenly give way under several tons of force can result in serious, even fatal, injury. Wear work gloves whenever possible, and replace any strap or cable as soon as it begins to fray.

The ideal pocket compass is liquid-filled to help its indicator settle quickly, but with a movement that turns smoothly, without sticking or jerking. Beware any new compass with a bubble of any size inside the indicator capsule. Small bubbles may occur after prolonged use afield, but a bubble in a new compass points to a leaky indicator capsule. If a bubble grows large enough, it can trap the indicator and prevent it from turning freely, or at all.

# ABCs OF ORIENTEERING

Human beings don't have a sense of direction, and anthropologists claim we most likely never did. The ferric deposit that acts as a compass in the beaks and noses of "lower" animals is present in our own noses, but we lack the sensory connections that permit them to feel the pull of earth's magnetic north pole. Because our species has no sense of direction, we need a compass to find our way through untracked wilderness. In prehistory, our nomadic ancestors depended on reliable natural indicators, like the sun, moon, and stars, prevailing winds, tall pines whose north-facing branches had been killed by winter winds, and the direction faced by some plants.

Creation of the first magnetic compass is credited to early Egyptians, who discovered that a free-floating magnet will always align itself with earth's magnetic north pole. With a single constant point of reference, travelers could always know which direction they were heading, making it possible to maintain a straight course across vast areas of land or water, regardless of weather. The beauty of a compass has always been its simplicity and almost absolute reliability. All the needle or dial of the most sophisticated compass really does is point toward magnetic north, all the time, without batteries or parts that need replacing. A magnet at the north end of the needle or dial is attracted toward our planet's magnetic north pole when the compass is held flat in the user's palm, parallel to the ground. By turning the compass body or rotating dial (bezel) so that the northern half of the indicator is in agreement with the N on the compass dial, you know east is to the right, west to the left, and south directly to your rear. (Putting the first letters of those four directions together also spells NEWS—information from all four directions).

Just knowing where the four directions lie is enough to keep hikers from making the very common mistake of wandering in circles. But if you want to use your compass to get back out of the woods in a place at least close to where you came in, you'll need to take a "bearing" before you start. That means aligning your compass with north as described above, then using the information it provides to determine which direction you'll be taking into (and back out of) the forest.

For example, if you're about to enter thick swamp from a two-track road, you need to know in which direction that road lies once it's out of sight. Landmarks like roads, trails, railroad grades, and power lines are the best targets for a "back-bearing" (the direction that leads out) because they span large areas and are difficult to miss. If you leave the road and walk eastward into a woods, then finding that road again is as simple as walking west until you hit it. For most situations, that's all the orienteering you'll need to know.

Likewise, most campers, fishermen, and hunters don't need the complexity and expense of precision navigation instruments like Brunton's 8099 prismatic compass ($80). Compasses like this are designed to precisely navigate through many miles of untracked wilderness, but fully exploiting their potential demands more advanced orienteering techniques than are generally needed for getting to and from a camp or deer blind.

The compass I use religiously for informal day hikes is a simple "pocket" compass, like Silva's Type 7 ($8), worn around my neck on a string and carried tucked inside the shirt. Don't get the idea that simple has to mean low quality, however, because a good pocket compass is as serious an orienteering tool as its more sophisticated counterparts; it just lacks the precision sights and other accessories that most day hikers don't need anyway.

Even better is a compass made for use with a map, like Coleman's Map Compass ($7), which has a see-through base with a ruler and map scales etched into the plastic. By laying the compass on top of a map and orienting both to north, you have a preview of the surrounding terrain. Even if you can't see it, that lake the map shows to be west of your position is there, and all you have to do to reach it is hike west over the distance shown on your map.

Whichever compass you use, it's a good idea to include a map of the area you'll be traveling. Detailed area maps are available from Department of Natural Resources field offices and most local bookstores for about $2, depending on the size of the area they cover. Even more precise topographical maps can be purchased from United States Geographical Survey (www.usgs.gov) for $4 each, plus $4 shipping and handling per order.

# ADVANCED ORIENTEERING

While a typical outdoorsman seldom needs his compass to do more than show the way to a nearby road, situations can arise that demand more advanced orienteering methods. Dodging new beaver floodings or broken bridges, making forced course changes to avoid hostile weather, or cutting cross-country to get medical help for an injured companion are all real-life possibilities.

More advanced navigation techniques require using a map and compass together, and here is where map compasses come into their own. Map compasses—including the prismatic sighting models—have see-through bases that allow you to place the instrument directly onto a map and read the two together. This makes course calculations faster and more precise than is possible with metal-body compasses.

The first step is to align both map and compass to magnetic north. To do this, place

the map flat on the ground, away from metal objects that might deflect the compass indicator, and lay the compass on top of it. Orient the compass to north, as if you were taking a bearing, and rotate the map beneath it until the two are in agreement. With both instruments aligned to north, the map becomes a microcosm of the surrounding country side; a mountain shown to your left (west) on the map will indeed be visible to your left, and the same applies to all other mapped landmarks.

It's also important to understand that there are two norths: true north, the one your map will probably be oriented to, and magnetic north, the one your compass points to. Depending on your geographic location, the difference between these two norths—called declination— in North America can range from 0 degrees in Ishpeming, Michigan, to a whopping 35 degrees along Alaska's Pacific shoreline. The 0–Declination line, where compass and map agree, is a narrow strip of land extending in an irregular line from Florida's tip through Michigan's Keweenaw Peninsula. The farther east or west you travel from the 0-declination line, the greater the difference between map north and compass north, and the more important it becomes to take this difference into account when plotting a course. .

Compensating for declination is easy, though. Locate your position as closely as possible using the declination chart, and if you're left (west) of the 0 line, subtract the number of degrees shown from the heading you arrived at with compass and map. If your position is right (east) of the 0 line, add the value indicated. For example, if you were in Idaho, which has a negative declination of 20 degrees, and wanted to follow a bearing of 270 degrees, the compass heading you'd follow would be at 250 degrees. Failure to compensate for declination would result in your being off course by ¾ mile after traveling just 2 miles in any direction. magnetic declination can thus have serious consequences if you're trying to reach a remote cabin in blinding snow, fog, or torrential rain.

A surprisingly common and potentially serious mistake made by hikers crossing country where identifiable landmarks are hidden by weather or terrain is not trusting their compasses. Not too long ago one of my backpacking companions, who should have known better, had to walk to the 2 miles he'd missed our rendezvous by because he'd decided his compass was lying. It can be unnerving to spend hours crossing trackless wilderness with only compass and map to show you the way, but always remember that a compass cannot give a false reading or be off by any amount (so long as it isn't being deflected by ferric metals). A compass either works all the time, or it's obviously broken.

A fairly rare exception to this rule occurs in iron country, when ferric ore deposits prove more attractive to your compass than the magnetic north pole. I've encountered this problem in Michigan's iron-rich Huron Mountains, but such places are generally small enough to merely inconvenience hikers, and if you've been minding your course the effect on your compass will be noticeable immediately. You can change course to escape these effects, but in most cases a map and the surrounding terrain will provide enough information to keep you on course until your compass reads true again.

There will be many times when traveling from one place to another requires breaking your trip into sections, or legs, each of which requires a new compass bearing. Ironically, this is easier in untracked wilderness, because the first trail intersection you come to might not be the same intersection shown on your map, but a new trail created after the map was printed. For this reason, it's imperative to have the means to calculate distances traveled with a workable degree of accuracy.

The most common map scales are 1:25,000 (1 inch equals 25,000 inches, or 694.44 yards); 1:50,000 (1 inch equals 50,000 inches, or 1,388.88 yards) and 1:62,000, which means 1 inch is equivalent to 1,722.22 yards, or just shy of a mile. All map compasses have at least two of these scales printed along the edges of their see-through bases, and most also have inch and millimeter scales for making conversions.

But hikers sometimes need a way to measure actual distances on the ground for correlation with map distances. An average adult covers about 3 miles in an hour of walking—a good guideline to remember—but when circumstances demand the precision necessary to locate a cabin, mountain pass, or the correct trail, you'll need a place counter.

The best such counter is the military model, which is essentially a heavy string with tight-fitting beads strung along its length. Unfortunately, every manufactured pace counter I've seen is calibrated to kilometers, while most maps are scaled in miles. I remedy this problem by threading 23 "beats" made from ¼-inch sections of plastic tubing with a ⅛-inch inside diameter onto a doubled shoelace. A simple overhand knot in the doubled end prevents the beads from sliding off. Another knot in the middle of the shoelace separates the beads into groups of 5 and 18, while a knot in the free ends holds them all together as a unit. Leave the shoelace at least an inch too long in either group so that you can clearly separate beads from the rest of the group by sliding them to the opposite knot. It's important to have enough friction to make the beads stay wherever you slide them.

Using the completed pace counter is simple. Starting with all the beads pushed to the inside, determine how many paces, on average, it takes you to cover 100 yards (the military says 62 paces, but I personally find that 100 steps equals 100 yards). If, for example, you determine that 75 of your paces equals 100 yards, then you'd slide one bead from the large group down to the end for each set of 75 paces. When all 18 have been pushed to the end, indicating 1,800 yards of travel, you know you've traveled approximately one mile (1,760 yards). At this point slide one bead from the smaller group to its outer end and reset all the beads in the larger group by sliding them back to the center. The process continues until all five beads in the smaller group have been pushed to the end, indicating 5 miles of travel. it's a good idea to now stop and mark your position on the map before you start the entire process over. For all its simplicity, the pace counter is surprisingly accurate, and I consider it an indispensable component of any orienteering kit.

Once, after we'd spent a whole day four-wheeling along an ancient, unmapped mountain trail, one of my companions asked me to show him our location on the map. He seemed a bit disconcerted when I told him I had no idea where we were. Sooner or later, everyone who explores the wilderness encounters this problem—you don't have to be lost to not know where you are. The solution, as I demonstrated to my anxious companion the new morning, is an orienteering exercise called triangulation, a complex-sounding technique that's actually quite simple to perform. The only requirements are two positively identifiable terrain features, a good map to reference them against, and a sighting compass that allows you to read precise bearings from these landmarks. Triangulation is of little or no use in deep forest where tall trees obscure vision, but in any open country where distant landmarks are visible, it's possible to determine within 100 yards your exact location on a map. That's important because if you don't know where you are right now—if you don't have a solid anchor upon which to base map headings—there's no way you can plot an intelligent course to anywhere else.

The first step is to find a place where you can visually identify two distant landmarks that are also identified on your map. The points should be as far away from one another as possible. Orient your map and compass to magnetic north, making certain to compensate

for magnetic declination, and sight a bearing from either point, jotting down both forward bearings and back bearings in the margins for use in the next step. Any compass can be used for triangulating, but the more precise the instrument's sighting system, the more accurate will be your calculations. This is where a prismatic (mirrored) compass shines.

Next, use the compass's protractor and straightedge to draw a line through each landmark on the map, extending these lines on the same angles as their back bearings. If your compass isn't equipped with a protractor, center its indicator post exactly on top of either reference point and use its bezel as a protractor.

You'll note that as you extend the back-bearing lines on the map back toward yourself, they draw closer together. The point where these lines intersect is your position.

# NIGHT NAVIGATION

As much as we try to convince ourselves otherwise, few of use are unafraid to be alone in the woods at night. There are many reasons behind this fear: humans have perhaps the lowest perception of ultraviolet light of any species, which means we can't see at night; the forest is already an alien environment where most civilized folks feel somewhat insecure in daylight; worse, all of us have been taught from childhood to fear what could be lurking in the darkness. The logical part of our brains may know that such fear is unfounded, but each of us carries a burden of childhood terror left over from tales about werewolves, vampires, and all sorts of sharp-clawed predators that wait to rend and tear unsuspecting humans in the darkness. While these stories probably sprang from an era when our distant ancestors huddled around a fire for protection from now-extinct predators that sometimes did eat them, almost every species on the planet has learned to avoid humans, none more so than in North America.

The trick to traveling at night is learning to rely less on your eyesight and more on your other senses. Your eyes will adjust better than you might think, but you must learn to use the hardness of a trail underfoot to guide your steps on moonless or cloudy nights. Condition yourself to step higher than normal to clear protruding roots and other tripping hazards. Learn to "see" movement around with your ears, not your eyes, listening for the rushing of water, the rustling of leaves, and other audible clues. Feel for minute changes in air currents with you extremely sensitive facial skin, and learn to recognize how these tactile differences relate to changes in terrain.

Night orienteering requires a small flashlight for map reading and taking bearings, but as with any battery-powered device, you'll want to use is sparingly. I recommend using a recognizable star as a bearing point—a fixed point that you can see and follow without the aid of artificial light.

# OTHER ORIENTEERING TRICKS

One persistent myth among outdoor lovers of all disciplines is the belief that moss prefers to grow on the northern sides of trees. The truth is that moss grows wherever conditions most favor it, regardless of direction. In fact, in the North Woods mosses actually tend

toward the southern side of their hosts, away from winter's killing north wind, but always keeping to shade.

In this same vein hikers in northern and mountain states can use the tallest spruce, hemlock, or other pine tree to find their way. Since this tree will rise above the surrounding forest to face winter's full fury, any buds that sprout on its northern side will literally be frozen to death each winter. Thus the branches growing on its opposite side will always point generally south.

If you can see it, the sun is a reliable indicator of direction because, as every kid from my generation knew, east is the land of the rising sun, and cowboys always ride west into the sunset. But it's also true that our sun is directly overhead only at the planet's equator. The farther north you travel from the sun, the more southerly becomes its east-to-west arc across the sky. The opposite is true in the southern latitudes.

Chronograph-type wristwatches can also serve as compasses in a pinch, but they too rely on a visible sun to work. In the morning, point the watch's hour hand at the sun, and at the point where the angle between it and the number 12 is bisected will be south. The same procedure applies when you're taking a bearing in the afternoon, except that A.M. bearings are always taken from the left (6-12) half of a watch, while P.M. bearings are read from the right (12-6) half. This method is neither accurate or reliable enough to replace a dedicated compass— changes in latitude and cloudy days can pose problems—but if something happens to your compass, a good watch can actually help you get home.

There are also a few miscellaneous tips I can give you about using terrain features to find a route through the wilderness. For example, it's good to know that most rivers flow southward generally, and that if you follow the flow of water downstream to its outlet, sooner or later you'll run across civilization. Also, prevailing winds across North America blow generally west to east, and downhill usually leads to water.

# Coping with Disasters

**W**hile many aspects of survival are generic—like the need to eat, drink, and sleep—different situations can demand different responses. Following are some of the disasters that are most anticipated by FEMA and DHL.

## FLOODS

Flooding is the most common natural disaster in every U.S. state, a statistic that has proved itself repeatedly in recent years. Some floods occur during heavy rains, some during a heavy snowmelt. Flash floods can strike quickly in mountain country, often from rains that fall many miles away, because even a light rain can run into rivulets that form into rivers that become torrents as they rush downhill over nonabsorbent rock. It is especially important to be prepared for flooding if you are in low-level terrain, near a river or creek, or downstream from a dam.

According to the Department of Homeland Security, the first step in safe-guarding against any type of flood is to "Get a Kit." DHS recommends an Emergency Supply Kit that includes a 3-day supply of nonperishable food, water, a battery-powered or hand-crank radio receiver, flashlights, and spare batteries.

DHS also suggests assembling a second kit for the car. This kit is more critical than a household emergency kit because there are fewer alterna-tives—if you don't have a 4-by-4 bandage, you can't go to the linen closet

Next, create a Family Emergency Plan. Members of your family might not be together when a disaster occurs, and it could be vital to have a strategy for contacting one another, a place where everyone will go to meet the others, and discuss contingency plans, in case things don't go as expected. Bear in mind that when phone lines or towers are down at ground-zero, it might be easier to make a telephone call long-distance than locally. Ask about emergency plans at your workplace, and at schools or daycare facilities attended by your children, and don't be embarrassed to share your own emergency plan with the staff there. And of course, pets should be included in any emergency strategy. If you'd like to become more involved, DHS sponsors Community Emergency Response Team (CERT) classes from local Citizen Corps chapters.

to make bandages from a sheet. This kit should contain photocopies of prescriptions so that you can get refills more easily when normalcy returns. It should include copies and photocopies of deeds, titles, and identification documents, as well as pertinent medical information—blood type, heart or other organ problems—medications being taken, and copies of financial records, all sealed in a watertight lockbox. A change of clothing, warm sleeping bag(s) and pillows sealed inside garbage bags help to ensure a restful night's sleep. You should have bottled water sufficient to provide each person in your family or intended group with at least one gallon of drinking water, and a water filter that enables you to make more from any ditch. An LED flashlight or headlamp with spare batteries provides cheap night-vision and can be used to signal for help from passing vehicles or aircraft at night. A battery-operated shortwave radio often provides international news that is more current and accurate than local broadcasts from a disaster area; Coleman's StormBeam incorporates a nice LED flashlight, an FM receiver, and multiple cell-phone adapters into a palm-size unit that seems made for automobile survival. An NOAA Weather Radio is also an asset.

## FLOOD WARNINGS

- Flood Watch: Flooding is possible. Tune in to NOAA or local weather broadcasts for the most current information.
- Flash Flood Watch: Flash flooding is possible; be ready to move to the highest elevation available; listen to NOAA and local weather broadcasts.
- Flood Warning: A flood is happening or is imminent; prepare to evacuate when advised to do so.
- Flash Flood Warning: A flash flood is occurring; do not attempt to drive, but seek out the highest elevation immediately.

# FREQUENT CAUSES OF FLOODING

**Tropical Storms and Hurricanes:** Hurricanes bring powerful winds, pounding rain, and dangerous flying debris. They can submerge coastlines and cause monsoon-like rains hundreds of miles inland. DHS claims that all coastlines are at risk, but some low-lying cities are especially vulnerable and could suffer damages even greater than those caused by Hurricane Katrina in 2005. When hurricanes slow to become tropical storms, their loss of impetus can concentrate copious amounts of rain onto a single area—like the 30 inches that Tropical Storm Allison dumped onto Houston, Texas, in 2001, flooding more than 70,000 homes

**Snowmelt:** During the spring melt in snow country, frozen earth prevents water from being absorbed into the ground. Like a flash flood in mountain country, the melted rivulets run together to form increasing larger streams that join on their way to the lowest geographical point. The result can be overflowing streams, rivers, and lakes, especially when meltwater is joined by spring rains.

**Heavy Rains:** Several areas of the country are at heightened risk for flooding due to heavy rains. The Northwest is at high risk due to La Niña conditions, which include an increased risk of extreme snowmelts, heavy rains, and wildfires. And The Northeast is at high risk due to heavy rains produced from Nor'easters. This excessive amount of rainfall can happen throughout the year, putting your property at risk.

**West Coast Threats:** The West Coast rainy season usually lasts from November to April, bringing heavy flooding and increased flood risks with it; however, flooding can happen at any time. Large wildfires have dramatically changed the landscape and ground

conditions, causing fire-scorched land to become mudflows under heavy rain. Experts say that it might take years for vegetation, which will help stabilize these areas, to return. The West Coast also has thousands of miles of levees, which are meant to help protect homes and their land in case of a flood. However, levees can erode, weaken, or overtop when waters rise, often causing catastrophic results.

**Levees and Dams:** Levees are designed to protect against a certain level of flooding. However, levees can and do decay over time, making maintenance a serious challenge. Levees can also be overtopped or even fail during large floods, creating more damage than if the levee wasn't even there. Because of the escalating flood risks in areas with levees, especially in the Midwest, FEMA strongly recommends flood insurance for all homeowners in these areas.

Flash Floods: Flash floods are the number one weather-related killer in the United States; they can roll boulders, tear out trees, and destroy buildings and bridges. A flash flood is a rapid flooding of low-lying areas in less than six hours, which is caused by intense rainfall from a thunderstorm or several thunderstorms. Flash floods can also occur from the collapse of a man-made structure or ice dam.

New Development: Construction and development can change the natural drainage and create brand-new flood risks. That's because new buildings, parking lots, and roads mean less land to absorb excess precipitation from heavy rains, hurricanes, and tropical storms.

## KNOW YOUR RISKS, KNOW YOUR SAFTEY

Find out if your home is at risk for flood and educate yourself on the impact a flood could have on you and your family. FEMA's Flood Insurance Study compiled statistical data on river flows, storm tides, hydrologic/hydraulic analyses, and rainfall and topographic surveys to create flood hazard maps that outline your community's different flood risk areas.

Most homeowners insurance does not cover flood damage. Talk to your insurance provider about your policy and consider if you need additional coverage. The National Flood Insurance Program (NFIP) can help provide a means for property owners to financially protect themselves if additional coverage is required. The NFIP offers flood insurance to homeowners, renters, and business owners if their community participates in the NFIP. To find out more about the NFIP visit www.FloodSmart.gov.

## PREPARE YOUR HOME
- Elevate the furnace, water heater, and electric panel in your home if you live in an area that has a high flood risk.
- Consider installing "check valves" to prevent floodwater from backing up into the drains of your home.
- If feasible, construct barriers to stop floodwater from entering the building and seal walls in basements with waterproofing compounds.
- Find out how to keep food safe during and after an emergency by visiting www.foodsafety.gov/keep/emergency/index.html

## PREPARE YOUR BUSINESS
- Plan to stay in business, talk to your employees, and protect your investment.

- Carefully assess how your company functions, both internally and externally, to determine which staff, materials, procedures and equipment are absolutely necessary to keep the business operating.

## IDENTIFY OPERATIONS CRITICAL TO SURVIVAL AND RECOVERY.
- Plan what you will do if your building, plant, or store is not accessible.
- Consider if you can run the business from a different location or from your home.
- Develop relationships with other companies to use their facilities in case a disaster makes your location unusable.
- Learn about programs, services, and resources at the U.S. Small Business Administration.

## LISTEN TO LOCAL OFFICIALS
Learn about the emergency plans that have been established in your area by your state and local government. In any emergency, always listen to the instructions given by local emergency management officials.

## FEDERAL AND NATIONAL RESOURCES
Find additional information on how to plan and prepare for floods, learn what to do during and after a flood, and explore other available resources by visiting the following:
Federal Emergency Management Agency
NOAA Watch
American Red Cross
U.S. Environmental Protection Agency
U.S. Department of Health and Human Services, Center for Disease Control
USA Freedom Corps Website
www.FloodSmart.gov

# MAN-MADE DISASTERS

A radiation threat, commonly referred to as a "dirty bomb" or "radiological dispersion device (RDD)," is the use of common explosives to spread radioactive materials over a targeted area. It is not a nuclear blast. The force of the explosion and radioactive contamination will be more localized. While the blast will be immediately obvious, the presence of radiation will not be clearly defined until trained personnel with specialized equipment are on the scene. As with any radiation, you want to try to limit exposure. It is important to avoid breathing radiological dust that may be released in the air.

### IF THERE IS A RADIATION THREAT OR "DIRTY BOMB":

- If you are outside and there is an explosion or authorities warn of a radiation release nearby, cover your nose and mouth and quickly go inside a building that has not been damaged. If you are already inside, check to see if your building has been damaged. If your building is stable, stay where you are.
- Close windows and doors; turn off air conditioners, heaters, or other ventilation systems.
- If you are inside and there is an explosion near where you are or you are warned of a radiation release inside, cover nose and mouth and go outside immediately. Look for a building or other shelter that has not been damaged and quickly get inside.
- Once you are inside, close windows and doors; turn off air conditioners, heaters, or other ventilation systems.
- If you think you have been exposed to radiation, take off your clothes and wash as soon as possible.
- Stay where you are, watch TV, listen to the radio, or check the Internet for official news as it becomes available.
- Remember: To limit the amount of radiation you are exposed to, think about time, distance, and shielding:
  - Time: Minimizing time spent exposed will also reduce your risk.
  - Distance: The farther away you are away from the blast and the fallout, the lower your exposure.
  - Shielding: If you have a thick shield between yourself and the radioactive materials, more of the radiation will be absorbed, and you will be exposed to less.

As with any emergency, local authorities may not be able to immediately provide information on what is happening and what you should do. However, you should watch TV, listen to the radio, or check the Internet often for official news and information as it becomes available.

## NUCLEAR BLAST

A nuclear blast is an explosion with intense light and heat, a damaging pressure wave, and widespread radioactive material that can contaminate the air, water, and ground surfaces for miles around. During a nuclear incident, it is important to avoid radioactive material, if possible. While experts may predict at this time that a nuclear attack is less likely than other types, terrorism by its nature is unpredictable.

If there is advanced warning of an attack, Take cover immediately, as far belowground as possible, though any shield or
shelter will help protect you from the immediate effects of the
blast and the pressure wave.

**IF THERE IS NO WARNING:**

- Quickly assess the situation.
- Consider if you can get out of the area or if it would
  be better to go inside a building to limit the amount of
  radioactive material you are exposed to.
- If you take shelter, go as far belowground as possible,
  close windows and doors, and turn off air conditioners,
  heaters, or other ventilation systems. Stay where you
  are, watch TV, listen to the radio, or check the Internet
  for official news as it becomes available.
- To limit the amount of radiation you are exposed to,
  think about shielding, distance, and time:
    - Shielding: If you have a thick shield between yourself and the radioactive
      materials, more of the radiation will be absorbed, and you will be exposed
      to less.
    - Distance: The farther away you are away from the blast and the fallout the
      lower your exposure.
    - Time: Minimizing time spent exposed will also reduce your risk.

Use available information to assess the situation. If there is a significant radiation
threat, health care authorities may or may not advise you to take potassium iodide. Potassium iodide is the same stuff added to your table salt to make it iodized. It may or may not
protect your thyroid gland, which is particularly vulnerable, from
radioactive iodine exposure. Plan to speak with your health care
provider in advance about what makes sense for your family.

For more information, see "Potassium Iodide" from the
Centers for Disease Control.

For more general information, see "Are you Ready?" from the
Federal Emergency Management Agency.

# BIOLOGICAL THREATS

A biological attack is the deliberate release of germs or other
biological substances that can make you sick. Many agents must
be inhaled, enter through a cut in the skin, or be eaten to make
you sick. Some biological agents, such as anthrax, do not cause
contagious diseases. Others, like the smallpox virus, can result
in diseases you can catch from other people.

## IF THERE IS A BIOLOGICAL THREAT:

Unlike an explosion, a biological attack may or may not be immediately obvious. While it is possible that you will see signs of a biological attack, as was sometimes the case with the anthrax mailings, it is perhaps more likely that local health care workers will report a pattern of unusual illness or there will be a wave of sick people seeking emergency medical attention. You will probably learn of the danger through an emergency radio or TV broadcast or some other signal used in your community. You might get a telephone call, or emergency response workers may come to your door.

In the event of a biological attack, public health officials may not immediately be able to provide information on what you should do. It will take time to determine exactly what the illness is, how it should be treated, and who is in danger. However, you should watch TV, listen to the radio, or check the Internet for official news including the following:

- Are you in the group or area authorities consider in danger?
- What are the signs and symptoms of the disease?
- Are medications or vaccines being distributed?
- Where? Who should get them?
- Where should you seek emergency medical care if you become sick?

During a declared biological emergency, if a family member becomes sick, it is important to be suspicious.

- Do not assume, however, that you should go to a hospital emergency room or that any illness is the result of the biological attack. Symptoms of many common illnesses may overlap.
- Use common sense, practice good hygiene and cleanliness to avoid spreading germs, and seek medical advice.
- Consider if you are in the group or area authorities believe to be in danger.
- If your symptoms match those described, and you are in the group considered at risk, immediately seek emergency medical attention.

## IF YOU ARE POTENTIALLY EXPOSED:

- Follow instructions given by doctors and other public health officials.
- If the disease is contagious expect to receive medical evaluation and treatment. You may be advised to stay away from others or even deliberately quarantined.
- For noncontagious diseases, expect to receive medical evaluation and treatment.

## IF YOU BECOME AWARE OF AN UNUSUAL AND SUSPICIOUS SUBSTANCE NEARBY:

- Quickly get away.

- Protect yourself. Cover your mouth and nose with layers of fabric that can filter the air but still allow breathing. Examples include two to three layers of cotton such as a T-shirt, handkerchief or towel. Otherwise, several layers of tissue or paper towels may help.
- Wash with soap and water.
- Contact authorities.
- Watch TV, listen to the radio, or check the Internet for official news and information including what the signs and symptoms of the disease are, if medications or vaccinations are being distributed, and where you should seek medical attention if you become sick.
- If you become sick, seek emergency medical attention.

# CHEMICAL THREATS

A chemical attack is the deliberate release of a toxic gas, liquid or solid that can poison people and the environment.

### POSSIBLE SIGNS OF CHEMICAL THREAT:

- Many people suffering from watery eyes, twitching, choking, having trouble breathing or losing coordination.
- Many sick or dead birds, fish, or small animals are also cause for suspicion.

### IF YOU SEE SIGNS OF CHEMICAL ATTACK: FIND CLEAN AIR QUICKLY

- Quickly try to define the impacted area or where the chemical is coming from, if possible.
- Take immediate action to get away.
- If the chemical is inside a building where you are, get out of the building without passing through the contaminated area, if possible.
- If you can't get out of the building or find clean air without passing through the area where you see signs of a chemical attack, it may be better to move as far away as possible and shelter in place.
- If you are outside, quickly decide what is the fastest way to find clean air. Consider if you can get out of the area or if you should go inside the closest building and shelter in place.

### IF YOU THINK YOU HAVE BEEN EXPOSED TO A CHEMICAL:

- If your eyes are watering, your skin is stinging, and you are having trouble breathing, you may have been exposed to a chemical.
- If you think you may have been exposed to a chemical, strip immediately and wash.
- Look for a hose, fountain, or any source of water, and wash with soap if possible, being sure not to scrub the chemical into your skin.
- Seek emergency medical attention.

For more information, see "Are you Ready?" from the Federal Emergency Management Agency.

# INFLUENZA PANDEMIC SWINE FLU INFO

You can prepare for an influenza pandemic now. You should know both the magnitude of what can happen during a pandemic outbreak and what actions you can take to help lessen the impact of an influenza pandemic on you and your family. This list will help you gather the information and resources you may need in case of a flu pandemic.

### PLAN FOR A PANDEMIC:

- Store a two-week supply of water and food. During a pandemic, if you cannot get to a store, or if stores are out of supplies, it will be important for you to have extra supplies on hand. This can be useful in other types of emergencies, such as power outages and disasters.
- Periodically check your regular prescription drugs to ensure a continuous supply in your home.
- Have any nonprescription drugs and other health supplies on hand, including pain relievers, stomach remedies, cough and cold medicines, fluids with electrolytes, and vitamins.
- Talk with family members and loved ones about how they would be cared for if they got sick, or what will be needed to care for them in your home.
- Volunteer with local groups to prepare and assist with emergency response.
- Get involved in your community as it works to prepare for an influenza pandemic.

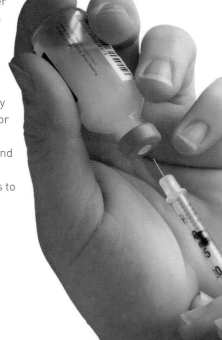

## LIMIT THE SPREAD OF GERMS AND PREVENT INFECTION:

- Avoid close contact with people who are sick. When you are sick, keep your distance from others to protect them from getting sick too.
- If possible, stay home from work, school, and errands when you are sick. You will help prevent others from catching your illness.
- Cover your mouth and nose with a tissue when coughing or sneezing. It may prevent those around you from getting sick.
- Wash your hands often; this will help protect you from germs.
- Avoid touching your eyes, nose, or mouth. Germs are often spread when a person touches something that is contaminated with germs and then touches his or her eyes, nose, or mouth.
- Practice other good health habits. Get plenty of sleep, be physically active, manage your stress, drink plenty of fluids, and eat nutritious food.

For more information on preparing for and responding to an influenza pandemic, visit the U.S. Department of Health and Human Service's website at www.pandemicflu.gov.

# TSUNAMIS

Tsunamis, also known as seismic sea waves, are most common along the Pacific coast, but can strike anywhere along the U.S. coastline. Tsunamis are enormous waves caused by an underground disturbance such as an earthquake. They can move hundreds of miles per hour and hit land with waves topping 100 feet in height.

Understand the difference between the terms that identify a tsunami hazard: advisory, watch, and warning. For a detailed explanation of these terms, see www.fema.gov/areyouready/tsunamis.shtm.

## PLAN TO ACT QUICKLY.

- If you are in coastal waters and notice a dramatic recession of water from the shoreline you should heed nature's warning that a tsunami is approaching.
- Move inland immediately and do not return to the flooded and damaged areas until officials say it is safe to do so.
- Visit NOAA for more weather-related information.
- Find out how to keep food safe during and after and emergency by visiting www.foodsafety.gov/keep/emergency/index.html

Stay informed. Local authorities may not immediately be able to provide information on what is happening and what you should do. However, you should listen to NOAA Weather Radio, watch TV, listen to the radio, or check the Internet often for official news and instructions as they become available.

# VOLCANOES

Potentially active volcanoes in the United States exist mainly in Hawaii, Alaska, and the Pacific Northwest. When pressure builds up within a volcano's molten rock, it has the potential to erupt, sending forth lava flows, poisonous gases, and flying rock and ash that can sometimes travel hundreds of miles downwind.

- Follow the instructions given by local emergency officials.
- Know your community's warning systems and disaster plans, including evacuation routes.
- Plan to evacuate quickly and to take your portable emergency supply kit with you.
- Plan ahead by adding extra goggles and something to cover your nose and mouth to your emergency supply kit. Include something to cover your nose and mouth for every member of your family.
- If you are unable to evacuate, and in order to protect yourself from falling ash, you should remain indoors with doors, windows, and ventilation closed until the ash settles.

Stay informed. Local authorities may not immediately be able to provide information on what is happening and what you should do. However, you should listen to NOAA Weather Radio, watch TV, listen to the radio or check the Internet often for official news and instructions as they become available.

For additional information on dealing with volcanic eruptions, please see:www.redcross.org/www-files/Documents/pdf/Preparedness/AreYou-Ready/PublicInformationVolcanoes.pdf and/or www.fema.gov/areyou-ready/volcanoes.shtm.

# WINTER STORMS AND EXTREME COLD

While the danger from winter weather varies across the country, nearly all Americans, regardless of where they live, are likely to face some type of severe winter weather at some point in their lives. That could mean snow or subfreezing temperatures, as well as strong winds or even ice or heavy rainstorms. One of the primary concerns is the winter weather's ability to knock out heat, power, and communications services to your home or office, sometimes for days at a time. The National Weather Service refers to winter storms as the "Deceptive Killers" because most deaths are indirectly related to the storm. Instead, people die in traffic accidents on icy roads and of hypothermia from prolonged exposure to cold. It is important to be prepared for winter weather before it strikes.

## STEP 1: GET A KIT
- Get an Emergency Supply Kit that includes items like nonperishable food, water, a battery-powered or hand-crank radio, extra flashlights, and batteries.
- Thoroughly check and update your family's Emergency Supply Kit before winter approaches, and add the following supplies in preparation for winter weather:
  - Rock salt to melt ice on walkways
  - Sand to improve traction
  - Snow shovels and other snow removal equipment
  - Adequate clothing and blankets to keep you warm

## STEP 2: MAKE A PLAN
### Prepare Your Family
Make a Family Emergency Plan. Your family may not be together when disaster strikes, so it is important to know how you will contact one another, how you will get back together, and what you will do in case of an emergency.
- Plan places where your family will meet, both within and outside your immediate neighborhood.
- It may be easier to make a long-distance phone call than to call across town, so an out-of-town contact may be in a better position to communicate among separated family members.

- You may also want to inquire about emergency plans at places where your family spends time: work, day care and school. If no plans exist, consider volunteering to help create one.
- Take a Community Emergency Response Team (CERT) class from your local Citizen Corps chapter. Keep your training current.

## STEP 3: BE INFORMED
### Prepare Your Home

- Make sure your home is well insulated and that you have weather stripping around your doors and windowsills to keep the warm air inside.
- Insulate pipes with insulation or newspapers and plastic and allow faucets to drip a little during cold weather to avoid freezing.
- Learn how to shut off water valves (in case a pipe bursts).
- Keep fire extinguishers on hand, and make sure everyone in your house knows how to use them. House fires pose an additional risk as more people turn to alternate heating sources without taking the necessary safety precautions.
- Know ahead of time what you should do to help elderly or disabled friends, neighbors, or employees.
- Hire a contractor to check the structural stability of the roof to sustain unusually heavy weight from the accumulation of snow—or water, if drains on flat roofs do not work.

**If you have a car, fill the gas tank in case you have to leave. In addition, check or have a mechanic check the following items on your car:**

- Antifreeze levels—ensure they are sufficient to avoid freezing.
- Battery and ignition system—should be in top condition, and battery terminals should be clean.
- Brakes—check for wear and fluid levels.
- Exhaust system—check for leaks and crimped pipes and repair or replace as necessary. Carbon monoxide is deadly and usually gives no warning.
- Fuel and air filters—replace and keep water out of the system by using additives and maintaining a full tank of gas.
- Heater and defroster—ensure they work properly.
- Lights and flashing hazard lights—check for serviceability.
- Oil—check for level and weight. Heavier oils congeal more at low temperatures and do not lubricate as well.
- Thermostat—ensure it works properly.

- Tires—make sure the tires have adequate tread. All-weather radials are usually adequate for most winter conditions. However, some jurisdictions require that to drive on their roads, vehicles must be equipped with chains or snow tires with studs.
- Windshield wiper equipment—repair any problems and maintain proper washer fluid level.

## FAMILIARIZE YOURSELF WITH THE TERMS THAT ARE USED TO IDENTIFY WINTER WEATHER:

- Freezing rain creates a coating of ice on roads and walkways.
- Sleet is rain that turns to ice pellets before reaching the ground. Sleet also causes roads to freeze and become slippery.
- Winter Weather Advisory means cold, ice, and snow are expected.
- Winter Storm Watch means severe weather such as heavy snow or ice is possible in the next day or two.
- Winter Storm Warning means severe winter conditions have begun or will begin very soon.
- Blizzard Warning means heavy snow and strong winds will produce a blinding snow, near zero visibility, deep drifts, and life-threatening windchill. Frost/Freeze Warning means below-freezing temperatures are expected.

## WHEN A WINTER STORM WATCH IS ISSUED:

- Listen to NOAA Weather Radio, local radio, and television stations, or cable television such as The Weather Channel for further updates.
- Be alert to changing weather conditions.
- Avoid unnecessary travel
- When a Winter Storm WARNING is issued
- Stay indoors during the storm.
- If you must go outside, several layers of lightweight clothing will keep you warmer than a single heavy coat. Gloves (or mittens) and a hat will prevent loss of body heat. Cover your mouth to protect your lungs.
- Walk carefully on snowy, icy walkways.
- If the pipes freeze, remove any insulation or layers of newspapers and wrap pipes in rags. Completely open all faucets and pour hot water over the pipes, starting where they were most exposed to the cold (or where the cold was most likely to penetrate).

- Maintain ventilation when using kerosene heaters to avoid buildup of toxic fumes. Refuel kerosene heaters outside and keep them at least 3 feet from flammable objects.

**Avoid traveling by car in a storm, but if you must . . .**

- Carry an Emergency Supply Kit in the trunk.
- Keep your car's gas tank full for emergency use and to keep the fuel line from freezing.
- Let someone know your destination, your route, and when you expect to arrive. If your car gets stuck along the way, help can be sent along your predetermined route.
- Eat regularly and drink ample fluids, but avoid caffeine and alcohol.
- Conserve fuel, if necessary, by keeping your residence cooler than normal. Temporarily close off heat to some rooms.

# LISTEN TO LOCAL OFFICIALS

Learn about the emergency plans that have been established in your area by your state and local government. In any emergency, always listen to the instructions given by local emergency management officials. For further information on how to plan and prepare for winter storms as well as what to do during and after a winter storm, visit the Web sites for the Federal Emergency Management Agency, NOAA Watch, or American Red Cross.

# APPENDICES

# Edible Plants

*I*n a survival situation, plants can provide food and medicine. Their safe usage requires absolutely positive identification, knowing how to prepare them for eating, and knowing any dangerous properties they might have. Familiarity with botanical structures of plants and information on where they grow will make them easier to locate and identify.

# ABAL

## *CALLIGONUM COMOSUM*

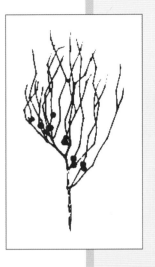

**Description:** The abal is one of the few shrubby plants that exists in the shady deserts. This plant grows to about 1.2 meters, and its branches look like wisps from a broom. The stiff, green branches produce an abundance of flowers in the early spring months (March, April).

**Habitat and Distribution:** This plant is found in desert scrub and waste in any climatic zone. It inhabits much of the North African desert. It may also be found on the desert sands of the Middle East and as far eastward as the Rajputana desert of westen India.

**Edible Parts:** This plant's general appearance would not indicate its usefulness to the survivor, but while this plant is flowering in the spring, its fresh flowers can be eaten. This plant is common in the areas where it is found. An analysis of the food value of this plant has shown it to be high in sugar and nitrogenous components.

# ACACIA

## *ACACIA FARNESIANA*

**Description:** Acacia is a spreading, usually short tree with spines and alternate compound leaves. Its individual leaflets are small. Its flowers are ball-shaped, bright yellow, and very fragrant. Its bark is a whitish-gray color. Its fruits are dark brown and podlike.

**Habitat and Distribution:** Acacia grows in open, sunny areas. It is found throughout all tropical regions.

*Note: There are about 500 species of acacia. These plants are especially prevalent in Africa, southern Asia, and Australia, but many species are found in the warmer and drier parts of America.*

**Edible Parts:** Its young leaves, flowers, and pods are edible raw or cooked.

# AGAVE

*AGAVE SPECIES*

**Description:** These plants have large clusters of thick, fleshy leaves borne close to the ground and surrounding a central stalk. The plants flower only once, then die. They produce a massive flower stalk.

**Habitat and Distribution:** Agaves prefer dry, open areas. They are found throughout Central America, the Caribbean, and parts of the western deserts of the United States and Mexico.

**Edible Parts:** Its flowers and flower buds are edible. Boil them before eating.

**Caution:** The juice of some species causes dermatitis in some individuals.

**Other Uses:** Cut the huge flower stalk and collect the juice for drinking. Some species have very fibrous leaves. Pound the leaves and remove the fibers for weaving and making ropes. Most species have thick, sharp needles at the tips of the leaves. Use them for sewing or making hacks. The sap of some species contains a chemical that makes the sap suitable for use as a soap.

# ALMOND

*PRUNUS AMYGDALUS*

**Description:** The almond tree, which sometimes grows to 12.2 meters, looks like a peach tree. The fresh almond fruit resembles a gnarled, unripe peach and grows in clusters. The stone (the almond itself) is covered with a thick, dry, woolly skin.

**Habitat and Distribution:** Almonds are found in the scrub and thorn forests of the tropics, the evergreen scrub forests of temperate areas, and in desert scrub and waste in all climatic zones. The almond tree is also found in the semidesert areas of the Old World in southern Europe, the eastern Mediterranean, Iran, the Middle East, China, Madeira, the Azores, and the Canary Islands.

**Edible Parts:** The mature almond fruit splits open lengthwise down the side, exposing the ripe almond nut. You can easily get the dry kernel by simply cracking open the stone. Almond meats are rich in food value, like all nuts. Gather them in large quantities and shell them for further use as survival food. You could live solely on almonds for rather long periods. When you boil them, the kernel's outer covering comes off and only the white meat remains.

# AMARANTH

### *AMARANTHUS SPECIES*

**Description:** These plants, which grow 90 centimeters to 150 centimeters tall, are abundant weeds in many parts of the world. All amaranth have alternate simple leaves. They may have some red color present on the stems. They bear minute, greenish flowers in dense clusters at the top of the plants. Their seeds may be brown or black in weedy species and light-colored in domestic species.

**Habitat and Distribution:** Look for amaranth along roadsides, in disturbed waste areas, or as weeds in crops throughout the world. Some amaranth species have been grown as a grain crop and a garden vegetable in various parts of the world, especially in South America.

**Edible Parts:** All parts are edible, but some may have sharp spines you should remove before eating. The young plants or the growing tips of alder plants are an excellent vegetable. Simply boil the young plants or eat them raw. Their seeds are very nutritious. Shake the tops of alder plants to get the seeds. Eat the seeds raw, boiled, ground into flour, or popped like popcorn.

# ARCTIC WILLOW

*SALIX ARCTICA*

**Description:** The arctic willow is a shrub that never exceeds more than 60 centimeters in height and grows in clumps that form dense mats on the tundra.

**Habitat and Distribution:** The arctic willow is common on tundras in North America. Europe, and Asia. You can also find it in some mountainous areas in temperate regions.

**Edible Parts:** You can collect the succulent, tender young shoots of the arctic willow in early spring. Strip off the outer bark of the new shoots and eat the inner portion raw. You can also peel and eat raw the young underground shoots of any of the various kinds of arctic willow. Young willow leaves are one of the richest sources of vitamin C, containing 7 to 10 times more than an orange.

# ARROWROOT

*MARANTA* AND *SAGITTARIA* SPECIES

**Description:** The arrowroot is an aquatic plant with arrow-shaped leaves and potatolike tubers in the mud.

**Habitat and Distribution:** Aroowroot is found worldwide in temperate zones and the tropics. It is found in moist to wet habitats.

**Edible Parts:** The rootstock is a rich source of high quality starch. Boil the rootstock and eat it as a vegetable.

## ASPARAGUS
### *ASPARAGUS OFFICINALIS*

**Description:** The spring growth of this plant resembles a cluster of green fingers. The mature plant has fernlike, wispy foliage and red berries. Its flowers are small and greenish in color. Several species have sharp, thornlike structures.

**Habitat and Distribution:** Asparagus is found worldwide in temperate areas. Look for it in fields, old homesites, and fence-rows.

**Edible Parts:** Eat the young stems before leaves form. Steam or boil them for 10 to 15 minutes before eating. Raw asparagus may cause nausea or diarrhea. The fleshy roots are a good source of starch.

## BAEL FRUIT
### *AEGLE MARMELOS*

**Description:** This is a tree that grows from 2.4 to 4.6 meters tall, with a dense spiny growth. The fruit is 5 to 10 centimeters in diameter, gray or yellowish, and full of seeds.

**Habitat and Distribution:** Bael fruit is found in rain forests and semievergreen seasonal forests of the tropics. It grows wild in India and Burma.

**Edible Parts:** The fruit, which ripens in December, is at its best when just turning ripe. The juice of the ripe fruit, diluted with water and mixed with a small amount of tamarind and sugar or honey, is sour but refreshing. Like other citrus fruits, it is rich in vitamin C.

# BAMBOO

*VARIOUS SPECIES INCLUDING BAMBUSA, DENDROCALAMUS, PHYLLOSTACHYS*

**Description:** Bamboos are woody grasses that grow up to 15 meters tall. The leaves are grasslike and the stems are the familiar bamboo used in furniture and fishing poles.

**Habitat and Distribution:** Look for bamboo in warm, moist regions in open or jungle country, in lowland, or on mountains. Bamboos are native to the Far East (temperate and tropical zones) but have bean widely planted around the world.

**Edible Parts:** The young shoots of almost all species are edible raw or cooked. Raw shoots have a slightly bitter taste that is removed by boiling. To prepare, remove the tough protective sheath that is coated with tawny or red hairs. The seed grain of the flowering bamboo is also edible. Boil the seeds like rice or pulverize them, mix with water, and make into cakes.

**Other Uses:** Use the mature bamboo to build structures or to make containers, ladles, spoons, and various other cooking utensils. Also use bamboo to make tools and weapons. You can make a strong bow by splitting the bamboo and putting several pieces together.

**CAUTION:** Green bamboo may explode in a fire. Green bamboo has an internal membrane you must remove before using it as a food or water container.

# BANANA AND PLANTAIN

*MUSA SPECIES*

**Description:** These are treelike plants with several large leaves at the top. Their flowers are borne in dense hanging clusters.

**Habitat and Distribution:** Look for bananas and plantains in open fields or margins of forests where they are grown as a crop. They grow in the humid tropics.

**Edible Parts:** Their fruits are edible raw or cooked. They may be boiled or baked. You can boil their flowers and eat them like a vegetable. You can cook and eat the rootstocks and leaf sheaths of many species. The center or "heart" or the plant is edible year-round, cooked or raw.

**Other Uses:** You can use the layers of the lower third of the plants to cover coals to roast food. You can also use their stumps to get water. You can use their leaves to wrap other foods for cooking or storage.

# BAOBAB

## *ADANSONIA DIGITATA*

**Description:** The baobab tree may grow as high as 18 meters and may have a trunk 9 meters in diameter. The tree has short, stubby branches and a gray, thick bark. Its leaves are compound and their segments are arranged like the palm of a hand. Its flowers, which are white and several centimeters across, hang from the higher branches. Its fruit is shaped like a football, measures up to 45 centimeters long, and is covered with short dense hair.

**Habitat and Distribution:** These trees grow in savannas. They are found in Africa, in parts of Australia, and on the island of Madagascar.

**Edible Parts:** You can use the young leaves as a soup vegetable. The tender root of the young baobab tree is edible. The pulp and seeds of the fruit are also edible. Use one handful of pulp to about one cup of water for a refreshing drink. To obtain flour, roast the seeds, then grind them.

**Other Uses:** Drinking a mixture of pulp and water will help cure diarrhea. Often the hollow trunks are good sources of fresh water. The bark can be cut into strips and pounded to obtain a strong fiber for making rope.

# BATOKO PLUM
### *FLACOURTIA INERMIS*

**Description:** This shrub or small tree has dark green, alternate, simple leaves. Its fruits are bright red and contain six or more seeds.

**Habitat and Distribution:** This plant is a native of the Philippines but is widely cultivated for its fruit in other areas. It can be found in clearings and at the edges of the tropical rain forests of Africa and Asia.

**Edible Parts:** Eat the fruit raw or cooked.

# BEARBERRY OR KINNIKINNICK
### *ARCTOSTAPHYLOS UVAURSI*

**Description:** This plant is a common evergreen shrub with reddish, scaly bark and thick, leathery leaves 4 centimeters long and 1 centimeter wide. It has white flowers and bright red fruits.

**Habitat and Distribution:** This plant is found in arctic, subarctic, and temperate regions, most often in sandy or rocky soil.

**Edible Parts:** Its berries are edible raw or cooked. You can make a refreshing tea from its young leaves.

# BEECH

## *FAGUS* SPECIES

**Description:** Beech trees are large (9 to 24 meters), symmetrical forest trees that have smooth, light-gray bark and dark green foliage. The character of its bark, plus its clusters of prickly seedpods, clearly distinguish the beech tree in the field.

**Habitat and Distribution:** This tree is found in the Temperate Zone. It grows wild in the eastern United States, Europe, Asia, and North Africa. It is found in moist areas, mainly in the forests. This tree is common throughout southeastern Europe and across temperate Asia. Beech relatives are also found in Chile, New Guinea, and New Zealand.

**Edible Parts:** The mature beechnuts readily fall out of the husklike seedpods. You can eat these dark brown triangular nuts by breaking the thin shell with your fingernail and removing the white, sweet kernel inside. Beechnuts are one of the most delicious of all wild nuts. They are a most useful survival food because of the kernel's high oil content. You can also use the beechnuts as a coffee substitue. Roast them so that the kernel becomes golden brown and quite hard. Then pulverize the kernel and, after boiling or steeping in hot water, you have a passable coffee substitute.

# BIGNAY

## *ANTIDESMA BUNIUS*

**Description:** Bignay is a shrub or small tree, 3 to 12 meters tall, with shiny, pointed leaves about 15 centimeters long. Its flowers are small, clustered, and green. It has fleshy, dark red or black fruit and a single seed. The fruit is about 1 centimeter in diameter.

**Habitat and Distribution:** This plant is found in rain forests and semievergreen seasonal forests in the tropics. It is found in open places and in secondary forests. It grows wild from the Himalayas to Ceylon and eastward through Indonesia to northern Australia. However, it may be found anywhere in the tropics in cultivated forms.

**Edible Parts:** The fruit is edible raw. Do not eat any other parts of the tree. In Africa, the roots are toxic. Other parts of the plant may be poisonous.

**CAUTION:** Eaten in large quantities, the fruit may have a laxative effect.

# BLACKBERRY, RASPBERRY, AND DEWBERRY
## *RUBUS* SPECIES

**Description:** These plants have prickly stems (canes) that grow upward, arching back toward the ground. They have alternate, usually compound leaves. Their fruits may be red, black, yellow, or orange.

**Habitat and Distribution:** These plants grow in open, sunny areas at the margin of woods, lakes, streams, and roads throughout temperate regions. There is also an arctic raspberry.

**Edible Parts:** The fruits and peeled young shoots are edible. Flavor varies greatly.

**Other Uses:** Use the leaves to make tea. To treat diarrhea, drink a tea made by brewing the dried root bark of the blackberry bush.

# BLUEBERRY AND HUCKLEBERRY
## *VACCINIUM* AND *GAYLUSSACIA* SPECIES

**Description:** These shrubs vary in size from 30 centimeters to 3.7 meters tall. All have alternate, simple leaves. Their fruits may be dark blue, black, or red and have many small seeds.

**Habitat and Distribution:** These plants prefer open, sunny areas. They are found throughout much of the north temperate regions and at higher elevations in Central America.

**Edible Parts:** Their fruits are edible raw.

# BREADFRUIT

### *ARTOCARPUS INCISA*

**Description:** This tree may grow up to 9 meters tall. It has dark green, deeply divided leaves that are 75 centimeters long and 30 centimeters wide. Its fruits are large, green, ball-like structures up to 30 centimeters across when mature.

**Habitat and Distribution:** Look for this tree at the margins of forests and homesites in the humid tropics. It is native to the South Pacific region but has been widely planted in the West Indies and parts of Polynesia.

**Edible Parts:** The fruit pulp is edible raw. The fruit can be sliced, dried, and ground into flour for later use. The seeds are edible cooked.

**Other Uses:** The thick sap can serve as glue and caulking material. You can also use it as birdlime (to entrap small birds by smearing the sap on twigs where they usually perch).

# BURDOCK

### *ARCTIUM LAPPA*

**Description:** This plant has wavy-edged, arrow-shaped leaves and flower heads in burrlike clusters. It grows up to 2 meters tall, with purple or pink flowers and a large, fleshy root.

**Habitat and Distribution:** Burdock is found worldwide in the North Temperate Zone. Look for it in open waste areas during the spring and summer.

**Edible Parts:** Peel the tender leaf stalks and eat them raw or cook them like greens. The roots are also edible boiled or baked.

**CAUTION:** Do not confuse burdock with rhubarb that has poisonous leaves.

**Other Uses:** A liquid made from the roots will help to produce sweating and increase urination. Dry the root, simmer it in water, strain the liquid, and then drink the strained liquid. Use the fiber from the dried stalk to weave cordage.

# BURI PALM
### *CORYPHA ELATA*

**Description:** This tree may reach 18 meters in height. It has large, fan-shaped leaves up to 3 meters long and split into about 100 narrow segments. It bears flowers in huge dusters at the top of the tree. The tree dies after flowering.

**Habitat and Distribution:** This tree grows in coastal areas of the East Indies.

**Edible Parts:** The trunk contains starch that is edible raw. The very tip of the trunk is also edible raw or cooked. You can get large quantities of liquid by bruising the flowering stalk. The kernels of the nuts are edible.

**CAUTION:** The seed covering may cause dermatitis in some individuals.

**Other Uses:** You can use the leaves as weaving material.

# CANNA LILY
### *CANNA INDICA*

**Description:** The canna lily is a coarse perennial herb, 90 centimeters to 3 meters tall. The plant grows from a large, thick, underground rootstock that is edible. Its large leaves resemble those of the banana plant but are not so large. The flowers of wild canna lily are usually small, relatively inconspicuous, and brightly colored reds, oranges, or yellows.

**Habitat and Distribution:** As a wild plant, the canna lily is found in all tropical areas, especially in moist places along streams, springs, ditches, and the margins of woods. It may also be found in wet temperate, mountainous regions. It is easy to recognize because it is commonly cultivated in flower gardens in the United States.

**Edible Parts:** The large and much branched rootstocks are full of edible starch. The younger parts may be finely chopped and then boiled or pulverized into a meal. Mix in the young shoots of palm cabbage for flavoring.

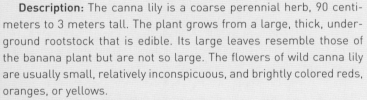

## CAROB TREE

*CERATONIA SILIQUA*

**Description:** This large tree has a spreading crown. Its leaves are compound and alternate. Its seedpods, also known as Saint John's bread, are up to 45 centimeters long and are filled with round, hard seeds and a thick pulp.

**Habitat and Distribution:** This tree is found throughout the Mediterranean, the Middle East, and parts of North Africa.

**Edible Parts:** The young tender pods are edible raw or boiled. You can pulverize the seeds in mature pods and cook as porridge.

## CASHEW NUT

*ANACARDIUM OCCIDENTALE*

**Description:** The cashew is a spreading evergreen tree growing to a height of 12 meters, with leaves up to 20 centimeters long and 10 centimeters wide. Its flowers are yellowish-pink. Its fruit is very easy to recognize because of its peculiar structure. The fruit is thick and pear-shaped, pulpy and red or yellow when ripe. This fruit bears a hard, green, kidney-shaped nut at its tip. This nut is smooth, shiny, and green or brown according to its maturity.

**Habitat and Distribution:** The cashew is native to the West Indies and northern South America, but transplantation has spread it to all tropical climates. In the Old World, it has escaped from cultivation and appears to be wild at least in parts of Africa and India.

**Edible Parts:** The nut encloses one seed. The seed is edible when roasted. The pear-shaped fruit is juicy, sweet-acid, and astringent. It is quite safe and considered delicious by most people who eat it.

**CAUTION:** The green hull surrounding the nut contains a resinous irritant poison that will blister the lips and tongue like poison ivy. Heat destroys this poison when roasting the nuts.

# CATTAIL
*TYPHA LATIFOLIA*

**Description:** Cattails are grasslike plants with strap-shaped leaves 1 to 5 centimeters wide and growing up to 1.8 meters tall. The male flowers are borne in a dense mass above the female flowers. These last only a short time, leaving the female flowers that develop into the brown cattail. Pollen from the male flowers is often abundant and bright yellow.

**Habitat and Distribution:** Cattails are found throughout most of the world. Look for them in full sun areas at the margins of lakes, streams, canals, rivers, and brackish water.

**Edible Parts:** The young tender shoots are edible raw or cooked. The rhizome is often very tough but is a rich source of starch. Pound the rhizome to remove the starch and use as a flour. The pollen is also an exceptional source of starch. When the cattail is immature and still green, you can boil the female portion and eat it like corn on the cob.

**Other Uses:** The dried leaves are an excellent source of weaving material you can use to make floats and rafts. The cottony seeds make good pillow stuffing and insulation. The fluff makes excellent tinder. Dried cattails are effective insect repellents when burned.

# CEREUS CACTUS
*CEREUS SPECIES*

**Description:** These cacti are tall and narrow with angled stems and numerous spines.

**Habitat and Distribution:** They may be found in true deserts and other dry, open, sunny areas throughout the Caribbean region, Central America, and the western United States.

**Edible Parts:** The fruits are edible, but some may have a laxative effect.

**Other Uses:** The pulp of the cactus is a good source of water. Break open the stem and scoop out the pulp.

# CHESTNUT

### *CASTANEA SATIVA*

**Description:** The European chestnut is usually a large tree, up to 18 meters in height.

**Habitat and Distribution:** In temperate regions, the chestnut is found in both hardwood and coniferous forests. In the tropics, it is found in semievergreen seasonal forests. They are found over all of middle and south Europe and across middle Asia to China and Japan. They are relatively abundant along the edge of meadows and as a forest tree. The European chestnut is one of the most common varieties. Wild chestnuts in Asia belong to the related chestnut species.

**Edible Parts:** Chestnuts are highly useful as survival food. Ripe nuts are usually picked in autumn, although unripe nuts picked while green may also be used for food. Perhaps the easiest way to prepare them is to roast the ripe nuts in embers. Cooked this way, they are quite tasty, and you can eat large quantities. Another way is to boil the kernels after removing the outer shell. After being boiled until fairly soft, you can mash the nuts like potatoes.

# CHICORY

### *CICHORIUM INTYBUS*

**Description:** This plant grows up to 1.8 meters tall. It has leaves clustered at the base of the stem and some leaves on the stem. The base leaves resemble those of the dandelion. The flowers are sky blue and stay open only on sunny days. Chicory has a milky juice.

**Habitat and Distribution:** Look for chicory in old fields, waste areas, weedy lots, and along roads. It is a native of Europe and Asia, but is also found in Africa and most of North America where it grows as a weed.

**Edible Parts:** All parts are edible. Eat the young leaves as a salad or boil to eat as a vegetable. Cook the roots as a vegetable. For use as a coffee substitute, roast the roots until they are dark brown and then pulverize them.

# CHUFA

## *CYPERUS ESCULENTUS*

**Description:** This very common plant has a triangular stem and grass-like leaves. It grows to a height of 20 to 60 centimeters. The mature plant has a soft furlike bloom that extends from a whorl of leaves. Tubers 1 to 2.5 centimeters in diameter grow at the ends of the roots.

**Habitat and Distribution:** Chufa grows in moist sandy areas throughout the world. It is often an abundant weed in cultivated fields.

**Edible Parts:** The tubers are edible raw, boiled, or baked. You can also grind them and use them as a coffee substitute.

# COCONUT

## *COCOS NUCIFERA*

**Description:** This tree has a single, narrow, tall trunk with a cluster of very large leaves at the top. Each leaf may be over 6 meters long with over 100 pairs of leaflets.

**Habitat and Distribution:** Coconut palms are found throughout the tropics. They are most abundant near coastal regions.

**Edible Parts:** The nut is a valuable source of food. The milk of the young coconut is rich in sugar and vitamins and is an excellent source of liquid. The nut meat is also nutritious but is rich in oil. To preserve the meat, spread it in the sun until it is completely dry.

**Other Uses:** Use coconut oil to cook and to protect metal objects from corrosion. Also use the oil to treat saltwater sores, sunburn, and dry skin. Use the oil in improvised torches. Use the tree trunk as building material and the leaves as thatch. Hollow out the large stump for use as a food container. The coconut husks are good flotation devices and the husk's fibers are used to weave ropes and other items. Use the gauzelike fibers at the leaf bases as strainers or use them to weave a bug net or to make a pad to use on wounds. The husk makes a good abrasive. Dried husk fiber is an excellent tinder. A smoldering husk helps to repel mosquitoes. Smoke caused by dripping coconut oil in a fire also repels mosquitoes. To render coconut oil, put the coconut meat in the sun, heat it over a slow fire, or boil it in a pot of water. Coconuts washed out to sea are a good source of fresh liquid for the sea survivor.

# COMMON JUJUBE
## *ZIZIPHUS JUJUBA*

**Description:** The common jujube is either a deciduous tree growing to a height of 12 meters or a large shrub, depending upon where it grows and how much water is available for growth. Its branches are usually spiny. Its reddish-brown to yellowish-green fruit is oblong to ovoid, 3 centimeters or less in diameter, smooth, and sweet in flavor, but has rather dry pulp around a comparatively large stone. Its flowers are green.

**Habitat and Distribution:** The jujube is found in forested areas of temperate regions and in desert scrub and waste areas worldwide. It is common in many of the tropical and subtropical areas of the Old World. In Africa, it is found mainly bordering the Mediterranean. In Asia, it is especially common in the drier parts of India and China. The jujube is also found throughout the East Indies. It can be found bordering some desert areas.

**Edible Parts:** The pulp, crushed in water, makes a refreshing beverage. If time permits, you can dry the ripe fruit in the sun like dates. Its fruits are high in vitamins A and C.

# CRANBERRY
## *VACCINIUM MACROCARPON*

**Description:** This plant has tiny leaves arranged alternately. Its stem creeps along the ground. Its fruits are red berries.

**Habitat and Distribution:** It only grows in open, sunny, wet areas in the colder regions of the Northern Hemisphere.

**Edible Parts:** The berries are very tart when eaten raw. Cook in a small amount of water and add sugar, if available, to make a jelly.

**Other Uses:** Cranberries may act as a diuretic. They are useful for treating urinary tract infections.

# CROWBERRY
### EMPETRUM NIGRUM

**Description:** This is a dwarf evergreen shrub with short needlelike leaves. It has small, shiny, black berries that remain on the bush throughout the winter.

**Habitat and Distribution:** Look for this plant in tundra throughout arctic regions of North America and Eurasia.

**Edible Parts:** The fruits are edible fresh or can be dried for later use.

# CUIPO TREE
### CAVANILLESIA PLATANIFOLIA

**Description:** This is a very dominant and easily detected tree because it extends above the other trees. Its height ranges from 45 to 60 meters. It has leaves only at the top and is bare 11 months out of the year. It has rings on its bark that extend to the top to make is easily recognizable. Its bark is reddish or gray in color. Its roots are light reddish-brown or yellowish-brown.

**Habitat and Distribution:** The cuipo tree is located primarily in Central American tropical rain forests in mountainous areas.

**Edible Parts:** To get water from this tree, cut a piece of the root and clean the dirt and bark off one end, keeping the root horizontal. Put the clean end to your mouth or canteen and raise the other. The water from this tree tastes like potato water.

**Other Uses:** Use young saplings and the branches' inner bark to make rope.

# DANDELION

### *TARAXACUM OFFICINALE*

**Description:** Dandelion leaves have a jagged edge, grow close to the ground, and are seldom more than 20 centimeters long. Its flowers are bright yellow. There are several dandelion species.

**Habitat and Distribution:** Dandelions grow in open, sunny locations throughout the Northern Hemisphere.

**Edible Parts:** All parts are edible. Eat the leaves raw or cooked. Boil the roots as a vegetable. Roots roasted and ground are a good coffee substitue. Dandelions are high in vitamins A and C and in calcium.

**Other Uses:** Use the white juice in the flower stems as glue.

# DATE PALM

### *PHOENIX DACTYLIFERA*

**Description:** The date palm is a tall, unbranched tree with a crown of huge, compound leaves. Its fruit is yellow when ripe.

**Habitat and Distribution:** This tree grows in arid semitropical regions. It is native to North Africa and the Middle East but has been planted in the arid semitropics in other parts of the world.

**Edible Parts:** Its fruit is edible fresh but is very bitter if eaten before it is ripe. You can dry the fruits in the sun and preserve them for a long time.

**Other Uses:** The trunks provide valuable building material in desert regions where few other treelike plants are found. The leaves are durable and you can use them for thatching and as weaving material. The base of the leaves resembles coarse cloth that you can use for scrubbing and cleaning.

# DAYLILY
### *HEMEROCALLIS FULVA*

**Description:** This plant has unspotted, tawny blossoms that open for 1 day only. It has long, swordlike, green basal leaves. Its root is a mass of swollen and elongated tubers.

**Habitat and Distribution:** Daylilies are found worldwide in Tropic and Temperate Zones. They are grown as a vegetable in parts of Asia and as an ornamental plant elsewhere.

**Edible Parts:** The young green leaves are edible raw or cooked. Tubers are also edible raw or cooked. You can eat its flowers raw, but they taste better cooked. You can also fry the flowers for storage.

**CAUTION:** Eating excessive amounts of raw flowers may cause diarrhea.

# DUCHESNEA OR INDIAN STRAWBERRY
### *DUCHESNEA INDICA*

**Description:** The duchesnea is a small plant that has runners and three-parted leaves. Its flowers are yellow and its fruit resembles a strawberry.

**Habitat and Distribution:** It is native to southern Asia but is a common weed in warmer temperate regions. Look for it in lawns, gardens, and along roads.

**Edible Parts:** Its fruit is edible. Eat it fresh.

# ELDERBERRY
## *SAMBUCUS CANADENSIS*

**Description:** Elderberry is a many-stemmed shrub with opposite, compound leaves. It grows to a height of 6 meters. Its flowers are fragrant, white, and borne in large flat-topped clusters up to 30 centimeters across. Its berrylike fruits are dark blue or black when ripe.

**Habitat and Distribution:** This plant is found in open, usually wet areas at the margins of marshes, rivers, ditches, and lakes. It grows throughout much of eastern North America and Canada.

**Edible Parts:** The flowers and fruits are edible. You can make a drink by soaking the flower heads for 8 hours, discarding the flowers, and drinking the liquid.

**CAUTION:** All other parts of the plant are poisonous and dangerous if eaten.

# FIREWEED
## *EPILOBIUM ANGUSTIFOLIUM*

**Description:** This plant grows up to 1.8 meters tall. It has large, showy, pink flowers and lance-shaped leaves. Its relative, the dwarf fireweed (Epilobium latifolium), grows 30 to 60 centimeters tall.

**Habitat and Ditstribution:** Tall fireweed is found in open woods, on hillsides, on stream banks, and near seashores in arctic regions. It is especially abundant in burned-over areas. Dwarf fireweed is found along streams, sandbars, and lakeshores and on alpine and arctic slopes.

**Edible Parts:** The leaves, stems, and flowers are edible in the spring but become tough in summer. You can split open the stems of old plants and eat the pith raw.

# FISHTAIL PALM

### *CARYOTA URENS*

**Description:** Fishtail palms are large trees, at least 18 meters tall. Their leaves are unlike those of any other palm; the leaflets are irregular and toothed on the upper margins. All other palms have either fan-shaped or featherlike leaves. Its massive flowering shoot is borne at the top of the tree and hangs downward.

**Habitat and Distribution:** The fishtail palm is native to the tropics of India, Assam, and Burma. Several related species also exist in Southeast Asia and the Philippines. These palms are found in open hill country and jungle areas.

**Edible Parts:** The chief food in this palm is the starch stored in large quantities in its trunk. The juice from the fishtail palm is very nourishing and you have to drink it shortly after getting it from the palm flower shoot. Boil the juice down to get a rich sugar syrup. Use the same method as for the sugar palm to get the juice. The palm cabbage may be eaten raw or cooked.

# FOXTAIL GRASS

### *SETARIA* SPECIES

**Description:** This weedy grass is readily recognized by the narrow, cylindrical head containing long hairs. Its grains are small, less than 6 millimeters long. The dense heads of grain often droop when ripe.

**Habitat and Distribution:** Look for foxtail grasses in open, sunny areas, along roads, and at the margins of fields. Some species occur in wet, marshy areas. Species of *Setaria* are found throughout the United States, Europe, western Asia, and tropical Africa. In some parts of the world, foxtail grasses are grown as a food crop.

**Edible Parts:** The grains are edible raw but are very hard and sometimes bitter. Boiling removes some of the bitterness and makes them easier to eat.

## GOA BEAN

*PSOPHOCARPUS TETRAGONOLOBUS*

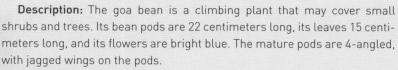

**Description:** The goa bean is a climbing plant that may cover small shrubs and trees. Its bean pods are 22 centimeters long, its leaves 15 centimeters long, and its flowers are bright blue. The mature pods are 4-angled, with jagged wings on the pods.

**Habitat and Distribution:** This plant grows in tropical Africa, Asia, the East Indies, the Philippines, and Taiwan. This member of the bean (legume) family serves to illustrate a kind of edible bean oommon in the tropics of the Old World. Wild edible beans of this sort are most frequently found in clearings and around abandoned garden sites. They are more rare in forested areas.

**Edible Parts:** You can eat the young pods like string beans. The mature seeds are a valuable source of protein after parching or roasting them over hot coals. You can germinate the seeds (as you can many kinds of beans) in damp moss and eat the resultant sprouts. The thickened roots are edible raw. They are slightly sweet, with the firmness of an apple. You can also eat the young leaves as a vegetable, raw or steamed.

## HACKBERRY

*CELTIS* **SPECIES**

**Description:** Hackberry trees have smooth, gray bark that often has corky warts or ridges. The tree may reach 39 meters in height. Hackberry trees have long-pointed leaves that grow in two rows. This tree bears small, round berries that can be eaten when they are ripe and fall from the tree. The wood of the hackberry is yellowish.

**Habitat and Distribution:** This plant is widespread in the United States, especially in and near ponds.

**Edible Parts:** Its berries are edible when they are ripe and fall from the tree.

# HAZELNUT OR WILD FILBERT
## *CORYLUS* SPECIES

**Description:** Hazelnuts grow on bushes 1.8 to 3.6 meters high. One species in Turkey and another in China are large trees. The nut itself grows in a very bristly husk that conspicuously contracts above the nut into a long neck. The different species vary in this respect as to size and shape.

**Habitat and Distribution:** Hazelnuts are found over wide areas in the United States, especially the eastern half of the country and along the Pacific coast. These nuts are also found in Europe where they are known as filberts. The hazelnut is common in Asia, especially in eastern Asia from the Himalayas to China and Japan. The hazelnut usually grows in the dense thickets along stream banks and open places. They are not plants of the dense forest.

**Edible Parts:** Hazelnuts ripen in the autumn when you can crack them open and eat the kernel. The dried nut is extremely delicious. The nut's high oil content makes it a good survival food. In the unripe stage, you can crack them open and eat the fresh kernel.

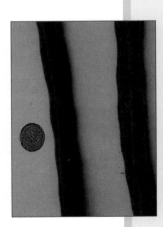

# HORSERADISH TREE
## *MORINGA PTERYGOSPERMA*

**Description:** This tree grows from 4.5 to 14 meters tall. Its leaves have a fernlike appearance. Its flowers and long, pendulous fruits grow on the ends of the branches. Its fruit (pod) looks like a giant bean. Its 25- to 60-centimeter-long pods are triangular in cross section, with strong ribs. Its roots have a pungent odor.

**Habitat and Distribution:** This tree is found in the rain forests and semievergreen seasonal forests of the tropical regions. It is widespread in India, Southeast Asia, Africa, and Central America. Look for it in abandoned fields and gardens and at the edges of forests.

**Edible Parts:** The leaves are edible raw or cooked, depending on their hardness. Cut the young seedpods into short lengths and cook them like string beans or fry them. You can get oil for frying by boiling the young fruits of palms and skimming the oil off the surface of the water. You can eat the flowers as part of a salad. You can chew fresh, young seedpods to eat the pulpy and soft seeds. The roots may be ground as a substitute for seasoning similar to horseradish.

# ICELAND MOSS

### *CETRARIA ISLANDICA*

**Description:** This moss grows only a few inches high. Its color may be gray, white, or even reddish.

**Habitat and Distribution:** Look for it in open areas. It is found only in the arctic.

**Edible Parts:** All parts of the Iceland moss are edible. During the winter or dry season, it is dry and crunchy but softens when soaked. Boil the moss to remove the bitterness. After boiling, eat by itself or add to milk or grains as a thickening agent. Dried plants store well.

# INDIAN POTATO OR ESKIMO POTATO

### *CLAYTONIA* **SPECIES**

**Description:** All *Claytonia* species are somewhat fleshy plants only a few centimeters tall, with showy flowers about 2.5 centimeters across.

**Habitat and Distribution:** Some species are found in rich forests where they are conspicuous before the leaves develop. Western species are found throughout most of the northern United States and in Canada.

**Edible Parts:** The tubers are edible but you should boil them before eating.

# JUNIPER
## *JUNIPERUS* SPECIES

**Description:** Junipers, sometimes called cedars, are trees or shurbs with very small, scalelike leaves densely crowded around the branches. Each leaf is less than 1.2 centimeters long. All species have a distinct aroma resembling the well-known cedar. The berrylike cones are usually blue and covered with a whitish wax.

**Habitat and Distribution:** Look for junipers in open, dry, sunny areas throughout North America and northern Europe. Some species are found in southeastern Europe, across Asia to Japan, and in the mountains of North Africa.

**Edible Parts:** The berries and twigs are edible. Eat the berries raw or roast the seeds to use as a coffee substitute. Use dried and crushed berries as a seasoning for meat. Gather young twigs to make a tea.

**CAUTION:** Many plants may be called cedars but are not related to junipers and may be harmful. Always look for the berrylike structures, neddle leaves, and resinous, fragrant sap to be sure the plant you have is a juniper.

# LOTUS
## *NELUMBO SPECIES*

**Description:** There are two species of lotus: one has yellow flowers and the other pink flowers. The flowers are large and showy. The leaves, which may float on or rise above the surface of the water, often reach 1.5 meters in radius. The fruit has a distinctive flattened shape and contains up to 20 hard seeds.

**Habitat and Distribution:** The yellow-flowered lotus is native to North America. The pink-flowered species, which is widespread in the Orient, is planted in many other areas of the world. Lotuses are found in quiet fresh water.

**Edible Parts:** All parts of the plant are edible raw or cooked. The underwater parts contain large quantities of starch. Dig the fleshy portions from the mud and bake or boil them. Boil the young leaves and eat them as a vegetable. The seeds have a pleasant flavor and are nutritious. Eat them raw, or parch and grind them into flour.

## MALANGA
### *XANTHOSOMA CARACU*

**Description:** This plant has soft, arrow-shaped leaves, up to 60 centimeters long. The leaves have no aboveground stems.

**Habitat and Distribution:** This plant grows widely in the Caribbean region. Look for it in open, sunny fields.

**Edible Parts:** The tubers are rich in starch. Cook them before eating to detroy a poison contained in all parts of the plant.

## MANGO
### *MANGIFERA INDICA*

**Description:** This tree may reach 30 meters in height. It has alternate, simple, shiny, dark green leaves. Its flowers are small and inconspicuous. Its fruits have a large single seed. There are many cultivated varieties of mango. Some have red flesh, others yellow or orange, often with many fibers and a kerosene taste.

**Habitat and Distribution:** This tree grows in warm, moist regions. It is native to northern India, Burma, and western Malaysia. It is now grown throughout the tropics.

**Edible Parts:** The fruits are nutritious food source. The unripe fruit can be peeled and its flesh eaten by shredding it and eating it like a salad. The ripe fruit can be peeled and eaten raw. Roasted seed kernels are edible.

**CAUTION:** If you are sensitive to poison ivy, avoid eating mangoes, as they cause a severe reaction in sensitive individuals.

# MANIOC
### *MANIHOT UTILLISSIMA*

**Description:** Manioc is a perennial shrubby plant, 1 to 3 meters tall, with jointed stems and deep green, fingerlike leaves. It has large, fleshy rootstocks.

**Habitat and Distribution:** Manioc is widespread in all tropical climates, particularly in moist areas. Although cultivated extensively, it may be found in abandoned gardens and growing wild in many areas.

**Edible Parts:** The rootstocks are full of starch and high in food value. Two kinds of manioc are known: bitter and sweet. Both are edible. The bitter type contains poisonous hydrocyanic acid. To prepare manioc, first grind the fresh manioc root into a pulp, then cook it for at least 1 hour to remove the bitter poison from the roots. Then flatten the pulp into cakes and bake as bread. Manioc cakes or flour will keep almost indefinitely if protected against insects and dampness. Wrap them in banana leaves for protection.

**CAUTION:** For safety, always cook the roots of either type.

# MARSH MARIGOLD
### *CALTHA PALUSTRIS*

**Description:** This plant has rounded, dark green leaves arising from a short stem. It has bright yellow flowers.

**Habitat and Distribution:** This plant is found in bogs, lakes, and slow-moving streams. It is abundant in arctic and subarctic regions and in much of the eastern region of the northern United States.

**Edible Parts:** All parts are edible if boiled.

**CAUTION:** As with all water plants, do not eat this plant raw. Raw water plants may carry dangerous organisms that are removed only by cooking.

# MULBERRY

## *MORUS* SPECIES

**Description:** This tree has alternate, simple, often lobed leaves with rough surfaces. Its fruits are blue or black and many-seeded.

**Habitat and Distribution:** Mulberry trees are found in forests, along roadsides, and in abandoned fields in Temperate and Tropical Zones of North America, South America, Europe, Asia, and Africa.

**Edible Parts:** The fruit is edible raw or cooked. It can be dried for eating later.

**CAUTION:** When eaten in quantity, mulberry fruit acts as a laxative. Green, unripe fruit can be hallucinogenic and cause extreme nausea and cramps.

**Other Uses:** You can shred the inner bark of the tree and use it to make twine or cord.

# NETTLE

## *URTICA* **AND** *LAPORTEA* SPECIES

**Description:** These plants grow several feet high. They have small, inconspicuous flowers. Fine, hairlike bristles cover the stems, leafstalks, and undersides of leaves. The bristles cause a stinging sensation when they touch the skin.

**Habitat and Distribution:** Nettles prefer moist areas along streams or at the margins of forests. They are found throughout North America, Central America, the Caribbean, and northern Europe.

**Edible Parts:** Young shoots and leaves are edible. Boiling the plant for 10 to 15 minutes destroys the stinging element of the bristles. This plant is very nutritious.

**Other Uses:** Mature stems have a fibrous layer that can be divided into individual fibers and used to weave string or twine.

# NIPA PALM
## *NYPA FRUTICANS*

**Description:** This palm has a short, mainly underground trunk and very large, erect leaves up to 6 meters tall. The leaves are divided into leaflets. A flowering head forms on a short erect stern that rises among the palm leaves. The fruiting (seed) head is dark brown and may be 30 centimeters in diameter.

**Habitat and Distribution:** This palm is common on muddy shores in coastal regions throughout eastern Asia.

**Edible Parts:** The young flower stalk and the seeds provide a good source of water and food. Cut the flower stalk and collect the juice. The juice is rich in sugar. The seeds are hard but edible.

**Other Uses:** The leaves are excellent as thatch and coarse weaving material.

# OAK
## *QUERCUS* SPECIES

**Description:** Oak trees have alternate leaves and acorn fruits. There are two main groups of oaks: red and white. The red oak group has leaves with bristles and smooth bark in the upper part of the tree. Red oak acorns take 2 years to mature. The white oak group has leaves without bristles and a rough bark in the upper portion of the tree. White oak acorns mature in 1 year.

**Habitat and Distribution:** Oak trees are found in many habitats throughout North America, Central America, and parts of Europe and Asia.

**Edible Parts:** All parts are edible, but often contain large quantities of bitter substances. White oak acorns usually have a better flavor than red oak acorns. Gather and shell the acorns. Soak red oak acorns in water for 1 to 2 days to remove the bitter substance. You can speed up this process by putting wood ashes in the water in which you soak the acorns. Boil the acorns or grind them into flour and use the flour for baking. You can use acorns that you baked until very dark as a coffee substitute.

**CAUTION:** Tannic acid gives the acorns their bitter taste. Eating an excessive amount of acorns high in tannic acid can lead to kidney failure. Before eating acorns, leach out this chemical.

**Other Uses:** Oak wood is excellent for building or burning. Small oaks can be split and cut into long thin strips (3 to 6 millimeters thick and 1.2 centimeters wide) used to weave mats, baskets, or frameworks for packs, sleds, furniture, etc. Oak bark soaked in water produces a tanning solution used to preserve leather.

## ORACH
### *ATRIPLEX* SPECIES

**Description:** This plant is vinelike in growth and has arrowhead-shaped, alternate leaves up to 5 cenitmeters long. Young leaves may be silver-colored. Its flowers and fruits are small and inconspicuous.

**Habitat and Distribution:** Orach species are entirely restricted to salty soils. They are found along North America's coasts and on the shores of alkaline lakes inland. They are also found along seashores from the Mediterranean countries to inland areas in North Africa and eastward to Turkey and central Siberia.

**Edible Parts:** The entire plant is edible raw or boiled.

# PALMETTO PALM

*SABAL PALMETTO*

**Description:** The palmetto palm is a tall, unbranched tree with persistent leaf bases on most of the trunk. The leaves are large, simple, and palmately lobed. Its fruits are dark blue or black with a hard seed.

**Habitat and Distribution:** The palmetto palm is found throughout the coastal regions of the southeastern United States.

**Edible Parts:** The fruits are edible raw. The hard seeds may be ground into flour. The heart of the palm is a nutritious food source at any time. Cut off the top of the tree to obtain the palm heart.

# PAPAYA OR PAWPAW

*CARICA PAPAYA*

**Description:** The papaya is a small tree 1.8 to 6 meters tall, with a soft, hollow trunk. When cut, the entire plant exudes a milky juice. The trunk is rough and the leaves are crowded at the trunk's apex. The fruit grows directly from the trunk, among and below the leaves. The fruit is green before ripening. When ripe, it turns yellow or remains greenish with a squashlike appearance.

**Habitat and Distribution:** Papaya is found in rain forests and semievergreen seasonal forests in tropical regions and in some temperate regions as well. Look for it in moist areas near clearings and former habitations. It is also found in open, sunny places in uninhabited jungle areas.

**Edible Parts:** The ripe fruit is high in vitamin C. Eat it raw or cook it like squash. Place green fruit in the sun to make it ripen quickly. Cook the young papaya leaves, flowers, and stems carefully, changing the water as for taro.

**CAUTION:** Be careful not to get the milky sap from the unripe fruit into your eyes. It will cause intense pain and temporary—sometimes even permanent—blindness.

**Other Uses:** Use the milky juice of the unripe fruit to tenderize tough meat. Rub the juice on the meat.

# PERSIMMON

### *DIOSPYROS VIRGINIANA* **AND OTHER SPECIES**

**Description:** These trees have alternate, dark green, elliptic leaves with entire margins. The flowers are inconspicuous. The fruits are orange, have a sticky consistency, and have several seeds.

**Habitat and Distribution:** The persimmon is a common forest margin tree. It is widespread in Africa, eastern North America, and the Far East.

**Edible Parts:** The leaves are a good source of vitamin C. The fruits are edible raw or baked. To make tea, dry the leaves and soak them in hot water. You can eat the roasted seeds.

**CAUTION:** Some persons are unable to digest persimmon pulp. Unripe persimmons are highly astringent and inedible.

# PINCUSHION CACTUS

### *MAMMILARIA* **SPECIES**

**Description:** Members of this cactus group are round, short, barrel-shaped, and without leaves. Sharp spines cover the entire plant.

**Habitat and Distribution:** These cacti are found throughout much of the desert regions of the western United States and parts of Central America.

**Edible Parts:** They are a good source of water in the desert.

# PINE
## *PINUS* SPECIES

**Description:** Pine trees are easily recognized by their needlelike leaves grouped in bundles. Each bundle may contain 1 to 5 needles, the number varying among species. The tree's odor and sticky sap provide a simple way to distinguish pines from similar looking trees with needlelike leaves.

**Habitat and Distribution:** Pines prefer open, sunny areas. They are found throughout North America, Central America, much of the Caribbean region, North Africa, the Middle East, Europe, and some places in Asia.

**Edible Parts:** The seeds of all species are edible. You can collect the young male cones, which grow only in the spring, as a survival food. Boil or bake the young cones. The bark of young twigs is edible. Peel off the bark of thin twigs. You can chew the juicy inner bark; it is rich in sugar and vitamins. Eat the seeds raw or cooked. Green pine needle tea is high in vitamin C.

**Other Uses:** Use the resin to waterproof articles. Also use it as glue. Collect the resin from the tree. If there is not enough resin on the tree, cut a notch in the bark so more sap will seep out. Put the resin in a container and heat it. The hot resin is your glue. Use it as is or add a small amount of ash dust to strengthen it. Use it immediately. You can use hardened pine resin as an emergency dental fillling.

# PLANTAIN, BROAD AND NARROW LEAF
## *PLANTAGO* SPECIES

**Description:** The broad leaf plantain has leaves over 2.5 centimeters across that grow close to the ground. The flowers are on a spike that rises from the middle of the cluster of leaves. The narrow leaf plantain has leaves up to 12 centimeters long and 2.5 centimeters wide, covered with hairs. The leaves form a rosette. The flowers are small and inconspicuous.

**Habitat and Distribution:** Look for these plants in lawns and along roads in the North Temperate Zone. This plant is a common weed throughout much of the world.

235

**Edible Parts:** The young tender leaves are edible raw. Older leaves should be cooked. Seeds are edible raw or roasted.

**Other Uses:** To relieve pain from wounds and sores, wash and soak the entire plant for a short time and apply it to the injured area. To treat diarrhea, drink tea made from 28 grams (1 ounce) of the plant leaves boiled in 0.5 liter of water. The seeds and seed husks act as laxatives.

# POKEWEED

*PHYTOLACCA AMERICANA*

**Description:** This plant may grow as high as 3 meters. Its leaves are elliptic and up to 1 meter in length. It produces many large clusters of purple fruits in late spring.

**Habitat and Distribution:** Look for this plant in open, sunny areas in forest clearings, in fields, and along roadsides in eastern North America, Central America, and the Caribbean.

**Edible Parts:** The young leaves and stems are edible cooked. Boil them twice, discarding the water from the first boiling. The fruits are edible if cooked.

**CAUTION:** All parts of this plant are poisonous if eaten raw. Never eat the underground portions of the plant as these contain the highest concentrations of the poisons. Do not eat any plant over 25 centimeters tall or when red is showing in the plant.

**Other Uses:** Use the juice of fresh berries as a dye.

# PRICKLY PEAR CACTUS
### *OPUNTIA* SPECIES

**Description:** This cactus has flat, padlike stems that are green. Many round, furry dots that contain sharp-pointed hairs cover these stems.

**Habitat and Distribution:** This cactus is found in arid and semi-arid regions and in dry, sandy areas of wetter regions throughout most of the United States and Central and South America. Some species are planted in arid and semiarid regions of other parts of the world.

**Edible Parts:** All parts of the plant are edible. Peel the fruits and eat them fresh or crush them to prepare a refreshing drink. Avoid the tiny, pointed hairs. Roast the seeds and grind them to a flour.

**CAUTION:** Avoid any prickly pear cactus like plant with milky sap.

**Other Uses:** The pad is a good source of water. Peel it carefully to remove all sharp hairs before putting it in your mouth. You can also use the pads to promote healing. Split them and apply the pulp to wounds.

# PURSLANE
### *PORTULACA OLERACEA*

**Description:** This plant grows close to the ground. It is seldom more than a few centimeters tall. Its stems and leaves are fleshy and often tinged with red. It has paddleshaped leaves, 2.5 centimeter or less long, clustered at the tips of the stems. Its flowers are yellow or pink. Its seeds are tiny and black.

**Habitat and Distribution:** It grows in full sun in cultivated fields, field margins, and other weedy areas throughout the world.

**Edible Parts:** All parts are edible. Wash and boil the plants for a tasty vegetable or eat them raw. Use the seeds as a flour substitute or eat them raw.

## RATTAN PALM
### *CALAMUS* SPECIES

**Description:** The rattan palm is a stout, robust climber. It has hooks on the midrib of its leaves that it uses to remain attached to trees on which it grows. Sometimes, mature stems grow to 90 meters. It has alternate, compound leaves and a whitish flower.

**Habitat and Distribution:** The rattan palm is found from tropical Africa through Asia to the East Indies and Australia. It grows mainly in rain forests.

**Edible Parts:** Rattan palms hold a considerable amount of starch in their young stem tips. You can eat them roasted or raw. In other kinds, a gelatinous pulp, either sweet or sour, surrounds the seeds. You can suck out this pulp. The palm heart is also edible raw or cooked.

**Other Uses:** You can obtain large amounts of potable water by cutting the ends of the long stems (see Chapter 6). The stems can be used to make baskets and fish traps.

## REED
### *PHRAGMITES AUSTRALIS*

**Description:** This tall, coarse grass grows to 3.5 meters tall and has gray-green leaves about 4 centimeters wide. It has large masses of brown flower branches in early summer. These rarely produce grain and become fluffy, gray masses late in the season.

**Habitat and Distribution:** Look for reed in any open, wet area, especially one that has been disturbed through dredging. Reed is found throughout the temperate regions of both the Northern and Southern Hemispheres.

**Edible Parts:** All parts of the plant are edible raw or cooked in any season. Harvest the stems as they emerge from the soil and boil them. You can also harvest them just before they produce flowers, then dry and beat them into flour. You can also dig up and boil the underground stems, but they are often tough. Seeds are edible raw or boiled, but they are rarely found.

## REINDEER MOSS

### *CLADONIA RANGIFERINA*

**Description:** Reindeer moss is a low-growing plant only a few centimeters tall. It does not flower but does produce bright red reproductive structures.

**Habitat and Distribution:** Look for this lichen in open, dry areas. It is very common in much of North America.

**Edible Parts:** The entire plant is edible but has a crunchy, brittle texture. Soak the plant in water with some wood ashes to remove the bitterness, then dry, crush, and add it to milk or to other food.

## ROCK TRIPE

### *UMBILICARIA* SPECIES

**Description:** This plant forms large patches with curling edges. The top of the plant is usually black. The underside is lighter in color.

**Habitat and Distribution:** Look on rocks and boulders for this plant. It is common throughout North America.

**Edible Parts:** The entire plant is edible. Scrape it off the rock and wash it to remove grit. The plant may be dry and crunchy; soak it in water until it becomes soft. Rock tripes may contain large quantities of bitter substances; soaking or boiling them in several changes of water will remove the bitterness.

**CAUTION:** There are some reports of poisoning from rock tripe, so apply the Universal Edibility Test.

## ROSE APPLE

*EUGENIA JAMBOS*

**Description:** This tree grows 3 to 9 meters high. It has opposite, simple, dark green, shiny leaves. When fresh, it has fluffy, yellowish-green flowers and red to purple egg-shaped fruit.

**Habitat and Distribution:** This tree is widely planted in all of the tropics. It can also be found in a semiwild state in thickets, waste places, and secondary forests.

**Edible Parts:** The entire fruit is edible raw or cooked.

## SAGO PALM

*METROXYLON SAGU*

**Description:** These palms are low trees, rarely over 9 meters tall, with a stout, spiny trunk. The outer rind is about 5 centimeters thick and hard as bamboo. The rind encloses a spongy inner pith containing a high proportion of starch. It has typical palmlike leaves clustered at the tip.

**Habitat and Distribution:** Sago palm is found in tropical rain forests. It flourishes in damp lowlands in the Malay Peninsula, New Guinea, Indonesia, the Philippines, and adjacent islands. It is found mainly in swamps and along streams, lakes, and rivers.

**Edible Parts:** These palms, when available, are of great use to the survivor. One trunk, cut just before it flowers, will yield enough sago to feed a person for 1 year. Obtain sago starch from nonflowering palms. To extract the edible sage, cut away the bark lengthwise from one half of the trunk, and pound the soft, whitish inner part (pith) as fine as possible. Knead the pith in water and strain it through a coarse cloth into a container. The fine, white sago will settle in the container. Once the sago settles, it is ready for use. Squeeze off the excess water and let it dry. Cook it as pancakes or oatmeal. Two kilograms of sago is the nutritional equivalent of 1.5 kilograms of rice. The upper part of the trunk's core does not yield sage, but you can roast it in lumps over a fire. You can also eat the young sago nuts and the growing shoots or palm cabbage.

**Other Uses:** Use the stems of tall sorghums as thatching materials.

# SASSAFRAS

*SASSAFRAS ALBIDUM*

**Description:** This shrub or small tree bears different leaves on the same plant. Some leaves will have one lobe, some two lobes, and some no lobes. The flowers, which appear in early spring, are small and yellow. The fruits are dark blue. The plant parts have a characteristics root beer smell.

**Habitat and Distribution:** Sassafras grows at the margins of roads and forests, usually in open, sunny areas. It is a common tree throughout eastern North America.

**Edible Parts:** The young twigs and leaves are edible fresh or dried. You can add dried young twigs and leaves to soups. Dig the underground portion, peel off the bark, and let it dry. Then boil it in water to prepare sassafras tea.

**Other Uses:** Shred the tender twigs for use as a toothbrush.

# SAXAUL

*HALOXYLON AMMONDENDRON*

**Description:** The saxaul is found either as a small tree or as a large shrub with heavy, coarse wood and spongy, water-soaked bark. The branches of the young trees are vivid green and pendulous. The flowers are small and yellow.

**Habitat and Distribution:** The saxaul is found in desert and arid areas. It is found on the arid salt deserts of Central Asia, particularly in the Turkestan region and east of the Caspian Sea.

**Edible Parts:** The thick bark acts as a water storage organ. You can get drinking water by pressing quantities of the bark. This plant is an important source of water in the arid regions in which it grows.

## SCREW PINE

### *PANDANUS SPECIES*

**Description:** The screw pine is a strange plant on stilts, or prop roots, that support the plant above-ground so that it appears more or less suspended in midair. These plants are either shrubby or treelike, 3 to 9 meters tall, with stiff leaves having sawlike edges. The fruits are large, roughened balls resembling pineapples, but without the tuft of leaves at the end.

**Habitat and Distribution:** The screw pine is a tropical plant that grows in rain forests and semievergreen seasonal forests. It is found mainly along seashores, although certain kinds occur inland for some distance, from Madagascar to southern Asia and the islands of the southwestern Pacific. There are about 180 types.

**Edible Parts:** Knock the ripe fruit to the ground to separate the fruit segments from the hard outer covering. Chew the inner fleshy part. Cook fruit that is not fully ripe in an earth oven. Before cooking, wrap the whole fruit in banana leaves, breadfruit leaves, or any other suitable thick, leathery leaves. After cooking for about 2 hours, you can chew fruit segments like ripe fruit. Green fruit is inedible.

## SEA ORACH

### *ATRIPLEX HALIMUS*

**Description:** The sea orach is a sparingly branched herbaceous plant with small, gray-colored leaves up to 2.5 centimeters long. Sea orach resembles lamb's quarter, a common weed in most gardens in the United States. It produces its flowers in narrow, densely compacted spikes at the tips of its branches.

**Habitat and Distribution:** The sea orach is found in highly alkaline and salty areas along seashores from the Mediterranean countries to inland areas in North Africa and eastward to Turkey and central Siberia. Generally, it can be found in tropical scrub and thorn forests, steppes in temperate regions, and most desert scrub and waste areas.

**Edible Parts:** Its leaves are edible. In the areas where it grows, it has the healthy reputation of being one of the few native plants that can sustain man in times of want.

# SHEEP SORREL
## *RUMEX ACETOSELLA*

**Description:** These plants are seldom more than 30 centimeters tall. They have alternate leaves, often with arrowlike bases, very small flowers, and frequently reddish stems.

**Habitat and Distribution:** Look for these plants in old fields and other disturbed areas in North America and Europe.

**Edible Parts:** The plants are edible raw or cooked.

**CAUTION:** These plants contain oxalic acid that can be damaging if too many plants are eaten raw. Cooking seems to destroy the chemical.

# SORGHUM
## *SORGHUM* SPECIES

**Description:** There are many different kinds of sorghum, all of which bear grains in heads at the top of the plants. The grains are brown, white, red, or black. Sorghum is the main food crop in many parts of the world.

**Habitat and Distribution:** Sorghum is found worldwide, usually in warmer climates. All species are found in open, sunny areas.

**Edible Parts:** The grains are edible at any stage of development. When young, the grains are milky and edible raw. Boil the older grains. Sorghum is a nutritious food.

**Other Uses:** Use the stems of tall sorghum as building materials.

# SPATTERDOCK OR YELLOW WATER LILY
## *NUPHAR* SPECIES

**Description:** This plant has leaves up to 60 centimeters long with a triangular notch at the base. The shape of the leaves is somewhat variable. The plant's yellow flowers are 2.5 centimeter across and develop into bottle-shaped fruits. The fruits are green when ripe.

**Habitat and Distribution:** These plants grow throughout most of North America. They are found in quiet, fresh, shallow water (never deeper than 1.8 meters).

**Edible Parts:** All parts of the plant are edible. The fruits contain several dark brown seeds you can parch or roast and then grind into flour. The large rootstock contains starch. Dig it out of the mud, peel off the outside, and boil the flesh. Sometimes the rootstock contains large quantities of a very bitter compound. Boiling in several changes of water may remove the bitterness.

# STERCULIA
## *STERCULIA FOETIDA*

**Description:** Sterculias are tall trees, rising in some instances to 30 meters. Their leaves are either undivided or palmately lobed. Their flowers are red or purple. The fruit of all sterculias is similar in aspect, with a red, segmented seedpod containing many edible black seeds.

**Habitat and Distribution:** There are over 100 species of sterculias distributed through all warm or tropical climates. They are mainly forest trees.

**Edible Parts:** The large, red pods produce a number of edible seeds. The seeds of all sterculias are edible and have a pleasant taste similar to cocoa. You can eat them like nuts, either raw or roasted.

**CAUTION:** Avoid eating large quantities. The seeds may have a laxative effect.

## STRAWBERRY
### *FRAGARIA* SPECIES

**Description:** Strawberry is a small plant with a three-leaved growth pattern. It has small, white flowers usually produced during the spring. Its fruit is red and fleshy.

**Habitat and Distribution:** Strawberries are found in the North Temperate Zone and also in the high mountains of the southern Western Hemisphere. Strawberries prefer open, sunny areas. They are commonly planted.

**Edible Parts:** The fruit is edible fresh, cooked, or dried. Strawberries are a good source of vitamin C. You can also eat the plant's leaves or dry them and make a tea with them.

## SUGARCANE
### *SACCHARUM OFFICINARUM*

**Description:** This plant grows up to 4.5 meters tall. It is a grass and has grasslike leaves. Its green or reddish stems are swollen where the leaves grow. Cultivated sugarcane seldom flowers.

**Habitat and Distribution:** Look for sugarcane in fields. It grows only in the tropics (throughout the world). Because it is a crop, it is often found in large numbers.

**Edible Parts:** The stem is an excellent source of sugar and is very nutritious. Peel the outer portion off with your teeth and eat the sugarcane raw. You can also squeeze juice out of the sugarcane.

## SUGAR PALM
### *ARENGA PINNATA*

**Description:** This tree grows about 15 meters high and has huge leaves up to 6 meters long. Needlelike structures stick out of the bases of the leaves. Flowers grow below the leaves and form large conspicuous dusters from which the fruits grow.

**Habitat and Distribution:** This palm is native to the East Indies but has been planted in many parts of the tropics. It can be found at the margins of forests.

**Edible Parts:** The chief use of this palm is for sugar. However, its seeds and the tip of its stems are a survival food. Bruise a young flower stalk with a stone or similar object and collect the juice as it comes out. It is an excellent source of sugar. Boil the seeds. Use the tip of the stems as a vegetable.

**CAUTION:** The flesh covering the seeds may cause dermatitis.

**Other Uses:** The shaggy material at the base of the leaves makes an excellent rope as it is strong and resists decay.

## SWEETSOP
### *ANNONA SQUAMOSA*

**Description:** This tree is small, seldom more than 6 meters tall, and multi-branched. It has alternate, simple, elongate, dark green leaves. Its fruit is green when ripe, round in shape, and covered with protruding bumps on its surface. The fruit's flesh is white and creamy.

**Habitat and Distribution:** Look for sweetsop at margins of fields, near villages, and around homesites in tropical regions.

**Edible Parts:** The fruit flesh is edible raw.

**Other Uses:** You can use the finely ground seeds as an insecticide.

**CAUTION:** The ground seeds are extremely dangerous to the eyes.

# TAMARIND

*TAMARINDUS INDICA*

**Description:** The tamarind is a large, densely branched tree, up to 25 meters tall. Its has pinnate leaves (divided like a feather) with 10 to 15 pairs of leaflets.

**Habitat and Distribution:** The tamarind grows in the drier parts of Africa, Asia, and the Philippines. Although it is thought to be a native of Africa, it has been cultivated in India for so long that it looks like a native tree. It is also found in the American tropics, the West Indies, Central America, and tropical South America.

**Edible Parts:** The pulp surrounding the seeds is rich in vitamin C and is an important survival food. You can make a pleasantly acid drink by mixing the pulp with water and sugar or honey and letting the mixture mature for several days. Suck the pulp to relieve thirst. Cook the young, unripe fruits or seedpods with meat. Use the young leaves in soup. You must cook the seeds. Roast them above a fire or in ashes. Another way is to remove the seed coat and soak the seeds in salted water and grated coconut for 24 hours, then cook them. You can peel the tamarind bark and chew it.

# TARO, COCOYAM, ELEPHANT EARS, EDDO, DASHEEN

*COLOCASIA* **AND** *ALOCASIA* **SPECIES**

**Description:** All plants in these groups have large leaves, sometimes up to 1.8 meters tall, that grow from a very short stem. The rootstock is thick and fleshy and filled with starch.

**Habitat and Distribution:** These plants grow in the humid tropics. Look for them in fields and near homesites and villages.

**Edible Parts:** All parts of the plant are edible when boiled or roasted. When boiling, change the water once to get rid of any poison.

**CAUTION:** If eaten raw, these plants will cause a serious inflammation of the mouth and throat.

# THISTLE
### *CIRSIUM* SPECIES

**Description:** This plant may grow as high as 1.5 meters. Its leaves are long-pointed, deeply lobed, and prickly.

**Habitat and Distribution:** Thistles grow worldwide in dry woods and fields.

**Edible Parts:** Peel the stalks, cut them into short sections, and boil them before eating. The roots are edible raw or cooked.

**CAUTION:** Some thistle species are poisonous.

**Other Uses:** Twist the tough fibers of the stems to make a strong twine.

# TI
### *CORDYLINE TERMINALIS*

**Description:** The ti has unbranched stems with straplike leaves often clustered at the tip of the stem. The leaves vary in color and may be green or reddish. The flowers grow at the plant's top in large, plumelike clusters. The ti may grow up to 4.5 meters tall.

**Habitat and Distribution:** Look for this plant at the margins of forests or near homesites in tropical areas. It is native to the Far East but is now widely planted in tropical areas worldwide.

**Edible Parts:** The roots and very tender young leaves are good survival food. Boil or bake the short, stout roots found at the base of the plant. They are a valuable source of starch. Boil the very young leaves to eat. You can use the leaves to wrap other food to cook over coals or to steam.

**Other Uses:** Use the leaves to cover shelters or to make a rain cloak. Cut the leaves into liners for shoes; this works especially well if you have a blister. Fashion temporary sandals from the ti leaves. The terminal leaf, if not completely unfurled, can be used as a sterile bandage. Cut the leaves into strips, then braid the strips into rope.

# TREE FERN
*VARIOUS GENERA*

**Description:** Tree ferns are tall trees with long, slender trunks that often have a very rough, barklike covering. Large, lacy leaves uncoil from the top of the trunk.

**Habitat and Distribution:** Tree ferns are found in wet, tropical forests.

**Edible Parts:** The young leaves and the soft inner portion of the trunk are edible. Boil the young leaves and eat as greens. Eat the inner portion of the trunk raw or bake it.

# TROPICAL ALMOND
*TERMINALIA CATAPPA*

**Description:** This tree grows up to 9 meters tall. Its leaves are evergreen, leathery, 45 centimeters long, 15 centimeters wide, and very shiny. It has small, yellowish-green flowers. Its fruit is flat, 10 centimeters long, and not quite as wide. The fruit is green when ripe.

**Habitat and Distribution:** This tree is usually found growing near the ocean. It is a common and often abundant tree in the Caribbean and Central and South America. It is also found in the tropical rain forests of southeastern Asia, northern Australia, and Polynesia.

**Edible Parts:** The seed is a good source of food. Remove the fleshy, green covering and eat the seed raw or cooked.

# WALNUT

### *JUGLANS* SPECIES

**Description:** Walnuts grow on very large trees, often reaching 18 meters tall. The divided leaves characterize all walnut spades. The walnut itself has a thick outer husk that must be removed to reach the hard inner shell of the nut.

**Habitat and Distribution:** The English walnut, in the wild state, is found from southeastern Europe across Asia to China and is abundant in the Himalayas. Several other species of walnut are found in China and Japan. The black walnut is common in the eastern United States.

**Edible Parts:** The nut kernel ripens in the autumn. You get the walnut meat by cracking the shell. Walnut meats are highly nutritious because of their protein and oil content.

**Other Uses:** You can boil walnuts and use the juice as an antifungal agent. The husks of "green" walnuts produce a dark brown dye for clothing or camouflage. Crush the husks of "green" black walnuts and sprinkle them into sluggish water or ponds for use as fish poison.

# WATER CHESTNUT

### *TRAPA NATANS*

**Description:** The water chestnut is an aquatic plant that roots in the mud and has finely divided leaves that grow underwater. Its floating leaves are much larger and coarsely toothed. The fruits, borne underwater, have four sharp spines on them.

**Habitat and Distribution:** The water chestnut is a freshwater plant only. It is a native of Asia but has spread to many parts of the world in both temperate and tropical areas.

**Edible Parts:** The fruits are edible raw and cooked. The seeds are also a source of food.

# WATER LETTUCE

### *CERATOPTERIS* SPECIES

**Description:** The leaves of water lettuce are much like lettuce and are very tender and succulent. One of the easiest ways of distinguishing water lettuce is by the little plantlets that grow from the margins of the leaves. These little plantlets grow in the shape of a rosette. Water lettuce plants often cover large areas in the regions where they are found.

**Habitat and Distribution:** Found in the tropics throughout the Old World in both Africa and Asia. Another kind is found in the New World tropics from Florida to South America. Water lettuce grows only in very wet places and often as a floating water plant. Look for water lettuce in still lakes, ponds, and the backwaters of rivers.

**Edible Parts:** Eat the fresh leaves like lettuce. Be careful not to dip the leaves in the contaminated water in which they are growing. Eat only the leaves that are well out of the water.

**CAUTION:** This plant has carcinogenic properties and should only be used as a last resort.

# WATER LILY

### *NYMPHAEA ODORATA*

**Description:** These plants have large, triangular leaves that float on the water's surface, large, fragrant flowers that are usually white, or red, and thick, fleshy rhizomes that grow in the mud.

**Habitat and Distribution:** Water lilies are found throughout much of the temperate and subtropical regions.

**Edible Parts:** The flowers, seeds, and rhizomes are edible raw or cooked. To prepare rhizomes for eating, peel off the corky rind. Eat raw, or slice thinly, allow to dry, and then grind into flour. Dry, parch, and grind the seeds into flour.

**Other Uses:** Use the liquid resulting from boiling the thickened root in water as a medicine for diarrhea and as a gargle for sore throats.

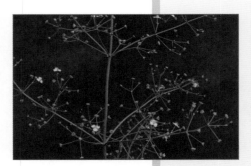

## WATER PLANTAIN
### *ALISMA PLANTAGO-AQUATICA*

**Description:** This plant has small, white flowers and heart-shaped leaves with pointed tips. The leaves are clustered at the base of the plant.

**Habitat and Distribution:** Look for this plant in fresh water and in wet, full sun areas in temperate and tropical zones.

**Edible Parts:** The rootstocks are a good source of starch. Boil or soak them in water to remove the bitter taste.

**CAUTION:** To avoid parasites, always cook aquatic plants.

## WILD CAPER
### *CAPPARIS APHYLLA*

**Description:** This is a thorny shrub that loses its leaves during the dry season. Its stems are gray-green and its flowers pink.

**Habitat and Distribution:** These shrubs form large stands in scrub and thorn forests and in desert scrub and waste. They are common throughout North Africa and the Middle East.

**Edible Parts:** The fruit and the buds of young shoots are edible raw.

# WILD CRAB APPLE OR WILD APPLE
## *MALUS SPECIES*

**Description:** Most wild apples look enough like domestic apples that the survivor can easily recognize them. Wild apple varieties are much smaller than cultivated kinds; the largest kinds usually do not exceed 5 to 7.5 centimeters in diameter, and most often less. They have small, alternate, simple leaves and often have thorns. Their flowers are white or pink and their fruits reddish or yellowish.

**Habitat and Distribution:** They are found in the savanna regions of the tropics. In temperate areas, wild apple varieties are found mainly in forested areas. Most frequently, they are found on the edge of woods or in fields. They are found throughout the Northern Hemisphere.

**Edible Parts:** Prepare wild apples for eating in the same manner as cultivated kinds. Eat them fresh, when ripe, or cooked. Should you need to store food, cut the apples into thin slices and dry them. They are a good source of vitamins.

**CAUTION:** Apple seeds contain cyanide compounds. Do not eat them.

# WILD DESERT GOURD OR COLOCYNTH
## *CITRULLUS COLOCYNTHIS*

**Description:** The wild desert gourd, a member of the watermelon family, produces a 2.4- to 3-meter-long ground-trailing vine. The perfectly round gourds are as large as an orange. They are yellow when ripe.

**Habitat and Distribution:** This creeping plant can be found in any climatic zone, generally in desert scrub and waste areas. It grows abundantly in the Sahara, in many Arab countries, on the southeastern coast of India, and on some of the islands of the Aegean Sea. The wild desert gourd will grow in the hottest localities.

**Edible Parts:** The seeds inside the ripe gourd are edible after they are completely separated from the very bitter pulp. Roast or boil the seeds—their kernels are rich in oil. The flowers are edible. The succulent stem tips can be chewed to obtain water.

## WILD DOCK AND WILD SORREL

*RUMEX CRISPUS* **AND** *RUMEX ACETOSELLA*

**Description:** Wild dock is a stout plant with most of its leaves at the base of its stem that is commonly 15 to 30 centimeters long. The plants usually develop from a strong, fleshy, carrotlike taproot. Its flowers are usually very small, growing in green to purplish plumelike clusters. Wild sorrel is similar to the wild dock but smaller. Many of the basal leaves are arrow-shaped but smaller than those of the dock and contain a sour juice.

**Habitat and Distribution:** These plants can be found in almost all climatic zones of the world, in areas of high as well as low rainfall. Many kinds are found as weeds in fields, along roadsides, and in waste places.

**Edible Parts:** Because of the tender nature of the foliage, the sorrel and the dock are useful plants, especially in desert areas. You can eat their succulent leaves fresh or slightly cooked. To take away the strong taste, change the water once or twice during cooking. This latter tip is a useful hint in preparing many kinds of wild greens.

## WILD FIG

*FICUS* **SPECIES**

**Description:** These trees have alternate, simple leaves with entire margins. Often, the leaves are dark green and shiny. All figs have a milky, sticky juice. The fruits vary in size depending on the species, but are usually yellow-brown when ripe.

**Habitat and Distribution:** Figs are plants of the tropics and semi-tropics. They grow in several different habitats, including dense forests, margins of forests, and around human settlements.

**Edible Parts:** The fruits are edible raw or cooked. Some figs have little flavor.

## WILD GOURD OR LUFFA SPONGE
### *LUFFA CYLINDRICA*

**Description:** The luffs sponge is widely distributed and fairly typical of a wild squash. There are several dozen kinds of wild squashes in tropical regions. Like most squashes, the luffa is a vine with leaves 7.5 to 20 centimeters across having 3 lobes. Some squashes have leaves twice this size. Luffs fruits are oblong or cylindrical, smooth, and many-seeded. Luffs flowers are bright yellow. The luffa fruit, when mature, is brown and resembles the cucumber.

**Habitat and Distribution:** A member of the squash family, which also includes the watermelon, cantaloupe, and cucumber, the luffa sponge is widely cultivated throughout the Tropical Zone. It may be found in a semiwild state in old clearings and abandoned gardens in rain forests and semievergreen seasonal forests.

**Edible Parts:** You can boil the young green (half-ripe) fruit and eat them as a vegetable. Adding coconut milk will improve the flavor. After ripening, the luffa sponge develops an inedible spongelike texture in the interior of the fruit. You can also eat the tender shoots, flowers, and young leaves after cooking them. Roast the mature seeds a little and eat them like peanuts.

## WILD GRAPE VINE
### *VITIS* SPECIES

**Description:** The wild grape vine climbs with the aid of tendrils. Most grape vines produce deeply lobed leaves similar to the cultivated grape. Wild grapes grow in pyramidal, hanging bunches and are black-blue to amber, or white when ripe.

**Habitat and Distribution:** Wild grapes are distributed worldwide. Some kinds are found in deserts, others in temperate forests, and others in tropical areas. Wild grapes are commonly found throughout the eastern United States as well as in the southwestern desert areas. Most kinds are rampant climbers over other vegetation. The best place to look for wild grapes is

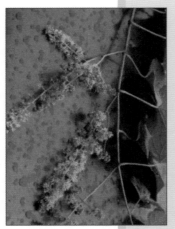

on the edges of forested areas. Wild grapes are also found in Mexico. In the Old World, wild grapes are found from the Mediterranean region eastward through Asia, the East Indies, and to Australia. Africa also has several kinds of wild grapes.

**Edible Parts:** The ripe grape is the portion eaten. Grapes are rich in natural sugars and, for this reason, are much sought after as a source of energy-giving wild food. None are poisonous.

**Other Uses:** You can obtain water from severed grape vine stems. Cut off the vine at the bottom and place the cut end in a container. Make a slant-wise cut into the vine about 1.8 meters upon the hanging part. This cut will allow water to flow from the bottom end. As water diminishes in volume, make additional cuts further down the vine.

**CAUTION:** To avoid poisoning, do not eat grapelike fruits with only a *single* seed (moonseed).

# WILD ONION AND GARLIC
### *ALLIUM* SPECIES

**Description:** *Allium cernuum* is an example of the many species of wild onions and garlics, all easily recognized by their distinctive odor.

**Habitat and Distribution:** Wild onions and garlics are found in open, sunny areas throughout the temperate regions. Cultivated varieties are found anywhere in the world.

**Edible Parts:** The bulbs and young leaves are edible raw or cooked. Use in soup or to flavor meat.

**CAUTION:** There are several plants with onionlike bulbs that are extremely poisonous. Be certain that the plant you are using is a true onion or garlic. Do not eat bulbs with no onion smell.

## WILD PISTACHIO

### *PISTACIA* SPECIES

**Description:** Some kinds of pistachio trees are evergreen, while others lose their leaves during the dry season. The leaves alternate on the stem and have either three large leaves or a number of leaflets. The fruits or nuts are usually hard and dry at maturity.

**Habitat and Distribution:** About seven kinds of wild pistachio nuts are found in desert, or semidesert areas surrounding the Mediterranean Sea to Turkey and Afghanistan. It is generally found in evergreen scrub forests or scrub and thorn forests.

**Edible Parts:** You can eat the oil nut kernels after parching them over coals.

## WILD RICE

### *ZIZANIA AQUATICA*

**Description:** Wild rice is a tall grass that averages 1 to 1.5 meters in height, but may reach 4.5 meters. Its grain grows in very loose heads at the top of the plant and is dark brown or blackish when ripe.

**Habitat and Distribution:** Wild rice grows only in very wet areas in tropical and temperate regions.

**Edible Parts:** During the spring and summer, the central portion of the lower sterns and root shoots are edible. Remove the tough covering before eating. During the late summer and fall, collect the straw-covered husks. Dry and parch the husks, break them, and remove the rice. Boil or roast the rice and then beat it into flour.

## WILD ROSE
### *ROSA* SPECIES

**Description:** This shrub grows 60 centimeters to 2.5 meters high. It has alternate leaves and sharp prickles. Its flowers may be red, pink, or yellow. Its fruit, called rose hip, stays on the shrub year-round.

**Habitat and Distribution:** Look for wild roses in dry fields and open woods throughout the Northern Hemisphere.

**Edible Parts:** The flowers and buds are edible raw or boiled. In an emergency, you can peel and eat the young shoots. You can boil fresh, young leaves in water to make a tea. After the flower petals fall, eat the rose hips; the pulp is highly nutritious and an excellent source of vitamin C. Crush or grind dried rose hips to make flour.

**CAUTION:** Eat only the outer portion of the fruit as the seeds of some species are quite prickly and can cause internal distress.

## WOOD SORREL
### *OXALIS* SPECIES

**Description:** Wood sorrel resembles shamrock or four-leaf clover, with a bell-shaped pink, yellow, or white flower.

**Habitat and Distribution:** Wood sorrel is found in Temperate Zones worldwide, in lawns, open areas, and sunny woods.

**Edible Parts:** Cook the entire plant.

**CAUTION:** Eat only small amounts of this plant as it contains a fairly high concentration of oxalic acid that can be harmful.

# YAM

### *DIOSCOREA* SPECIES

**Description:** These plants are vines that creep along the ground. They have alternate, heart- or arrow-shaped leaves. Their rootstock may be very large and weigh many kilograms.

**Habitat and Distribution:** True yams are restricted to tropical regions where they are an important food crop. Look for yams in fields, clearings, and abandoned gardens. They are found in rain forests, semievergreen seasonal forests, and scrub and thorn forests in the tropics. In warm temperate areas, they are found in seasonal hardwood or mixed hardwood-coniferous forests, as well as some mountainous areas.

**Edible Parts:** Boil the rootstock and eat it as a vegetable.

# YAM BEAN

### *PACHYRHIZUS EROSUS*

**Description:** The yam bean is a climbing plant of the bean family, with alternate, threeparted leaves and a turniplike root. The bluish or purplish flowers are pealike in shape. The plants are often so rampant that they cover the vegetation upon which they are growing.

**Habitat and Distribution:** The yam bean is native to the American tropics, but it was carried by man years ago to Asia and the Pacific islands. Now it is commonly cultivated in these places, and is also found growing wild in forested areas. This plant grows in wet areas of tropical regions.

**Edible Parts:** The tubers are about the size of a turnip and they are crisp, sweet, and juicy and have a nutty flavor. They are nourishing and at the same time quench the thirst. Eat them raw or boiled. To make flour, slice the raw tubers, let them dry in the sun, and grind into a flour that is high in starch and may be used to thicken soup.

259

# Poisonous Plants

*Plants basically poison on contact, through ingestion, or by absorption or inhalation. They cause painful skin irritations upon contact, they cause internal poisoning when eaten, and they poison through skin absorption or inhalation in respiratory system. Many edible plants have deadly relatives and look-alikes. Preparation for military missions includes learning to identify those harmful plants in the target area. Positive identification of edible plants will eliminate the danger of accidental poisoning. There is no room for experimentation where plants are concerned, especially in unfamiliar territory.*

# CASTOR BEAN, CASTOR-OIL PLANT, PALMA CHRISTI

## *RICINUS COMMUNIS*

**Spurge** *(Euphorbiaceae)* **Family**

**Description:** The castor bean is a semiwoody plant with large, alternate, starlike leaves that grows as a tree in tropical regions and as an annual in temperate regions. Its flowers are very small and inconspicuous. Its fruits grow in clusters at the tops of the plants.

**CAUTION:** All parts of the plant are very poisonous to eat. The seeds are large and may be mistaken for a beanlike food.

**Habitat and Distribution:** This plant is found in all tropical regions and has been introduced to temperate regions.

# CHINABERRY

## *MELIA AZEDARACH*

**Mahogany** *(Meliaceae)* **Family**

**Description:** This tree has a spreading crown and grows up to 14 meters tall. It has alternate, compound leaves with toothed leaflets. Its flowers are light purple with a dark center and grow in ball-like masses. It has marble-sized fruits that are light orange when first formed but turn lighter as they become older.

**CAUTION:** All parts of the tree should be considered dangerous if eaten. Its leaves are a natural insecticide and will repel insects from stored fruits and grains. Take care not to eat leaves mixed with the stored food.

**Habitat and Distribution:** Chinaberry is native to the Himalayas and eastern Asia but is now planted as an ornamental tree throughout the tropical and subtropical regions. It has been introduced to the southern United States and has escaped to thickets, old fields, and disturbed areas.

## COWHAGE, COWAGE, COWITCH
### *MUCUNA PRURITUM*

**Leguminosae** *(Fabaceae)* **Family**

**Description:** A vinelike plant that has oval leaflets in groups of three and hairy spikes with dull purplish flowers. The seeds are brown, hairy pods.

**CAUTION:** Contact with the pods and flowers causes irritation and blindness if in the eyes.

## DEATH CAMAS, DEATH LILY
### *ZIGADENUS* SPECIES

**Lily** *(Liliaceae)* **Family**

**Description:** This plant arises from a bulb and may be mistaken for an onionlike plant. Its leaves are grasslike. Its flowers are six-parted and the petals have a green, heart-shaped structure on them. The flowers grow on showy stalks above the leaves.

**CAUTION:** All parts of this plant are very poisonous. Death camas does not have the onion smell.

**Habitat and Distribution:** Death camas is found in wet, open, sunny habitats, although some species favor dry, rocky slopes. They are common in parts of the western United States. Some species are found in the eastern United States and in parts of the North American western subarctic and eastern Siberia.

# LANTANA

*LANTANA CAMARA*

**Vervain** *(Verbenaceae)* **Family**

**Description:** Lantana is a shrublike plant that may grow up to 45 centimeters high. It has opposite, round leaves and flowers borne in flat-topped clusters. The flower color (which varies in different areas) maybe white, yellow, orange, pink, or red. It has a dark blue or black berrylike fruit. A distinctive feature of all parts of this plant is its strong scent.

**CAUTION:** All parts of this plant are poisonous if eaten and can be fatal. This plant causes dermatitis in some individuals.

**Habitat and Distribution:** Lantana is grown as an omamental in tropical and temperate areas and has escaped cultivation as a weed along roads and old fields.

# MANCHINEEL

*HIPPOMANE MANCINELLA*

**Spurge** *(Euphorbiaceae)* **Family**

**Description:** Manchineel is a tree reaching up to 15 meters high with alternate, shiny green leaves and spikes of small greenish flowers. Its fruits are green or greenish-yellow when ripe.

**CAUTION:** This tree is extremly toxic. It causes severe dermatitis in most individuals after only .5 hour. Even water dripping from the leaves may cause dermatitis. The smoke from burning it irritates the eyes. No part of this plant should be considered a food.

**Habitat and Distribution:** The tree prefers coastal regions. Found in south Florida, the Caribbean, Central America, and northern South America.

# OLEANDER
## *NERIUM OLEANDER*

**Dogbane** *(Apocynaceae)* **Family**

**Description:** This shrub or small tree grows to about 9 meters, with alternate, very straight, dark green leaves. Its flowers may be white, yellow, red, pink, or intermediate colors. Its fruit is a brown, podlike structure with many small seeds.

**CAUTION:** All parts of the plant are very poisonous. Do not use the wood for cooking; it gives off poisonous fumes that can poison food.

**Habitat and Distribution:** This native of the Mediterranean area is now grown as an ornamental in tropical and temperate regions.

# PANGI
## *PANGIUM EDULE*

**Pangi Family**

**Description:** This tree, with heart-shaped leaves in spirals, reaches a height of 18 meters. Its flowers grow in spikes and are green in color. Its large, brownish, pear-shaped fruits grow in clusters.

**CAUTION:** All parts are poisonous, especially the fruit.

**Habitat and Distribution:** Pangi trees grow in southeast Asia

## PHYSIC NUT
### *JATROPHA CURCAS*

**Spurge** *(Euphoriaceae)* **Family**

**Description:** This shrub or small tree has large, 3- to 5-parted alternate leaves. It has small, greenish-yelllow flowers and its yellow, apple-sized fruits contain three large seeds.

**CAUTION:** The seeds taste sweet but their oil is violently purgative. All parts of the physic nut are poisonous.

**Habitat and Distribution:** Throughout the tropics and southern United States.

## POISON HEMLOCK, FOOL'S PARSLEY
### *CONIUM MACULATUM*

**Parsley** *(Apiaceae)* **Family**

**Description:** This biennial herb may grow to 2.5 meters high. The smooth, hollow stem may or may not be purple or red striped or mottled. Its white flowers are small and grow in small groups that tend to form flat umbels. Its long, turniplike taproot is solid.

**CAUTION:** This plant is very poisonous and even a very small amount may cause death. This plant is easy to confuse with wild carrot or Queen Anne's lace, especially in its first stage of growth. Wild carrot or Queen Anne's lace has hairy leaves and stems and smells like carrot. Poison hemlook does not.

**Habitat and Distribution:** Poison hemlock grows in wet or moist ground like swamps, wet meadows, stream banks, and ditches. Native to Eurasia, it has been introduced to the United States and Canada.

266

## POISON IVY AND POISON OAK

*TOXICODENDRON RADICANS AND TOXICODENDRON DIVERSIBBA*

**Cashew** *(Anacardiacese)* **Family**

**Description:** These two plants are quite similar in appearance and will often crossbreed to make a hybrid. Both have alternate, compound leaves with three leaflets. The leaves of poison ivy are smooth or serrated. Poison oak's leaves are lobed and resemble oak leaves. Poison ivy grows as a vine along the ground or climbs by red feeder roots (see page 260 for photograph). Poison oak grows like a bush. The greenish-white flowers are small and inconspicuous and are followed by waxy green berries that turn waxy white or yellow, then gray.

**CAUTION:** All parts, at all times of the year, can cause serious contact dermatitis.

**Habitat and Distribution:** Poison ivy and oak can be found in almost any habitat in North America.

## POISON SUMAC

*TOXICODENDRON VERNIX*

**Cashew** *(Anacardiacese)* **Family**

**Description:** Poison sumac is a shrub that grows to 8.5 meters tall. It has alternate, pinnately compound leafstalks with 7 to 13 leaflets. Flowers are greenish-yellow and inconspicuous and are followed by white or pale yellow berries.

**CAUTION:** All parts can cause serious contact dermatitis at all times of the year.

**Habitat and Distribution:** Poison sumac grows only in wet, acid swamps in North America.

## RENGHAS TREE, RENGAS TREE, MARKING NUT, BLACK-VARNISH TREE

*GLUTA*

**Cashew** *(Anacardiacese)* **Family**

**Description:** This family comprises about 48 species of trees or shrubs with alternating leaves in terminal or axillary panicles. Flowers are similar to those of poison ivy and oak.

**CAUTION:** Can cause contact dermatitis similar to poison ivy and oak.

**Habitat and Distribution:** India, east to Southeast Asia.

## ROSARY PEA OR CRAB'S EYES

*ABRUS PRECATORIUS*

**Leguminosae** *(Fabaceae)* **Family**

**Description:** This plant is a vine with alternate compound leaves, light purple flowers, and beautiful seeds that are red and black.

**CAUTION:** This plant is one of the most danderous plants. One seed may contain enough poison to kill an adult.

**Habitat and Distribution:** This is a common weed in parts of Africa, southern Florida, Hawaii, Guam, the Caribbean, and Central and South America.

# STRYCHNINE TREE
### NUX VOMICA

**Logania** *(Loganiaceae)* **Family**

**Description:** The strychnine tree is a medium-sized evergreen, reaching a height of about 12 meters, with a thick, frequently crooked trunk. Its deeply veined oval leaves grow in alternate pairs. Small, loose clusters of greenish flowers appear at the ends of branches and are followed by fleshy, orange-red berries about 4 centimeters in diameter.

**CAUTION:** The berries contain the dislike seeds that yield the poisonous substance strychnine. All parts of the plant are poisonous.

**Habitat and Distribution:** A native of the tropics and subtropics of southeastern Asia and Australia.

# TRUMPET VINE OR TRUMPET CREEPER
### CAMPSIS RADICANS

**Trumpet creeper** *(Bignoniaceae)* **Family**

**Description:** This woody vine may climb to 15 meters high. It has pealike fruit capsules. The leaves are pinnately compound, 7 to 11 toothed leaves per leaf stock. The trumpet-shaped flowers are orange to scarlet in color.

**CAUTION:** This plant causes contact dermatitis.

**Habitat and Distribution:** This vine is found in wet woods and thickets throughout eastern and central North America.

# WATER HEMLOCK OR SPOTTED COWBANE
## *CICUTA MACULATA*

**Parsley** *(Apiaceae)* **Family**

**Description:** This perennial herb may grow to 1.8 meters high. The stem is hollow and sectioned off like bamboo. It may or may not be purple or red striped or mottled. Its flowers are small, white, and grow in groups that tend to form flat umbels. Its roots may have hollow air chambers and, when cut, may produce drops of yellow oil.

**CAUTION:** This plant is very poisonous and even a very small amount of this plant may cause death. Its roots have been mistaken for parsnips.

**Habitat and Distribution:** Water hemlock grows in wet or moist ground like swamps, wet meadows, stream banks, and ditches throughout the Unites States and Canada.

# Knots

# SIMPLE OVERHAND KNOT

## PURPOSE

This basic knot is used to stop any kind of line, from a cotton thread to a heavy-duty tow-rope, from pulling out of whatever work it is employed to do, whether that is assembling a block-and-tackle, attaching cord to a toddler's pull-along toy, or re-stringing a musical instrument. It can also act in a first aid capacity to prevent a line from fraying.

## TYING

Simply make a loop, pull the working end through and then tighten the resulting knot (figures 1–3). Observe how the twin knot parts spiral to the right or clockwise. All knots have a mirror image; in this instance, it is one in which the knot parts spiral to the left or counter-clockwise (figures 4–6). Tie whichever comes naturally. It is essential to recognize and be able to reproduce whichever is required, however, as some knots (such as the fisherman's knot) must only be tied with a pair of overhand knots of identical handedness. Others—such as the reef knot (page 40)—need a couple of half-knots of opposite-handedness.

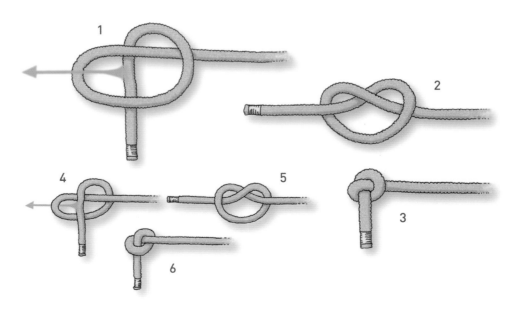

# FISHERMAN'S KNOT

## PURPOSE

To join (or bend) two lines of similar size and construction together, this regular standby is a compact knot with both ends streamlined to lie alongside their adjacent standing parts.

## TYING

Bring both working ends together, parallel and pointing in opposite directions. With one end tie an overhand knot around the adjacent standing part (figure 1). With the other end, tie an identical overhand knot; that is, if one is left-handed, the other must be left-handed, or vice versa (figure 2). Tighten each individual knot, then pull on both standing parts of the line so that the knots slide together (figures 3–4).

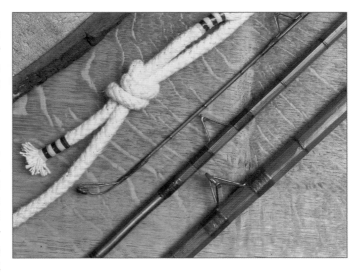

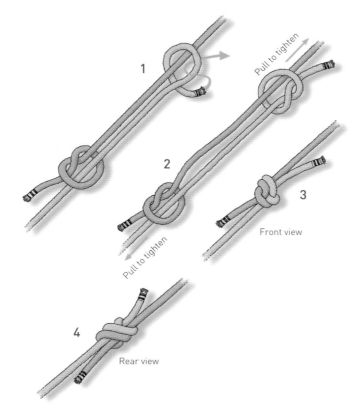

1

Pull to tighten

2

Pull to tighten

3

Front view

4

Rear view

# REEF (OR SQUARE) KNOT

## PURPOSE

This is a binding knot for use in threads, string, and other small cords. Use it only to fasten both ends of the same piece of small stuff, when it is strictly for bandages and packages, including the reefing of sails aboard dinghies and yachts that have traditional reefing points. With twin draw-loops it is the knot used to tie shoe laces (when it is called a double reef bow). It relies for its security upon bearing against whatever it is tied around, and is also a weak knot (reducing the breaking strength of whatever it is tied in by as much as a half). For these reasons it must never be used as a bend to join two working ropes.

## TYING

When an overhand knot is tied in two ends of the same twine or cord around some foundation (or a space) it is known as a half-knot. Half-knots, like overhand knots, may be left-handed or right-handed depending upon the direction in which their knot parts helix. To make a reef knot, tie a single half-knot (figure 1), then add a second half-knot of opposite handedness (figure 2). In this example repeat the instruction: "Left over right, then right over left." The result is a flat knot, consisting of two interlocked bights, with both working ends emerging on the same side of the knot (figure 3).

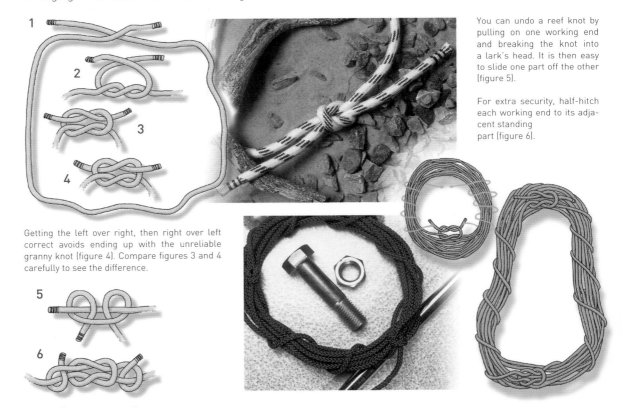

You can undo a reef knot by pulling on one working end and breaking the knot into a lark's head. It is then easy to slide one part off the other (figure 5).

For extra security, half-hitch each working end to its adjacent standing part (figure 6).

Getting the left over right, then right over left correct avoids ending up with the unreliable granny knot (figure 4). Compare figures 3 and 4 carefully to see the difference.

# ROUND TURN & TWO HALF-HITCHES

## PURPOSE

This is a tried-and-trusted, relatively strong and secure, attachment for a line of any kind to a fixed anchorage point.

## TYING

Insert a ring, rail, post or other object through an overhand knot and what results is known as a half-hitch (figure 1). A single half-hitch is inadequate, but add a second identical one for a satisfactory hitch (figure 2). For greater strength and reliability, first form a round turn and then add the two half-hitches (figure 3).

## KNOT LORE

The first mention of this knot was by David Steel in his Elements and Practice of Rigging and Seamanship (1794).

# STRANGLE KNOT

### PURPOSE

This is a binding knot, for use in jobs as diverse as seizing a hose pipe to a water source, holding a roll of carpet, or embellishing a presentation scroll.

### TYING

Tie a double overhand knot and slide it over the object as shown (figure 1). Pull as tight as required (figure 2). It will also hold together a coil of rope (figure 3) so that it might be carried on the shoulder or slung diagonally across one's chest.

### KNOT LORE

In his book Om Knutar (1916) the Swedish knot expert Hjalmar Öhrvall preferred this knot to the constrictor knot (pages 94–95) because its turns bedded down more snugly together. In the March 1997 issue of Knotting Matters (the quarterly magazine of the International Guild of Knot Tyers), a contributor writing under the pen-name of Jack Fidspike confirmed:

The Bag, Sack or Miller's knots
Are rudimentary bindings,
But often ropework jobs need lots
Of more elaborate windings.
The aptly named Constrictor
Will cling and grip like glue, Sir!
While the Strangle knot's a stricture
Some deem neater—and no looser.

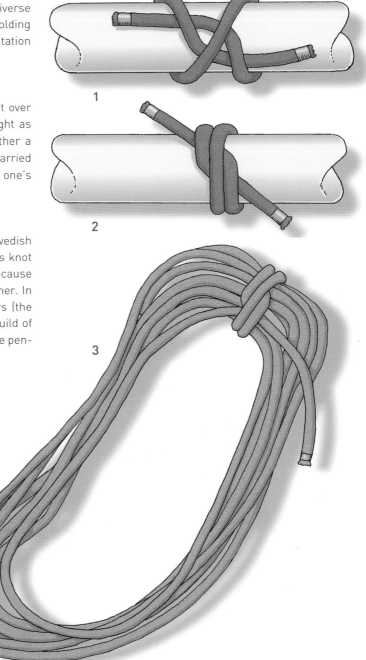

# FIGURE EIGHT KNOT

## PURPOSE

The basic knot is a stopper knot. It is easily untied after use and is recommended for any rope work that will be repeatedly assembled and dismantled. Note that, despite its bulkier appearance, it will not stop up a larger hole or slot than either the overhand or double overhand knots. As advised earlier, if a larger stopper knot is needed, use Ashley's stopper knot.

## TYING

Make a loop and impart an extra twist (figure 1). Tuck the working end as shown to create the characteristic figure eight layout that gives this family of knots its name (figures 2–3). Tighten the knot, taking care to push the bight furthest from the end of the line up as far as it will go, while at the same time pulling down on the standing part of the line to bend and trap the working end (figure 4).

When only the most temporary use will be made of this knot, consider incorporating a quick-release draw-loop (figure 5).

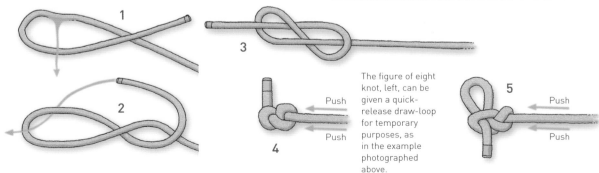

**1**

**2**

**3**

**4**

The figure of eight knot, left, can be given a quick-release draw-loop for temporary purposes, as in the example photographed above.

Push

Push

**5**

Push

Push

# COMMON BOWLINE

## PURPOSE

Pronounced boh-linn, the common bowline forms a single fixed loop. It is a classic knot but neither strong (about 60%) nor very secure unless the tail end is taped or tied to its adjacent loop leg.

## TYING

Make a loop and grasp it in one hand (palm down), then turn that hand palm up to trip or roll a loop into the standing part, through which the working end is automatically inserted (figures 1–2). Tuck the working end as indicated to complete this knot (figures 3–4). In tightening the knot ensure that the tail end is as long as a moderate sized loop.

## KNOT LORE

At sea the bow line was a rope used to hold the weather leech of a square sail forward closer to the wind, to prevent it from being taken aback (that is, unintentionally blown inside out, impeding the ship's progress), so the knot that secured it was literally a bow line knot; but it has since become diminished, and its pronunciation altered.

A.P. (later Sir Alan) Herbert, the English playwright, lyricist and wit—and Member of Parliament for the University of Oxford, when that academic and august institution had its own parliamentary representative—wrote in his poem The Bowline that it was the King of Knots, and many knot tyers (some unaware of the source) still use that sobriquet.

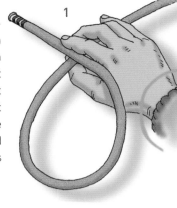

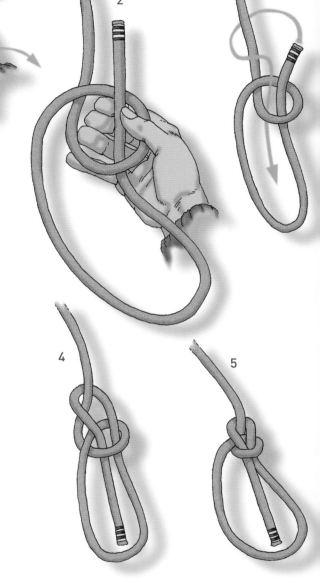

# SHEET BEND

## PURPOSE

Use this knot to join two lines together, or a line to a loop of some kind (when it is called a becket hitch). It will also cope with two lengths of cordage of somewhat dissimilar size and construction, in which case the bight must be made in the larger or stiffer material.

## TYING

Form a bight in one end and insert the other through it (figure 1). Wrap and tuck the working end as shown, taking care that both ends emerge on the same side of the knot (figure 2) since the knot seems in some materials to be more secure that way. Tighten it (figure 3). For a temporary hold-fast, and a quick-release, incorporate a draw-loop (figure 4).

## KNOT LORE

Remnants of nets from the Neolithic period have been found with mesh knots that resemble sheet bends.

A "sheet" was—and still is—a rope that controls or trims the lower corner of a sail (to "sheet home" or "sheet flat" is to pull the sheet taut, and so haul in the sail), from which comes the name sheet bend. David Steel used the name sheet bend in his Elements and Practice of Rigging and Seamanship (1794).

Some knot experts campaign against the use of this bend for lines of different sizes, pointing out that (if they are too dissimilar) a thick and stiff rope could overcome its weaker partner, straighten out and spill the knot. While this is a valid concern, it would be throwing the baby out with the bath water to discard this knot (since the property of accommodating dissimilar lines is a useful one).

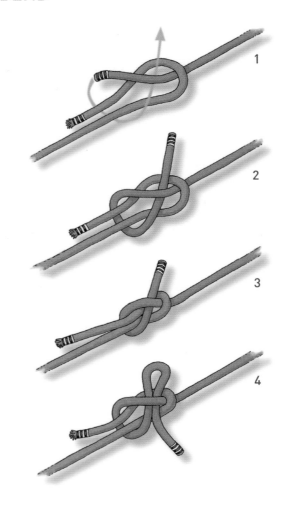

Knot craftsman and writer Stuart E. Grainger struck the right note:

*Use a Sheet Bend*
*To join on an end*
*To another of different size;*
*Also to tie through a thimble or eye,*
*But insure against trouble,*
*Tie it double.*

# CLOVE HITCH

## PURPOSE

The simplicity of this much-used hitch limits its application, for it can be trusted only as long as the pull is a steady one from a direction that is mostly at right-angles to the point of attachment. Otherwise it can prove unreliable. Provided this shortcoming is borne in mind, however, it is a knot worth knowing, one that can be tied by several different methods (the two most handy ones being described below).

## TYING #1

Take a turn with the working end around the intended anchorage and then cross over the standing part of the line (figure 1). Tuck as shown (figure 2). To suspend items by a lanyard—from a fender on a boat to a string of onions in the cellar—leave a draw-loop for later easy release (figure 3).

## TYING #2

To tie this knot quickly and simply in the bight—even when a working end is available—form a pair of alternate loops and overlap them (figure 4), then slip the resulting layout over the post or other point of attachment (figure 5).

## KNOT LORE

On land this was once known as the builder's knot. The name clove hitch seems to have been published first in the Universal Dictionary of the Marine (1769) by William Falconer.

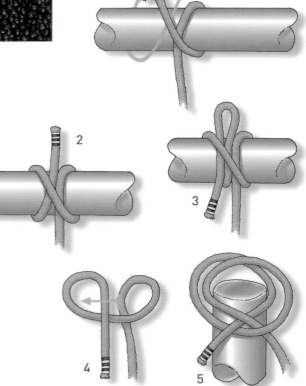

# TIMBER & KILLICK HITCHES

## PURPOSE

These two forms of the same basic knot are intended to haul or hoist logs or entire tree trunks. They will also drag or tow wooden piling, lengths of conduit pipe or any other similar objects.

## TYING

Take the working end once around the standing part of the rope and improvise a running eye by wrapping (dogging) the end several times around itself. Pull tight and a timber hitch results (figure 1). To ensure the load drags or tows in a straight line, add one (or more) half hitches some distance from the initial knot. This is a killick hitch (figure 2).

## KNOT LORE

The timber hitch was mentioned in A Treatise on Rigging (c.1625) and was illustrated in the Encyclopédie (1762) of Denis Diderot. It is an old knot. A killick was the naval term for a small anchor, and for any odd weight (such as a lump of stone) that might be employed on the end of a line (secured by a killick hitch) to anchor a dinghy, buoy or fisherman's lobster pot to the sea-bed. The killick hitch was named and illustrated in Elements and Practice of Rigging and Seamanship (1794) by David Steel.

# Tracking

## TRACKING WILDLIFE

Tracking is a skill that everyone with an interest in wild animals should possess to some degree. By learning to recognize a species' tracks and other signs, you can piece together enough clues left by its passing to form a very good picture of what the animal was, where it had been, where it was going, its size, its diet, and sometimes its sex.

Generic tracking tips include the knowledge that nearly all four-footed animals designed for running walk weight-forward, on the toes, and sometimes their heels print lightly or not at all. Hind prints normally register on top of fore tracks, an almost universal characteristic that allows forefeet to be placed visually, and that precise spot stepped onto by the hind foot on that same side, important when you have four legs in rough terrain. Another trait common to 4-legged animals is a little toe on the inside of the foot, opposite our own, and forefeet that are noticeably larger than hind paws. Nearly all 4-legged animals run with a "rocking-horse" gait, in which the forelegs print close together and slightly behind more widely-separated hind prints.

Recognizing prints is only the first step in learning to track, and while that seems simple enough, most beginners are surprised at how little they actually have to work with. Clear, complete impressions are rare except in mud, wet sand, and fresh snow, so what a tracker follows are not clear footprints but marks made by the animal's passing. Partial tracks—where toes, claws, or the edge of a hoof have pressed noticeably into the earth—can help you identify the species and sometimes the individual, but you might need to follow a trail some distance to get a complete track picture. Of course, you first need to know what a perfect track looks like to recognize partial prints, and the accompanying track identification table provides this information.

Easier to follow and usually more obvious are disturbances left by an animal's feet and body. A half circle of four or five perforations in leafy humus tells you a clawed animal stepped there; twin scrape marks on a moss-covered log show where a deer's hoof slipped; broom-like sweepings on sand denote the wagging of a porcupine's tail as it waddled along; a trough-shaped furrow in grass leading to the water's edge was made by beavers; larger furrows through tall grass tell where a dear or bear crossed; a twisted spiral of crushed grass stems was made when a heavy animal changed direction abruptly by spinning on one foot. Try to imagine yourself as the animal you're trailing, able to slip over low branches or leap over high ones, stopping to nibble a plant here, abruptly changing direction in response to a scent on the breeze.

Trackers who make their job look easy also employ a technique I call "looking wide." The trick is to avoid focusing your eyes on the ground, trees, or any single component of the surrounding terrain; instead, take in all of these components as a single picture. Allow your eyes to settle naturally on discontinuities and disturbances left by an animal's passing. You don't need tracks if you can follow a trail. Intersections may still require detective work to discern which prints belong to the animal you're tracking, but a practiced ability to look wide makes following any trail much faster.

Look, too, for territorial marks left by dominant animals advertising their claim to an area, its foods, and any potential mates living there. Most territorial sign is left by dominant males, and all of it is meant to be conspicuous. Bobcats scratch tree trunks with their claws, then urinate on the trunks to leave a pungent, distinctly feline aroma that even humans can smell at some distance. Bears leave proportionately larger claw marks on wooden bridges and standing trees, communicating their size and strength to fellow bruins by reaching as high up the trunk as they can. most territorial animals employ a variety of visual and olfactory markings to attract mates and warn off competitors, usually accompanied by a musky, vaguely skunk-like scent that animal watchers should always be alert for.

Animal droppings, known collectively as scat, can also reveal a good deal about their makers, including species, diet, and likely feeding grounds,. Territorial predators, from bobcats and coyotes to bears and wolves, use scat to mark the perimeter of their domains, typically leaving fresh scat very near older deposits to refresh their claim every day or so. Members of the deer family evacuate their bowels whenever the urge takes them, usually on well-traveled trails, to disperse their scent widely and to confuse predators. If you can conquer your natural aversion to examining poop, breaking scat apart to reveal its contents will tell you what the animal has eaten and, through deduction, where it was feeding.

# BEARS (FAMILY URSIDAE)

With these generalities in mind let's move on to individual species, starting with bears. No wild animal in North America is more feared by humans, and none has suffered more at the hands of fiction writers seeking to create thrills by painting bears as aggressive, bloodthirsty man killers. Early settlers armed with muzzleloading smoothbores feared these most powerful of land carnivores because of their tremendous strength and sometimes enormous size. Adult brown, or grizzly, bears can exceed half a ton by age five; black bears, which may be black, brown, blond, or even mostly white on Alaska's Gribble Island, can reach mature weights of more than 600 pounds. In either species females are usually about 20 percent smaller than males.

Long canines identify black and brown bears as carnivores, but their feeding habits and lack of hunting prowess classify them as omnivorous, with a diet that consists largely, or at some times of year entirely, of grasses, roots, berries, and other vegetation. Newborn deer fawns and elk or moose calves are frequently stalked along overgrown trails in late spring, and occasionally a hapless ground squirrel is dug from its burrow, but meat is a highly prized delicacy in the diets of both black and brown bears. Polar bears, being adapted to a habitat with almost no vegetation, are almost wholly carnivorous, but their darker-colored brethren normally have to settle for carrion they appropriate from more skilled but less powerful hunters.

Aside from a brief midsummer mating season, or rut, all bears are solitary and concerned only with gaining the layer of fat—about 25 percent of their body weights—they'll need to nourish them through a five-month winter denning period. To accomplish that, these large animals must feed constantly, following seasonal foods on an annual trek that might encompass more than 100 miles.

Active mainly from late afternoon to midmorning, bears bed down in secluded thickets to sleep away the warmest part of the day. A nomadic lifestyle makes them less territorial than animals with smaller, permanent domains, but all bears are known to have a "personal space" inside which intruders won't be tolerated.

Few hikers ever see a bear in the midst of prime bear country because both black and brown bears typically withdraw at the first scent or sound of a human, but there are instances where you might suddenly find yourself facing a bear. Approaching from downwind, which is what you'd want to do when stalking deer and other harmless animals, may be a bad idea in bear country. A bear's nose is as sensitive as any, but no animal can detect scent from upwind. Adding to the ease with which you might catch a bear unawares are small ears with a sense of hearing not much better than our own, and myopic, color-blind vision.

Surprising a bear is never good, regardless of its species. Black bears can be counted on to hightail it into the bushes, and so will most grizzlies, but occasionally there comes a bear that refuses to withdraw. These animals are always large, dominant adults, and nearly always have something worth defending, like cubs, a bee tree, or a deer carcass.

Stumbling onto an obstinate bear doesn't mean you'll be attacked, and even a grizzly mother is reluctant to risk possible injury if she can avoid a fight. The first rule in any surprise encounter with any animal is, don't run. By running, you identify yourself as prey, which may excite the bear's hunting instincts and cause it to give chase. Stand your ground, then slowly back away, never turning your back on the animal until at least 100 yards stand between you. The objective is to convince the bear that you're a potentially dangerous foe, regardless of how untrue that may be, but also that you're willing to with-draw without conflict.

Current bear-avoidance strategy recommends never looking an animal directly in the eye, ostensibly because this conveys a willingness for confrontation. Where more aggres-sive brown bears are concerned, I must defer to experts like fellow Michigander Doug Peacock, author of the book, *Grizzly Years*. But if the animal is a black bear, an exhibition of anything but total dominance over the beast goes against the teachings of my Indian mentors. I've always locked gazes with every aggressive animal I've encountered, from bears and dogs to moose and elk, and I'll continue using that technique so long as it works.

Be aware, too, that dominant bears especially have been known to charge humans during surprise encounters. Having experienced black bear charges several times, I can attest to the sheer terror inspired by 500 pounds of growling bruin moving toward you at high speed, but once again it's essential that you stand your ground. No human can outrun a bear, but enough have come through bear charges unscathed to prove that nearly every one is a bluff, meant to determine whether you're frightened prey or formi-dable foe.

Bear tracks are distinctive. Every species has five toes on every foot, each toe termi-nating in a thick functional claw. Brown bear claws are long and nearly straight, well suited to digging and inflicting mortal wounds, while black bears have shorter, hooked claws that are better suited for climbing trees to escape brown bears, the black's only natural predator.

Most striking are a bear's hind feet, which look nearly human if you discount claws and the fact that bears, like most animals, walk heavily on the outsides of their feet, so their big and little toes are opposite our own. Tracks are typically toe-in, a trait common to powerfully built, flat-footed animals not designed for speed, a group that includes badgers, raccoons, wolverines, and humans. At a relaxed walk all four feet usually leave individual prints, with front paws registering slightly behind hind feet on the same side. At a run the forepaws still register behind rear paws, but this time both front and hind feet print in pairs, next to or slightly diagonal to one another. Typical of all running animals, the bear's toes will be dug in more heavily than its heels, often with a spray of loose soil thrown to the rear.

## WILD CANDIS

The family Canidae includes the coyote, gray wolf, gray fox, the imported red fox and man's best friend, the dog (*Canis domesticus*). There has always been a strong bond between humans and the dog family and, tall tales notwithstanding, no non-rabid wild wolf or coyote has ever posed a danger to humans of any age or size. I've been spending nights alone in the woods with wolves and coyotes since boyhood, and my personal experience has been that any fear of these wild dogs is totally unfounded. Being near these wild hunters, listening to them howl messages across the forest to one another, is a thrill not to be missed.

## COYOTE (CANDIS IATRANS).

Coyotes are the most common and widespread wild dogs in the Americas. Smallest of the wolves, coyotes share their long-legged, lanky build, but stand only 24 inches at the shoulder and weigh just 30 to 45 pounds, with males slightly larger than females. At a top running speed of about 45 mph, they're natural predators of rabbits and hares, but carrion and rodents—the latter stunned by pouncing onto them with both front paws—make up the majority of any coyote's diet. Fawns and chickens are occasionally taken, but coyotes mostly respect human boundaries, and healthy deer are too much for the little wolf to handle, even in a pack of up to seven adults.

Because a large portion of their diet is rodents, many adults fit the Old West image of

a lone coyote. But when winters get tough in the North, five to seven adult family members may form a pack to bring down already dying deer. The little wolf isn't keen on tackling prey several times its own size, even with the help of its kin, but deer too weak to use their lethal hooves effectively are sometimes dispatched and eaten quickly, before larger carrion eaters (wolves) find and appropriate the carcass.

Coyotes are normally shy, staying well away from campers and human habitation, although there are places and instances where human practices cause them to become pests. In the late 1950s and 60s, during the paving of California, homeowners who'd settled in what were to become suburbs discovered that local coyotes were smart. They learned not only the milkman's delivery schedules but also how to uncap glass bottles and dump the milk onto concrete—the only nonabsorbent medium available—where it could then be lapped up. Today, as new housing continues to gobble up wilderness, rural homeowners are having similar problems with trash left outside for pickup.

No coyote has ever approached any camp I know of, whether people were there at the time or not, probably due to the shoot-on-sight status coyotes have always enjoyed with hunters. If you should happen upon a pack of coyotes that show reluctance at leaving, say, a fresh-killed fawn, simply brandishing a stick will set the entire pack to running. Be aware, however, that early spring (March and April) is a time when rabies takes a lethal toll on overcrowded animal populations, especially coyotes, raccoons, and skunks. Never, ever approach any wild animal that exhibits no fear, seems disoriented, or has greasy-looking, matted fur. Foaming at the mouth, that classic symptom of hydrophobia (rabies), is seen only at the disease's latter stages, just before the victim dies.

Although such a lightweight and soft-footed animal rarely leaves a clear, whole print, coyote tracks are unique. Like all dog tracks, front and hind prints show four toes with fixed claws, all pointing forward, but the heel pads of the rear feet leave distinctive forward-pointing winged impressions rather like a mustache on each side of their imprints.

## GRAY WOLF (CANIS LUPUS).

It has always seemed a bitter irony that the dog should be considered mankind's best friend while the wolf, which has never been known to attack any human being, has been

used to frighten small children and hunted to extinction over most of its range. Native Americans revered the wolf for the way a pack worked together for its own preservation, for the way pairs mated till death did them part, and for the drill-team hunting maneuvers a pack used to bring down prey much larger than themselves. With a running speed of more than 40 mph and body weights that can exceed 140 pounds for males (about 120 pounds for females), wolves running in packs of from two to more than six members are a formidable hunting machine for prey as large as a yearling moose.

In fact wolf and coyote packs are always formed of family members. Some offspring elect not to mate in order to stay with the strength of the pack, where only the original parents, the alpha male and the alpha female, are allowed to breed. Offspring that remain for a year or more take an active role as babysitters after the next generation of siblings has been weaned, feeding the pups on demand with regurgitated stomach contents and defending them from predation.

But for all their savage efficiency against animals they intend to eat, wolves, like coyotes, pose zero threat to humans, and there is not one verifiable report of a wolf or wolves attacking any human being for any reason at any time in history. I've spent many nights in woods where wolf packs were hunting, listening as they made kills; once I even managed to call an entire curious pack to the perimeter of my camp, but they refused to approach further. Put simply, there is no reason to fear brother wolf.

Wolf tracks can be confusing, even to trained biologists, because they are virtually identical to the tracks of dog breeds that have close ties to their wild cousins. Typical of the dog family, wolf tracks have four forward-pointing toes with thick fixed claws, but the heel pads of front and hind paws may be indistinguishable from those of the husky breeds, like Samoyeds, malamutes, and Siberian huskies. Differences include size, because the tracks of a full-grown gray wolf may reach 5 inches long by 4 inches wide, with front paws larger than hind paws. Note too that man's best friend is considered a prey animal by timber wolves. Dog tracks found in wolf country, which is by definition remote, were almost certainly made by a wolf or coyote.

## RACCOON (PROCYON LOTOR)

Everyone can recognize a raccoon, with its distinctive masked face, fluffy ringed tail, and long, monkeylike fingers that are notorious for being able to manipulate catches and locks on henhouse doors. The common name stems from the Algonquan Indian name *ah-roo-cown*, which translates roughly to "scratches with hands." *Lotor*, the suffix of its scientific name, is Latin for "washer," an allusion to the omnivorous species' habit of

washing food in a stream or pond before eating. The truth is that raccoons, like humans and primates, use their sensitive fingers to separate edible flesh from inedible bones, seeds, and rinds—why eat undigestible matter when you don't have to?

Officially raccoons can reach weights of 12 to 48 pounds, but in the fur-trading days of my youth I took two that topped 60 pounds. Preferred habitat may range from hardwoods to swamp, but always near a source of fresh water, which also provides delicacies like crayfish and clams. They don't hibernate, but in the hardest parts of

winter in the Far North, raccoons may den for several days at a time, living off stored body fat.

Cartoonists and movie directors have always opted to portray the raccoon as a cute little imp, capable of property damage but always friendly to humans. This simply isn't true. The once popular *Grizzly Adams* TV series was canceled after several youngsters, ostensibly influenced by cute and cuddly trained animal actors, were injured while attempting to handle raccoons drawn to campground garbage cans.

No healthy raccoon has ever attacked a human in my experience, but all are fierce, willing fighters when cornered, and numerous campers have had to endure rabies vaccinations after learning the hard way that a fearless animal isn't necessarily friendly. Raccoon hunters, who typically love their coon dogs like children, are careful to protect their much-larger bluetick, walker, and redbone hounds from the sometimes serious injuries a cornered raccoon can inflict on them. Most feared is that a dog might pursue a coon into deep water, where the raccoon can be counted on to turn and climb onto the stricken dog's head, drowning it. Never approach any wild raccoon, no matter how tame it might appear.

Raccoon tracks are typical of other plantigrade animals, like bears and humans, with elongated hind feet and five toes on each paw. All toes are extraordinarily long, like fingers, and these are perhaps the most distinctive identifying feature of raccoon tracks. Also, remember that nocturnal raccoons always frequent shorelines after dark, and wet sand or mud near the water will often yield plaster-cast-quality tracks.

# BEAVER (CASTOR CANADENSIS)

This uniquely American rodent is a marvel of nature. Many Indian cultures credit the beaver with teaching humans to build houses, French voyageurs believed the foul-smelling castoreum glands on the beaver's anus were a cure-all, and no animal in the world does more to promote the health of its own habitat. Today beavers sometimes run afoul of man by flooding power lines and real estate, by toppling commercially valuable

birch trees on vacation properties, and by diminishing water flow to cattle farmers on the downstream side of dammed waterways.

In the natural sense, however, beavers do only good: creating ponds and excellent fish habitat where forest once dominated and providing nesting and feeding areas for all types of waterfowl and other birds. Thinning fast-growing trees like poplar, aspen, and birch, the bark of which serves as the beaver's main source of nourishment year-round, promotes new growth and health in the surrounding forest, and every animal in the area will visit the pond to drink at some point every day. Years later, when the largest food trees are exhausted and the beavers move on to establish new ponds, the abandoned pond will dry up and become a rich garden of lush growth.

Largest of North America's rodents, beavers can officially reach weights in excess of 100 pounds, though 30 to 40 pounds is average for adults. None poses a danger to humans unless cornered on land, but never underestimate a beaver's ability to fight. The famed Lewis and Clark Expedition suffered its first near-fatal casualty when Captain Meriwether Lewis's huge Newfoundland retriever had its throat torn open by a cornered beaver.

Despite a plethora of tracks along muddy or sandy shorelines, easily recognizable beaver tracks are rare. Reasons for that odd scarcity include the fact that beavers seldom walk along a shoreline; instead they travel straight from water to work area, leaving a wide, flattened, furrowlike trail through tall grasses at the water's edge. Webbed hind paws help make beavers among the best swimmers in the mammal world, but print only faintly because of their wide surface area. Fortunately, gnawed trees with bark stripped off, dams, lodges, and, of course, ponds are proof enough that beavers live there.

When tracks are in evidence, there are five toes on every foot, although the small inside toe of the hind feet may not print at all. Front tracks look remarkably like a small human hand with fingers and thumb spread wide. The walking gait is a toe-in waddling pace in which all four feet register independently.

# WHITE-TAILED DEER (ODOCOILEUS VIRGINIANUS)

No wild animal in history has been more studied, manipulated, or revered than the white-tailed deer, and the strangest part is that all the money used to accomplish those things comes from people whose stated goal is to kill deer. Nearly exterminated by the mid-20th century because of unrestricted hunting, whitetails have made a phenomenal

comeback, even to the point of becoming agricultural pests and serious driving hazards, especially after dark. Few species have adapted to the crush of civilization better than the whitetail.

Whitetails are one of five native species in North America belonging to the family Cervidae, which also includes mule deer, caribou, elk, and moose. All are ungulates (hoofed animals) of the order Artiodactyla, meaning they have an even number of toes. Other shared characteristics include antlers that are shed by males in winter,

cloven hooves, a darker grizzled coat in winter, a purely vegetarian diet, a lack of top teeth, and twins born in early spring.

While I've heard some pretty tall tales from overexcited nimrods, I feel secure in saying that wild white-tailed deer are absolutely harmless to any human. The same applies to mule deer and caribou. Bull elk in the grip of raging hormones during the October rut, or mating season, have been known to charge photographers who got too close, but such instances are rare and roundly deserved. Moose, however, are scary; cows with calves are more protective than any other deer species, and rutting bulls have been known to charge anything up to and including locomotives. Once again, the safest rule of thumb is to give a wide berth to any large deer that seems reluctant to flee at your approach.

Whitetail tracks are typical of deer tracks, printing in the classic split-heart pattern. Each half of the cloven hoof is actually a modified toenail; paired dewclaws located above the hooves to the rear of each ankle are another pair of apparently useless toes that will probably disappear one day. Like those of most four-leggers, hind prints register precisely on top of foreprints at a casual walk. At a fast run of 35 mph, whitetails and other deer adopt a rocking-horse gait, with paired foreprints registering between and slightly behind more widely spaced hind prints.

## WILDCATS (FAMILY FELIDAE)

Discounting the jaguar, ocelot, and jaguarondi of Mexico, there are three wildcats in North America: the bobcat (*Lynx rufus*), the mountain lion (*Felis concolor*), and the long-legged lynx (*Lynx Canadensis*). All are superb hunters with pinpoint hearing, very good

vision, and some of the most lethal armament in nature. These cats have the stealth to stalk small rodents, the speed to catch a rabbit, and the teeth and claws to bring down prey much larger than themselves. Unlike wild candies, all cats prefer to kill their own food, and none will eat carrion unless very hungry.

Mountain lions are the largest of American wildcats, reaching weights of more than 250 pounds, followed by the muscular little bobcat at 65 pounds and the long-legged lynx at 40. Each of these was once far more widespread than it is today, but people have never been fond of wildcats in their backyards, and now all of them are more or less cornered in small pockets of wilderness.

While there have been tales of lynx and bobcats attacking humans, I find such stories very difficult to swallow—even a child is physically too large to be considered prey by such small felines. Mountain lions, though, have earned a good deal of prejudice by infrequently killing or mauling small-framed people, sometimes actually eating the bodies. As with bears, the culprits are always old, arthritic cats whose hunting skills are no longer sufficient to supply game. Humans are at the bottom of the list of wildcat food choices.

A chance meeting with a large mountain lion can be frightening. Most will hightail it for cover; if you should meet a cougar that seems reluctant to leave, it probably has a fresh kill or cubs that it's defending. As with a bear, the protocol for safe withdrawal includes maintaining constant eye contact while backing off slowly. Never turn your back on the cat, regardless of what it does, until you've put a minimum of 100 yards between you. barring this, a blank pistol, a compressed-air horn, or even a loud whistle has been sufficient to set even large cats to running.

Like canids, all felines have four toes on each foot, but while dogs have paws designed for digging, with stout fixed claws and forward-pointing toes, cats have retractable claws in toes that are arrayed in a semicircle. Cats can partially close their paws like a human fist, and widely spaced toes permit a better grip against flesh while needlelike fangs deliver a killing bite to the victim's throat.

Tracks of the three American wildcats are easily distinguished from one another. Mountain lion tracks are of course much larger and deeper than tracks from its two smaller cousins. Lynx tracks are disproportionately large and show long, widely splayed toes with almost formless heel pads; bobcats are unusual in that all four feet are nearly equal in size, while most animals have larger forefeet. Being retractable, claws are normally absent from the tracks of all species. An exception is on slippery surfaces like wet clay or ice where cats, like people, feel insecure about walking.

# TRACKS AT – A – GLANCE

## DEER FAMILY (CERVIDAE)

### FAMILY SPECIES:

**White-Tailed Deer** (*Odocoileus virginianus*)**- shown**
**Mule Deer** (*Odocoileus hemionus*)
**Elk** (*Cervus Canadensis*)
**Moose** (*Alces alces*)
**Caribou** (*Rangifer tarandus*)

### FAMILY CHARACTERISTICS:

Cloven hooves front & hind, 2 dewclaws per ankle
Large directional ears
No upper incisors
Males wear antlers most of the year
All species strictly herbivorous

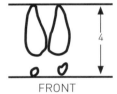
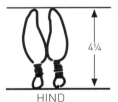

FRONT                    HIND

## SWINE FAMILY (SUIDAE)

### FAMILY SPECIES:

**European Wild Boar** (*Sus scrofa*)**- shown**
**Domestic Hog**

### FAMILY CHARACTERISTICS:

Cloven hooves front & hind, 2 dewclaws per ankle
Generally travel everywhere at a trot
Large snouts for rooting up food plants
Omnivorous diet
Fond of rolling in mud

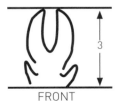
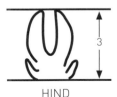

FRONT                    HIND

# PECCARY FAMILY (TAYASSUIDAE)

## FAMILY SPECIES:

    Collared Peccary (Dicotyles tajacu) – shown
    White-Lipped Peccary (Tayassu pecari) – S.America

## FAMILY CHARACTERISTICS

    Cloven hooves front & hind, no dewclaws
    Generally travel everywhere at a trot
    Large snouts for rooting up food plants
    Omnivorous diet
    Generally dislikes water, but swims well

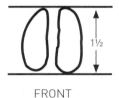 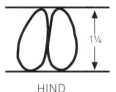

FRONT          HIND

# AMERICAN ANTELOPE FAMILY (ANTILOCAPRIDAE)

## FAMILY SPECIES

    Pronghorn Antelope (*Antilocapra americana*)
    Lone survivor of a 20-million-year old family

## FAMILY CHARACTERISTICS

    Cloven hooves resemble those of deer species
    No dewclaws streamlines legs for faster running speed
    Good vision – some say exceptional
    Herbivorous diet of ground plants & prairie grasses Social,
    travels in herds of mostly relatives
    70 mph running speed, fastest animal in N.America
    Black marks on buck's muzzles lacking on does
    Bucks & does grow horns, does usually without prongs

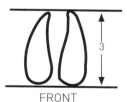 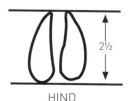

FRONT          HIND

## BEAR SPECIES:

### FAMILY SPECIES:

**Brown or Grizzly Bear** (*Ursus arctos horribilis*)
**Black Bear** (*Ursus americanus*) **– shown**
**Polar Bear** (*Ursus maritimus*)

### FAMILY CHARACTERISTICS:

5 toes front & hind feet, small toes innermost
Plantigrade (flat – footed) walk, shuffling gait
Excellent sense of smell, fair hearing, poor vision
Omnivorous diet includes carrion, fish, fruits
Sleep through winter months, but none hibernate
All species superb swimmers

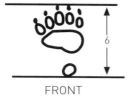

FRONT

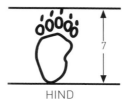

HIND

## WILD DOG FAMILY (CANIDAE)

### FAMILY SPECIES:

**Gray or Timber Wolf** (*Canis lupus*)
**Coyote** (*Canis latrans*) **– shown**
**Gray Fox** (*Urocyon cinereoargenteus*)
**Red Fox** (*Vulpes vulpes*)

### FAMILY CHARACTERISTICS:

4 toes front & hind feet, claws show in tracks
Pointed ears, excellent sense of smell, good vision
Lithe bodies, long furry tails
Both parents take part in rearing young
Pairs believed to mate for life
Mostly carnivorous diet includes carrion, fruits

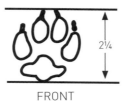

FRONT

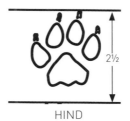

HIND

## WILDCAT FAMILY (FELIDAE)

FAMILY SPECIES:

Puma or Mountain Lion (Felis concolor)
Bobcat (*Lynx rufus*) - shown
Lynx (*Lynx canadensis*)
Jaguar (*Felis onca*)

FAMILY CHARACTERISTICS:

4 toes front & hind feet, retractable claws
Lithe, muscular bodies, tail length varies
Excellent sense of smell, fair hearing, good vision
Carnivorous diet includes fish, mammals, fruits
Solitary except when mating, only females rear young
Rarely eat carrion unless starving, prefer to hunt
All cats strong swimmers, but only jaguars like water

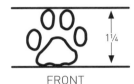 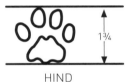

FRONT            HIND

## WEASEL FAMILY (MUSTELIDAE)

FAMILY SPECIES:

Wolverine (*Gulo gulo*)
Badger (*Taxiden taxus*)
River Otter (*Lutra Canadensis*)
Mink (*Mustela vison*) – shown
Ermine (*Mustela erminea*)
Striped Skunk (*Mepbitis mephitis*)

FAMILY CHARACTERISTICS:

5 toes front & hind feet, claws show in tracks
Small toes innermost, may not register in tracks
Perineal (anal) scent glands
Excellent sense of smell, fair hearing, fair vision
Carnivorous diet includes fish, mammals, insects
Slow runners, fierce & willing fighters

FRONT            HIND

## RACCOON FAMILY (PROCYONIDAE)

FAMILY SPECIES:
  Raccoon (*Procyon lotor*) – shown
  Ringtail (Bassariscus astutus)
  Coatimundi (Nasua nasua)

FAMILY CHARACTERISTICS:
  5 toes front & hind feet, small toes innermost
  Plantigrade (flat-footed) walk
  Long, ringed tail
  Omnivorous diet includes meat, fish, insects, fruits
  Solitary, mostly nocturnal
  Good senses of smell & vision, hearing fair
  All species good climbers, ferocious when cornered

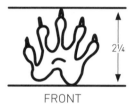
FRONT

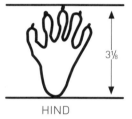
HIND

## OPOSSUM FAMILY (DIDELPHIDAE)

FAMILY SPECIES:
  Virginia Opossum (*Didelphis virginiana*)
  N. america's only native marsupial

FAMILY CHARACTERISTICS:
  5 toes front & hind feet, thumblike toe on hind feet
  Poor vision, fair hearing, excellent sense of smell
  Carnivorous diet of mostly carrion, some plants
  Solitary except when mating, only females rear young
  Mostly nocturnal, sometimes active by day
  Often plays dead when threatened, prefers to tree
  Beaver Family (Castoridae)

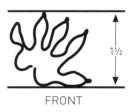
FRONT

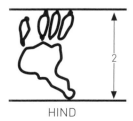
HIND

# BEAVER FAMILY (CASTORIDAE)

FAMILY SPECIES:

Beaver (*Castor Canadensis*)

FAMILY CHARACTERISTICS:

5 toes front & hind feet
Poor vision, fair hearing, excellent sense of smell
Perineal (anal) scent glands, obvious scent mounds
Strictly herbivorous, eats bark of aspen, willow
Slow runners, very strong & capable swimmers
Always lives on flowing freshwater streams
Social, family colonies of up to 18 animals

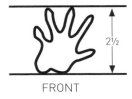

FRONT

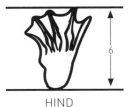

HIND

# PORCUPINE FAMILY (ERETHIZONTIDAE)

FAMILY SPECIES:

Porcupine (*Erethizon dorsatum*)
Single species in N. America

FAMILY CHARACTERISTICS:

4 toes front, 5 toes hind, unique pebbled soles
Plantigrade (flat-footed) walk
Long, heavily quilled tail
Coarse fur with 30,000 quills on back
Solitary, mostly nocturnal
Good sense of smell, poor vision, hearing fair
Always found in forested areas, cedar swamps

FRONT

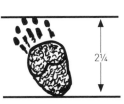

HIND

301

## HARE & RABBIT FAMILY (LEPORIDAE)

FAMILY SPECIES:

Snowshoe Hare (*Lepus americanus*) – shown
Cottontail Rabbit (*Sylvilagus floridanus*)
White-Tailed Jack Rabbit (*Lepus townsendii*)
Black-Tailed Jack Rabbit (*Lepus californicus*)
Nuttall's Cottontail (*Sylvilagus nuttallii*)
Desert Cottontail (*Sylvilagus audonbonii*)

FAMILY CHARACTERISTICS:

4 toes front & hind feet
Poor vision, fair hearing, excellent senses of smell & hearing
Fast runners, but only for short distances
Herbiverous diet of ground plants, buds, some bark
Solitary, mostly nocturnal
No fixed mating season, breeds prodigiously

FRONT

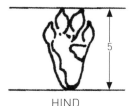

HIND

## MUSKRAT FAMILY (ZIBEHTICIDAE)

FAMILY SPECIES:

Common Muskrat (*Ondatra zibethica*)

FAMILY CHARACTERISTICS:

5 toes front & hind, vestigial inner toe
Black, scaly, ratlike tail
Much larger than rat species
Herbiverous diet also includes crustaceans, insects
Solitary, mostly nocturnal
Good sense of smell, poor vision, fair hearing

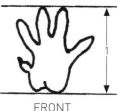

FRONT

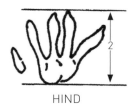

HIND

# SQUIRREL FAMILY (SCIURIDAE)

## FAMILY SPECIES:

**Fox Squirrel** (*Sciurus niger*)
**Gray Squirrel** (*Sciurus carolinensis*)—**shown**
**Red Squirrel** (*Tamiasciurus hudsonicus*)
**Eastern Woodchuck** (*Marmota monax*)
**Yellowbellied Marmot** (*Marmota flaviventris*)

## FAMILY CHARACTERISTICS:

4 toes front. 5 toes hind, elongated hind feet
Good vision, fair hearing, excellent sense of smell
Tree squirrels build cup-shaped nests high in trees
Ground squirrels dig burrows, most hibernate
Herbiverous diet of mostly nuts, some eat insects

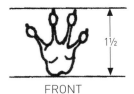

FRONT

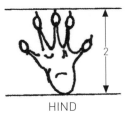

HIND

# Index

Analgesics, 131–132
Antihistamines, 132–133
Arteriosclerosis, 49
Basic solar still, 35
Bed warmers, 24
Beriberi
    Wet and dry, 50
Biological threat, 187–189
Black Talon, 85
Boot heel stove, *see trench stove*
Botulism, 52
Bow-and-drill
    Making a bow–and–drill, 18, 19
Bracken fern, 59
    "Fiddleheads," 59
Broadleaf cattail, 61
    Russian asparagus, 62
Brush pistols, 83
Bugging–out, 149–150
    Bag, 150–151
    Building the bag, 151
Calcium deficiency, 50
Canned foods, 51
    Hazards in canned foods, 52, 53
    Storing canned goods, 52
Canteens, 44
Cavity, *see Dentistry*
Chainsaw, 166, 167
Chemical threat, 189–190

Chlorine bleach, 47
Cholera, 1
Clostridium botulinum
    spores, 52
Coal bed, 23
Compass, see Orienteering
Condensation stills, 35–36
Conserving water, 44
Cooking, 20
Debris shelter, 112–116
Dehydration, 29, 135–136
Dentistry, 136–139
Dirty bomb, see Man-made
    disasters
Divining rod, 37
Divination, 37, 38, 39
Dried foods, 54
    Beans, 54
    Bulk foods, 55, 56
    Dehydrated potatoes, 55
    Pasta, 55
    Rice, 54
Dried water holes, 42
Driven well, 38
Driving method, 39–42
Dry reindeer moss, 62
Dysentery, 50
Earthquakes
    Port-au-Prince, Haiti, 1
Edible plants, 201–259
Enhancing digestibility, 57
    Cooking with wood
        ashes, 57
Estimating food needs, 56
Exotoxin, 52
Extreme cold, see Winter
    storms
Fire, 11
    Banking a fire, 24
    Building a fire, 16, 17
    Butane lighters, 13
    Cooking fire, 20

Flint–and–steel, 12
    Heating fire, 20
    Making fire, 12
    Matches, 14
    Smudge fire, 23
    Sparking tools, 12
Firewood, 17
    Gathering firewood, 17
First–Aid kits, 129–130
Fish bait
    Where to find it, 75
Fishing Floats
    "Bobbers," 73, 74
Fishing for food, 69
Fishing kits, 69, 70
Floods, 181–185
    Business preparation,
        184–185
    Causes, 183–184
    Home preparation, 184
    Insurance, 184
    Warnings, 182
Golden saber, 85
Gunslinging, 88–89
Handfishing, 70
Health maintenance, 130, 134
Heated condensation still, 36
Hemostatic dressings, 134
Home canning, 53
    Pressure cooker, 53
Hunting weapons, 77
    Air guns, 79
    Bow–and–arrow, 77, 78
    Crossbows, 79
Hurricanes
    Katrina, New Orleans, 1
Hypoglycemia, 49
Hypothermia, 11, 12
Ice–fishing, 72
Influenza, 190–191
Iodine, 47
Kevlar body armor, 85
Knife fishing, 76

Knots,
    Clove hitch, 282
    Common bowline, 280
    Figure-eight knot, 279
    Fisherman's knot, 275
    Reef knot, 276
    Round turn & two half-
        hitches, 277
    Sheet bend, 281
    Simple overhand knot, 274
    Square knot, see Reef knot
    Strangle knot, 278
    Timber & killick hitches,
        283
Lacerations, 133
Leprosy, 46
Listeria, 52
Lumberjacking, 160–168
    Clearing roadways, 165–168
    With an axe, 163–165
Man–made disasters, 184–186
Manufactured shelters,
    109–112
Meat hunting, 76, 77
Multivitamins, 130–131
Nalgenes, 44
Native Americans, 60
Navigation, see Orienteering
Nuclear blast, 186–187
Orienteering, 170–178
    Nighttime orienteering, 177
Osteomalacia, 50
Pencil snare, 66, 67, 68
Personal defense
    Chemical, 144–145
    Dirks, 148
    Edged weapons, 146
    Escape and evasion, 149
    Fixed–blade fighting
        knives, 147–148
    Non–lethal, 144
    Striking weapons, 145–146
    Tactical folding knives,

146–147
Personal survival kits, 151–153
    Belt knife survival kit, 152
    Pocket survival kit, 152
    Survival parka shell, 152
    Survival day pack, 153
Phosphate deficiency, 50
Pitcher pump, 41
Plaintains, 57
Poisonous plants, 261–270
Pole fishing, 71
Pot hunting, 95–97
Preparing game, 100–101, 103
Radiation threat, *see Man-
    made disasters*
Ranger sling (rifle sling),
    86–88
Reindeer moss lichens, 63
    For treatment of
    methicillin–resistant
    MRSA, 64
    For treatment of topical
    infections, 64
    For treatment of
    tuberculosis, 64
Rickets, 50
Riflescope sighting, 89–93
Salmonella, 52
Scurvy, 50
Seepage wells, 36–38
Sharpening edged tools,
    155–158
Shelter–in–place, 106–109
Simple snares, 65
Snare placement, 68, 69
Snow storms, *see Winter*

*storms*
Sodium chlorite tablet, 47
Spring snares, 65, 66
Squirrel hunting, 97–100
Storing water, 46
Stuck vehicles, 168–170
Survival boat, 158–160
Sutures, 133–134
Swine flu, *see Influenza*
Teeth, *see Dentistry*
Telescopic sight, 82
Tinder materials, 14
    Fire wick, 15
    Manufactured tinders, 16
Tracking
    Bears, 287–289, 298
    Beaver, 292–293, 301
    Coyote, 289–290, 298
    Gray wolf, 290–291, 298
    In general, 285–286
    Raccoon, 291–292, 300
    Track sketches, 296–303
    White–tailed deer, 293–294,
    296
    Wildcats, 294–295, 299
Trench foot, 13
Trench stove, 24, 25
Triage, 139, 141
Trigger line, 74
Tsunamis, 191–192
Ultimate Survival Firearm, 80
    .22 Long Rifle/"Squirrel
    Sniper," 80, 81
    Hydrostatic shock, 81
Urban cookfires, 27
Vitamin C deficiency, 50

Vitamin D deficiency, 50
Vitamin B deficiency, 50
Volcanoes, 192–193
Water, 29
    Chemical disinfectants,
    31–32
    Collecting water from
    precipitation, 29, 30
    Dangers of untreated
    water, 30–31
    Disinfecting water by
    boiling, 32–33
    Distilled water, 34
    Filters, 33–34
    From automobile
    radiators, 43
    From hot water heaters, 43
    From toilet, 42
Water bladder, 44
Water bottle warmer, 24
Water bottles, 44
Water table, 36–41
Wearable shelter, 116–120
Weather
    Identifying approaching
    weather, 121–122
    Lightning, 123
    Problems, 123–127
    Snow, 125, 127
    Tornadoes, 123–125
Well point, 39, 41
Wernicke–Korsakoff
    syndrome, 50
Wild foods, 56, 57
Wilderness survival kit, 12
Winter storms, 193–197